I0616347

TRIALS AND TRIBULATIONS OF

# TIN CAN LIZZIE

# TRIALS AND TRIBULATIONS OF

# TIN CAN LIZZIE

Elizabeth Catherine Stupansky Seither
June 3, 1940 to June 29, 2020

Stories She told about Her Life, Her Family, and Her Escape
To Freedom and Eternal Happiness as They Learned to Overcome Their Trials and Tribulations Through Christ Jesus

WRITTEN BY:

DR. RITA STUPAVSKY COLASENT

**ARPress**
ILLUMINATING IDEAS,
EMPOWERING VOICES

Copyright © 2024 by  Dr. Rita Colasent

All rights reserved. No part of this publication may be reproduced, distributed, or transmitted in any form or by any means, including, photocopying,recording, or other electronic or mechanical methods, without the prior written permission of the copyright owner and the publisher, except in the case of brief quotations embodied in critical reviews and certain other noncommercial uses permitted by copyright law. For permission requests, write to the publisher, addressed "Attention: Permissions Coordinator," at the address below.

**ARPress**
45 Dan Road Suite 5
Canton MA 02021
Hotline:          1(888) 821-0229
Fax:              1(508) 545-7580

Ordering Information:
Quantity sales. Special discounts are available on quantity purchases by corporations, associations, and others. For details, contact the publisher at the address above.

Printed in the United States of America.

| ISBN-13: | Softcover | 979-8-89330-156-4 |
|---|---|---|
|  | eBook | 979-8-89330-158-8 |
|  | Hardback | 979-8-89330-157-1 |

Library of Congress Control Number:  2024920432

# TABLE OF CONTENTS

The Previous Publisher has recognized that this book deserves recognition and respect in the literary world! Therefore, they award this book The Golden Plume Seal of Literary Excellence—a prestigious title awarded to authors with exceptional and extraordinary writing styles to draw the readers' attention!

The Golden Plume Seal of Literary Excellence is proof of support for this book, **"THE TRIALS AND TRIBULATIONS OF TIN CAN LIZZIE,"** which contains superior and exceptional literary work!

This book contributes to humanity through this dynamic true-life story, written primarily during a worldwide pandemic!

The Previous Publisher acknowledges and is proud that this book deserves recognition and respect in the literary world and to reach millions of readers across the globe. Indeed, this story genuinely **"Honors"** the family of Elizabeth Stupansky Seither and her sister, the author of this book, Dr. Rita Stupavsky Colasent. Dr. Rita brought this unique, warm, genuine, and wholehearted true story of her sister and their struggling family to fruition in the written word, especially during a life-and-death health crisis.

### Congratulations to the Stupavsky/Stupansky Family!

Your lives have been a testimony to your strong faith and determination to survive in a world of poverty while growing up with parents who were both **DEAF!** You each had a tempestuous and blustery life, but they gained much strength to **OVERCOME** your challenges and succeed in life! Now, you can encourage others to **OVERCOME** The **Trials and Tribulations** in their lives, as well!

# A Glimpse Into The Story

**THE TRIALS AND TRIBULATIONS OF TIN CAN LIZZIE** is not just a memoir but an emotionally charged journey that offers an intimate glimpse into the life and legacy of a woman named Liz, as seen through the eyes of her sister, Rita. This book is a tribute to Liz's life and a profound exploration of grief, love, and the relentless passage of **TIME**, inviting you to share in their emotional journey.

The story centers on Liz's final days, revealing her deep love for her family and her unfulfilled desire to spend more **TIME** with them. Liz's voice echoes throughout the narrative, emphasizing her belief in the strength needed to survive life's challenges. Her moto, "In life, you have to be strong to survive," poignantly reminds readers of the resilience required in the face of life's trials and inspires them with hope and courage.

The author's central theme is that you can **OVERCOME YOUR TRIALS AND TRIBULATIONS THROUGH CHRIST JESUS.** Liz stresses that you shouldn't let **TIME ESCAPE** from you or miss out on the opportunities God has planned for you, inspiring readers with a message of hope and courage!

Rita's account is deeply personal and raw, detailing her profound struggle to come to terms with her sister's sudden death. The narrative shifts between Liz's reflections on her life and Rita's experiences following Liz's passing, creating a layered and multifaceted portrait of two sisters bound by love and shared history. Rita's journey to Florida and her supernatural experiences adds a unique dimension to the story, blending the ordinary with the extraordinary.

The book's exploration of time as an antagonist is both powerful and relatable. **TIME** is depicted as a thief, mercilessly cutting short

Liz's life and leaving her family grappling with unfinished stories and unsaid goodbyes. Rita's poignant questions—why there wasn't more **TIME** , why they couldn't say goodbye—resonate with anyone who has experienced the sudden loss of a loved one, making the book a poignant and relevant read.

**THE TRIALS AND TRIBULATIONS OF TIN CAN LIZZIE** is not just a memoir; it's a testament to the enduring power of family, faith, and the human spirit. Liz's wish for her family's story to be told is beautifully realized in Rita's heartfelt writing. The book is a source of comfort and inspiration, offering readers the courage to face their **TRIALS** and the **FAITH** to believe in miracles.

Rita's narrative is a tribute to her sister and a universal story of love, loss, and the struggle to find meaning in life's inevitable hardships. This book will resonate with anyone who has experienced loss, reminding them of the importance of cherishing the **TIME** they have with their loved ones and the strength that comes from enduring life's Trials and Tribulations.

This book especially relates to those families who experienced Grief and Hardships during the Pandemic of the COVID-19 virus to many families worldwide. A **TIME** the world will never forget! You will not want to miss this true story and pass it down to future generations.

# SUMMARY OF THE BOOK

## THE TRIALS AND TRIBULATIONS OF TIN CAN LIZZIE

## WRITTEN BY: DR. RITA COLASENT

When Elizabeth Seither went into her doctor's office in June 2020, she suffered a mild stroke and was taken to a nearby hospital. While in the hospital and upon a complete physical examination, the doctors learned that she needed a relatively routine colonoscopy, even at age 80. This book tells the story of what happened while Liz was in the hospital during the COVID-19 CRISIS and the promise she elicited from her younger sister, Rita, asking her to write a book on her and her family's lives.

Since no visitors were allowed during this crisis, these two sisters had **TIME** to talk extensively on the phone over five days. Liz had difficulty concentrating and was very nervous because she was waiting for this procedure to be completed before returning home. However, the two sisters had many phone conversations in which Liz opened up the doors and windows of her entire life!

From their humble beginnings in Cleveland, Ohio, Liz and her four siblings, Dorothy, Victor, Rita, and Richard, faced numerous hardships. However, their shared resilience and determination led them to successful and fulfilling lives, a testament to the power of perseverance.

Liz had strong determination, stubbornness, and wit, and she was very smart, as all the Stupavsky members were. She was such a friendly character and had a lot of charisma. Everyone loved Liz, and she was so kind-hearted! She had one big secret about becoming **"Tin Can Lizzie"** in her younger years! She shared that secret with her sister Rita and looked forward to sharing it with all the family members, especially her children, grandchildren, and siblings. Liz made Rita promise not to tell anyone her secret(s) until their book was finished and published. Liz had faith in her sister Rita to gather and write all these conversations and snippets of the family history and get it published! Liz told Rita that many readers across the globe would read her book. Liz believed her story and her family's stories would help others **OVERCOME** their **Trials and Tribulations** worldwide!

Liz said she had many more secrets to tell and wanted them all out before she passed away. But **TIME** won out, and Liz was called home very unexpectedly by our Lord. Liz was so determined that she would make it through this last hospital procedure and return home, but **TIME** gave her and her family no warning, and she was "**Gone!**"

Liz told Rita secrets about her younger life growing up in the inner city of Cleveland and how she survived living in poverty with parents who were Deaf. Liz told Rita about how she named herself **"Tin Can Lizzie"** and told her she tossed pennies on the streets of the inner-city neighborhood as an **ESCAPE** to get out of the house. Rita promised Liz that she would write and publish the story. Liz felt that her story needed to be available to everyone for encouragement, strength, and courage so that families and readers would never give up in life, just as she never gave up as she experienced many struggles and hard **TIMES**. Upon Liz's passing, Rita immediately went to Florida for Liz's memorial, spent quality **TIME** with her family, and returned to Ohio to write her sister's story.

This story ventures into a woman's last days, revealing who she was, her love for her family, and her biggest desire to spend more **TIME** with her family. She also wanted her sister Rita to write and publish this book! She said that life is this way, and we do what we have to do to survive in this world. Liz repeatedly said, *"In Life, you have to be strong to survive!"* This book also contains many of Rita's circumstances, explaining natural, authentic, miraculous, and supernatural experiences after her sister Liz passed away and on her journey to and back from Florida. These experiences were pretty remarkable!

Liz said that her story could help others **OVERCOME** the most challenging **TIMES** when they are at the lowest stages of their lives, and it would seem there is no hope left for them. The reader will learn how Liz and her family overcame some of their Trials and Tribulations and their many struggles as they grew up in the inner city of Cleveland, Ohio, with their parents, who were both deaf.

This book contains Liz's story and her rendition of the stages of her life before she passed away! Liz made her **FINAL ESCAPE! TIME** won the battle and the race to continue so Liz could live longer and finish her and her family's story. Liz's **TIME** ran out, and she had so much more to tell and more Love to give!

This story is also Rita's day-by-day account of how she experienced her sister's shocking death. It was a challenging part of Rita's life that she had to walk through, and writing these accounts were very difficult for her. Rita kept asking herself, "Why, Lord? Why didn't we have enough **TIME** to dig deeper into these accounts/stories, and why couldn't Liz and Rita have more **TIME TOGETHER?** Why didn't the family have enough **TIME** to say "Goodbye" to their beloved mother and sister? Unfortunately, **TIME** was the antagonist in this storyline, and **TIME** showed no "**Mercy**" to Liz as she unfairly was taken to the heavens as quickly as a *"Thief in the night!"*

Liz wanted her family and others to hear the story of her younger days, and she felt that this book was the only way to happen! She said so many times, "Rita, you can do it! I know what you can do! What you wrote about our mother's miraculous birth as one of the first Incubator Babies was incredible! Our mother made history! This book can help many people by giving them the faith, courage, hope, and strength to keep living and trusting in God!

This book is about a family's story and their heart-breaking cry that the family members will never forget. It tells about their lives growing up on the East side of Cleveland, Ohio, with tremendous, caring, and loving parents who were DEAF. Hopefully, these stories will live on forever and linger through the minds and hearts of this family and other readers worldwide! Rita compares her sister Liz's death, her trip to Florida, and the process of writing her sister Liz's book as an **INCREDIBLE JOURNEY!**

Yes, the coronavirus pandemic has tremendously impacted people's lives worldwide. It surely did not pass the Stupansky/Stupavsky family, as Liz was lying in a Florida hospital waiting for a health procedure to be done amid this pandemic and was constantly overlooked. Ultimately, **TIME** was not handing out "exceptions." Liz never received the care she deserved and waited days without food or nourishment. **TIME** got her before the medical help could reach her and saved her life by giving her the treatment she needed. It was a very critical, senseless, and ruthless **TIME** in our world that unnecessarily took the lives of many people.

You will love reading and learning about this remarkable woman and her family's hardships, struggles, and victories! Life was tough for Liz and her family, but they miraculously made it through as they put their faith in our Lord Jesus Christ. However, during this worldwide pandemic, there was no **"SAVING GRACE."** Most of the world had to bear massive changes in their lives as well as the loss of many of their loved ones who were scooped by the massive spreading Pandemic tragedy and had to die all alone in this senseless affliction that showed no recourse and no mercy.

# DEDICATION

I DEDICATE THIS BOOK TO THE LOVING MEMORY OF MY SISTER
ELIZABETH CATHERINE STUPANSKY SEITHER
June 3, 1940, to June 29, 2020

To My Dear Sister: I fulfilled my promise to you and published your and our family's stories for the world to read and understand who we are!

## WE ARE STRONG SURVIVORS!

My sister dreamed that her life experiences and snippets of our family's stories would be published in a book for all to read. This book can encourage others as they attempt to **OVERCOME** their Trials and Tribulations in life as we did!

Hopefully, after reading this book, the readers will have a fresh new outlook and a renewed faith that our Lord will see them through their hardships and bring them peace!

My fondest hopes and dreams are that my sister Liz's memory and our family's legacy will live on forever in the years to come and for our younger generations.

This book was written with the utmost love and thanks to our Lord for helping our family endure a life of troubled times and uncertainties. We have so much to be thankful for, and we survived to tell our stories!

Liz, you are much loved and will remain in our hearts and minds forever until we see you again!

# THEME

There are many themes, as a writer, I could have used in the creation of this story. I could have written several themes, such as:

STRUGGLES OF A FAMILY WHOSE PARENTS WERE DEAF SURVIVING IN A LIFE AND WORLD OF POVERTY

STRUGGLES OF ONE CHILD LIVING IN POVERTY AND TRYING TO PROVIDE

LEADERSHIP TO HER SIBLINGS AND OTHERS IN HER LIFE

DON'T ALLOW **TIME** TO GET AWAY FROM YOU!

DO WHAT YOU HAVE TO DO BEFORE YOUR **TIME** ON EARTH RUNS OUT AND YOUR

CLOCK STOPS TICKING!

NEVER ALLOW **TIME** TO BE YOUR "**ENEMY**" FIGHT TO "**OVERCOME**" YOUR OBSTACLES TODAY!

BUT MOST FITTING TO THIS STORYLINE IS THE
FOLLOWING THEME:

WHEN LIFE GETS UNBEARABLE
THERE IS ALWAYS A WAY OUT!
YOU WILL **OVERCOME**!

# ABOUT THIS STORY
# AMID THE CORONAVIRUS

## THE ENEMY OF "TIME" JUST RACING AWAY

> *THIS BOOK IS DEDICATED*
>
> *TO THE LOVING MEMORY OF MY SISTER*
>
> *ELIZABETH CATHERINE STUPANSKY SEITHER*

The story you are about to read is about my oldest sister, liz, and her desire for her true self-story to come out, revealing secrets about her life before she passed away.

She had wanted to do this before **TIME** rolled away and believed she must fulfill this intense passion.

I intended to try to put down these occurrences of her life in writing and tell of my journey before she passed away, her actual death, and the odyssey of this entire adventure! It was an amazing pilgrimage with many earth-shattering and unusual (or miraculous) surprises, stories, and experiences.

Stories can transfer minds, hearts, and beliefs from one person to another or entire families. But it takes **TIME**. Storytelling is a powerful tool to relate one's world to another. That is how it was with my sister Liz as she poured out snippets of her life to me in just a few short days.

My daughter, Pam, remembers me talking about **TIME** as I wept the night Liz passed away. I said, "I didn't expect Auntie Liz to pass away. We both were working as fast as we could to write her story. I kept saying I needed more **TIME** and more **TIME**, and it just didn't happen! Why Lord? She had been ill, but she shouldn't have died! We did what we could do, but "**TIME**" just raced away from us both!"

Liz had been ill, but she didn't know she would die, and how she died so quickly surprised us all. Her story takes place amid the COVID-19 crisis, or as it is called, the CORONAVIRUS, as she lay in the hospital. Even though she did not have the virus herself, the times were difficult during the pandemic because of additional restrictions. It was a **TIME** during which a person wouldn't want to be sick in the hospital—or worse yet, be dying there. Patients were under strict isolation and were all alone during their hospital stays. If the patients were close to death in most hospitals, they would die alone with only the essential workers at their bedsides holding their hands.

The tale I am about to reveal took almost five days for my sister to share snippets of her life, from the first phone call to the sad, exhausting end, which took about 120 hours. I knew I was at war with **TIME**, as most of us are, but she wasn't planning on passing away. I felt **TIME** breathing down my neck like a cold winter wind, but **TIME** did give me the **GIFT OF KNOWING MORE OF HER LIFE** within those five days of hearing the last words of my sister, Liz.

We traveled together in those 120 hours—a lifetime of joy, sadness, the discovery of secrets, and more with our phone calls. We came as close as two sisters could be as we teamed up, racing against **TIME**. We were always hoping for more **TIME**, and I was selfish; I wanted every minute I could get with her—yes, **TIME** passed quickly in those few short days. We spent every second conversing, writing notes, and trying to plan out the next day's topics that were to be discussed. Even when I slept, I was dreaming about how I would approach her the next day and what she would tell me.

I felt as close as ever to my sister and felt her relief that I could keep us on the topic and write it all down while pulling from my brain what we talked about on the previous call. We all know that **TIME** doesn't bargain with anyone, and it doesn't matter if people are rich, poor, smart, dull, fast, slow, or lying in a hospital bed. **TIME** became my enemy but my gift as well. **TIME** did give me many seconds with Liz on this hospital phone. It was in our world of hope, spiritual healing, and forgiveness with COVID-19 whipping around us. I knew I was fighting **TIME**, and Liz and I felt deep within our minds and spirits that it was a battle! I hoped she would improve so we could continue writing our families' and her stories together. But **TIME** raced away from us, and then her **TIME** ran out. The clock stopped ticking, so our story was left for me to write all alone. I knew it would be a challenging and overwhelming task, but what could I do? How could I complete the task at hand without her?

Our country was going through a massive pandemic that changed the world. People who were lucky enough to make it out of the hospital had to follow strict guidelines, and for those who were not so fortunate, their funeral would not be like they would want it to become, without saying goodbye to their loved ones. There were massive restrictions, especially in Florida, where many seniors were dying of the virus. Patients were all alone, except for the medical staff, who were the only ones at their bedsides. They were overwhelmed, and some procedures didn't go as planned or as they should have been conducted. The only connection to one's family was by phone if patients were lucky enough to get through the busy hospital phone lines. But trust me, this was a **TIME** in history when a person wouldn't want to get sick or, worse yet, die.

Such was my sister Liz's story as I wrote about it during the **TIME** of her hospital stay, her ultimate death, and me trying to cope with these experiences. Her story is how she told it to me, as shocking and implausible as some parts were. As her story unravels, please realize that she jumped from her early childhood to highlights of her adult life as she was in the hospital in her last days. I had to keep alert to follow her, for her mind was so sharp!

She recollected the people in her life and how they related to her as a daughter, a sister, a single young girl, a wife, a mother, and a business world member. It was challenging for me to understand what she was saying in her low voice due to the noise and necessary interruptions of the medical staff. I was unsure about writing this story, for I could foresee many roadblocks along the way, even from family members. But I kept up with her the best I could, and by day four, I could feel my sister's exhaustion. She physically felt weak, but she held on to revealing her stories. I only wished that we had known she only had nearly 24 hours left; **TIME** and **DEATH** gave us no such luxury! I kept pushing her, and she felt the need to continue talking so that I could take notes and type them later. I had to recall every word she said, and it was not easy, but I did the best I could. It was a challenge, and I put my whole heart, soul, and every strength I had to follow along and get it all right!

I even yelled out to her, "Liz, hold on! In no **TIME**, this procedure will get done, and in a short **TIME**, you will return home!"

I could picture her sitting alone in the hospital room, with nice bedclothes and her long, pretty blonde hair neatly combed and tied back in a ponytail as she had been wearing it lately. I am sure her sense of humor came through as she complimented all the cute doctors as she often did. She kept calm yet had a sophisticated demeanor, a prim smile, and her big brown eyes twinkling. She was always amazed at all who came across her path, even when hospitalized.

I didn't always know how to make sense of what she was saying at times because of her situation, but at least I was familiar and knew most of the people she was talking about, so it was a little easier to get a grip on her tales. As a reader, you may not know what she recalled from her past or the people in her life. She often said that her story might help others when they are at the lowest stages of their lives when it seems there is no hope left for them and their **TRIALS AND TRIBULATIONS** plague them. She said her story would help them **OVERCOME** their most challenging times, just as her story helped her make it through her darkest times when she saw no other end in sight. Liz felt all alone again in her life, and she only had the hospital staff to talk to and me and her daughters calling her on the hospital phone, which was hard getting phone calls through.

I am only writing on the positive sides that she spoke. She sometimes commented negatively about others, but I knew most of the background. I only added bits of information in her recollections for clarity, but I only wrote how she said it. I just wanted to make it easier for the reader to follow along with the storyline's primary gist. I filled in the history of the lives of our family members as she wanted me to. I heard her speak on these rolling parts of her life (as she called them) and said many times when I was trying to slow her, she would tell me, "I can't stop! Please don't stop me! I am on such a roll!"

In writing this story, I am trying to give the audience a fuller, more complete picture of her incredible stories of how she survived and what she had to do to keep her sanity and freedom. I only wrote about how she told this story. Therefore, if you disagree with what she said upon reading these brief testimonies, that is between you and her. Someday, when you meet her again, you can ask her to clarify, but until then, this is her story and her rendition of the stages of her life as far as we could make it through before the clock stopped ticking and she was gone. She had so much more to tell me but never got that chance. I am sure you will discover her and draw conclusions and opinions. My only regret is that we didn't complete these stories, and we didn't have the **TIME** together for her to clarify these accounts and for me to ask her more questions.

This story is also my day-by-day account of how I experienced Liz's **SHOCKING** and **UNTIMELY** death. It is about how I walked these remarkable last days she had on earth—me going to Florida to say my goodbyes at her memorial, seeing my Florida family, and then coming home again to my family in Ohio. It was a challenging part of my life that I had to walk through, and writing these accounts was very difficult. I kept asking myself, "Why, Lord? Why didn't we have enough **TIME** to dig deeper into these accounts?" The most challenging **TIME** was the day she passed away. It was my prayer to ask for more **TIME** to grasp better what and who she was. However, the Lord called her home.

As these accounts of her life are read, her determination, stubbornness, and wit can be felt, as well as her secrets. Liz did tell me there were many more secrets in her life, and she wanted them all out before it was **TIME** to see our Lord. Liz was determined to make it through this last hospital stay and this final routine procedure, but she did not. The enemy of **TIME** won the race! She knew she didn't have much **TIME** and did so many little things to prove it. She asked me frequently to pray for her to make it through this last procedure, make it right with individuals in her life, and say her "Goodbyes" and kiss and hug them one last **TIME**. I kept telling her, "Liz, stop talking like that! You have made it through so much, and God will see and know that you are not finished yet."

It was all about natural, genuine experiences. They were all pretty remarkable, as I think you will agree as you venture into this woman's last days, revealing who she was. She would tell me that life is that way… we do what we have to do to survive. We establish our priorities and go forth, doing what we need to do for our family to endure, including our tragedies. Yes, she mentioned many regrets in her four marriages and with her live-in partners that she would have done differently, but isn't that the case with all of us? We all make bad decisions at times and try to compensate later. Liz told me her biggest regret was not spending more **TIME** with her girls and grandchildren, whom she loved so much. Instead, she went for the next deal or house to sell. It was a bit of selfishness, not seeing the reality of her deeds, and poor decision-making, especially when she loved to go shopping, which was her downfall!

Her youngest daughter, Gina, lived on the east coast of Florida, and Liz and her other daughter, Kim, lived on the west coast. Liz was always going through a business venture, which took all her strength. She told me, though, that she was always planning to make it up to the girls, and somehow, she wanted to make a difference in success and happiness in their lives. She said that my writing this book was the only way she could do that.

She said so many times, "Rita, you can do it! I have your work, and I know what you can do." This is another reason I must follow my promise: I would write about and share what she said with our family—especially her children and grandchildren. Hopefully, they will be willing to take the **TIME** to read these accounts and listen to what she has to say. She loved them very much and wanted to tell them about her life and all her **Trials and Tribulations** to help them endure their tough times.

This story goes along with the old saying that as people come close to death, they recollect their past and most vivid memories. I often read back to her what I wrote, and she said, "It's perfect, but you have a much longer way to go before we finish, and there is never an ending to my stories—they will live on forever! They will linger through the minds and hearts of our family and other readers. Therefore, this book isn't much, but it is all I have, and whoever takes the **TIME** to read about me will begin to understand a bit of my life and who I was."

The shame and travesty of it all are that I never had the chance to continue hearing all that she was planning to tell me to make everyone know how much she regretted many choices but loved her family very much.

Liz told me how much she loved my daughter, Pam, who would go down to Florida, and I would take my sisters, Kim and Pam, on a cruise. Liz said those experiences were some of the best days of her life. She loved to cruise and went on several. Pam would always say that her Aunt Liz was so wonderful and loved her Auntie dearly. Pam said when she stayed with Liz in Florida, Liz always made her feel comfortable, and they had so much fun! Pam recalled that Liz would take her to a store and spend her last penny on her to buy her things for the cruise. She said someone always knew her wherever they went, and she had charisma and a comfortable outreach to them.

Pam said, "Aunt Liz was always trying to make a deal to buy a piece of property that she was selling. She had guts—big guts and was not afraid to take a risk; even when all else failed and she lost everything she had, she would start up again. She always wanted to help others, and she sure did!"

If one is serious about getting to know this heroic woman, her true character can be picked up, whether or not some of the testimony and fashion I wrote about are understood. The main person who was to understand what she was saying at the **TIME** was me! The more I wrote, the more I remembered, and I could bring these outpourings she had via the written word.

Liz poured her heart out to me as we talked daily on the phone. I took her death very hard, and it will be a long **TIME** before I can **OVERCOME** my grief. If no one reads this final product and never gets to a known or unknown audience, it's O.K. This whole procedure is a growing process to help us know who we are and take inventory of our lives to prepare for when the Lord calls us home.

As I write, I can unveil my blinders and see who I am and my life with more precise knowledge of my sister. Liz wanted our family's remarkable, miraculous stories to be told, and she wanted me to tell the whole story. I have researched our mother, so I always knew there were missing pieces in our family's lives. I uncovered one big, massive find about our mother being born prematurely. I am also learning that there were missing pieces in my sister's life. I would beat all odds of racing against **TIME** and discover them.

In February 2020, I gave a PowerPoint on my mother's early life. Liz was touched and completely enthralled by that tribute to our mother, and she said she trusted me to do the same for her in her story. Liz's story is not quite like my mother's heroic story, but it is truly an amazing piece to read. Liz told me that our mom's revelation gave her the idea of asking me to write her story as I did my mother's presentation, but she wanted it in book form. She said that is why she is bringing her life and story to me and trusting me to "make good" on my promise. So, I will never give up until the book is published. After sharing some information, Liz always said, "Rita, I can't wait; I can't wait to have everyone read this story about our family and me!" Of course, she would also say, "I can't wait to read it myself!"

Unfortunately, she never got that chance.

For my sister Liz, this story is a start, and it is only bits and pieces, but it is all true, and I only wish she could tell us more- especially of the many secrets she wanted to get to but didn't have the chance. I wanted to know those secrets, and I was supposed to tell everyone in this content what they were. Enjoy and picture my sister Liz as you read her small and impressive beginning account of her life. You will find pictures of her in different stages and ages of her life and the lives of our family members. She desperately wanted me to write some family history; you will discover how her legend will live forever! I wouldn't allow the enemy of "**TIME**" ever to win the victory! **I am determined to get Liz's and our family's story out to others so they can OVERCOME TRIALS AND TRIBULATIONS IN THEIR LIVES!**

Meet the splendid Lady, Ms. Lizzie! She was the **"Belle of the Ball."** Wherever she went, in whatever era, she was rolling. She was one Classy Lady, as you soon will learn, from her younger days as the **"Tin Can Lizzie"** or the **"Tin Can Queen"** to her older days as a swanky and fashionable senior, ready to roll!

# THE TRIALS AND TRIBULATIONS

# OF

# "TIN CAN LIZZIE"

## TRUE LIFE STORY OF HER LIFE AND
## THE LIFE OF HER FAMILY

STORIES TOLD BY ELIZABETH CATHERINE
STUPANSKY SEITHER
June 2, 1940 to June 29, 2020

WRITTEN BY HER SISTER,
DR. RITA STUPAVSKY COLASENT

# PREFACE

It is said that everyone has a story to tell before they pass away or think they are passing away. They say their whole life goes before them, and they can remember everything so vividly, especially from the earliest **TIME** of their lives. This is one of those stories my oldest sister, Liz, told me as she was going through some health problems. When one has severe health issues going on, it truly makes you stop and think of who you are and what you have been through in your life. This is just a phenomenon of being born in this world and returning to the world of where you came from.

We never thought our sister Liz would make it through all the health issues she went through over the past several years, but she did! I never gave up on her many of her many illnesses, even when she suffered a terrible fall in the bathroom before she passed away. You wouldn't even have recognized her. During these last bouts of hospital visits, she always seemed to make it back home. I believed that God would heal her, for I knew she had much to share in her life. She had many **TRIALS and TRIBULATIONS,** as she titled this book, that she persevered through during her lifetime, as many people's experiences in life can be traumatic and painful at times. She had some rough times, but she always survived, as all of us kids did growing up in the old neighborhood. We had to know and learn how to survive to keep on living.

Liz made it to her 80th birthday, and it was a fine day of celebration. Her daughter, Kim, threw a wonderful party with her brother Richard's anniversary and Liz's granddaughter Sophia's Sweet 16th birthday. It was a glorious day, and I helped as much as possible with the planning. Her daughter Kim and I designed the cake for this special day. I prayed that sister Liz would make it through to that 80th birthday, and God granted my wish and fulfilled my prayers, for she made it farther than we ever imagined, and she looked gorgeous on that special celebration day.

Liz had cirrhosis of the liver but never was a drinker. She had kidney issues and a weak heart; then she suffered from a terrible fall she had in the bathroom, and it was a miracle she was able to make it through that fall. Liz also suffered as she went through cervical cancer involving massive radiation treatments that burned her stomach, colon, and bladder linings.

Shortly after her 80th celebration, she went to the doctor, and a PET SCAN was ordered to determine where the cancer was located in her body because her tumor markers were high. Everyone thought for sure she had some cancer again, but I firmly believed that she was going to be cancer-free, and she was. Liz even thought for sure that the odds were against her- that she would die of some cancer and what made her believe that she had cancer before; therefore, she knew how it felt. She couldn't go through it again, for she said she would rather die than have cancer again, but that indeed was not the case because there was no cancer.

This story evolves shortly after that gloomy day when Liz goes to the doctor to get the PET scan results, and there it is. She was sitting on the table in the doctor's office, and she had a stroke right there! Her tensions of possibly knowing she had cancer again were too frightening for her. It was shocking as Liz's eyes rolled back in her head and her face distorted and blue. Liz's daughter, Regina, was on FaceTime with her sister, Kim, and saw the whole thing. It was very traumatizing for all who witnessed this stroke, and even for the doctor who was going to read the PET scan results of the findings of her cancer and location within her body.

The doctor's office called 911, and Liz was rushed to the nearest Stroke Emergency hospital. Now, this was amid the COVID-19 Virus, where the whole country and world had suffered severe tribulations, which only compounded when one had to go to the Emergency Room for a stroke or any sudden sickness. Liz's daughter, Kim, followed the ambulance as she was rushed to a particular hospital for neurological and stroke victims. Liz was incoherent the whole **TIME**, and upon arriving, the doctors began to examine her to see how severe this stroke was. Liz had other strokes before, so this was not the first occurrence.

Liz made it through the night, and her daughter, Kim, was allowed to stay in the Emergency Room with her because she was her Power of Attorney. Liz had suffered three strokes within that short period. Everyone in the family thought the worst was going to happen, but we ALL prayed and prayed and believed she would survive, and she did. The ironic thing was that when her daughter Kim took her to the doctor's office to hear where her cancer was, she was told that she never had cancer at all and was declared "cancer-free." However, Liz was so uptight about the possibility of having cancer again that it was too much for her to even get to the results from the doctor, even though the results all turned out very good.

While Liz was in the hospital, I played my old voicemail messages on my home phone, and I heard Liz's voice thanking me for helping with the 80th birthday party. She also thanked me for the beautiful birthday wish that I wrote to her. I usually wrote homemade birthday cards for her, and I knew she loved them. She asked me to write a book about her and our family's lives. Liz 's message about her big birthday celebration on June 3rd was right. Now, this was before the strokes happened, and it was the first **TIME** I had ever heard of such a request. I was so shocked by my sister on my voice machine asking me to write her life story! It was one thing to ask me to write a poem or a story, but a book! It was overwhelming, but I agreed I would try doing this for her because she was determined, and I wanted to fulfill her wishes and make her happy. Lizzie was my sister; she was always good to me, and I loved her!

Liz was free to live again! Now, she will be ready to tell me her story so we can write and publish it. When the doctor said that Liz didn't have cancer, Liz had a stroke right there in the doctor's office. Yes, Liz did have three strokes in a short amount of **TIME**, but she was determined to get out of the hospital and be with her family, and, more importantly, she was waiting for me to call her to begin telling me her story, and we did just that!

The following day, while she was waiting in her room, I called Liz in her hospital room. She said she was so happy to hear from me and awaited my call. I texted Kim and told her to tell her mother I would write her book as she requested of me in the voice message to write a life story on her life, and I told her I would try to do it.

As the intro states, sometimes, right before you pass on to God's heavenly level, your life starts flashing before your eyes, and it indeed was for my sister, but I was hoping and thinking that wasn't the case this **TIME**. Since Liz had health problems, I always pictured how she was going to die- as terrible as those sounds. I would stop and pray she would not have to be stuck recovering from an illness in a nursing home as she once was after suffering a broken collar bone and arm from a fall in the shower in the middle of a hurricane a few years ago. She said it was awful there, and she was right next to her friend, who actually was in the Rehab facility from a massive stroke and never returned home.

Now Liz had a strong will to live again, knowing that she didn't have cancer at all. She had it once before in her life and went through hell. She said she couldn't do it again. Liz told me she has had this burning desire, especially after the birthday celebration, that her life story needs to be told and many secrets must come out. Liz was rolling her life story out as fast as she could, and it was hard for me to remember everything she said over the phone. I had to tell her to slow down, slow down, but she did not and kept rolling out more and more information, and some pieces were precious and some very shocking. I told Liz to hold on to this dream to get this story out, but she insisted, "No, I want you to start writing now.!" Then she told me that I already have a name for my book, and she told me it will be called **"Trials and Tribulations of Tin Can Lizzie!"**

I was shocked and asked her, "Tin Can Lizzie—what kind of name is that?" I laughed as she got mad at me as she did often, and Liz said, "Stop it and listen!" I asked her, "Where did you get that name from?" Liz said, "I named myself! I gave it to me while on Sophia Ave. That is my name, and I want to return to everyone calling me that again, and in that life I had. I was the happiest I ever was when **"Tin Can Lizzie"**—was the greatest adventure of my entire life! Tell everyone in our family about this life I had, and please write it all in the book. I will tell you the whole story. My name was **"Tin Can,"** and I want to return to being that happy and carefree person again, with no pain, hunger, family problems, or sadness. Nothing negative happened to me when I was Tin Can. I was the true helper of the kids in the street and helped them solve their life issues. It was truly an ESCAPE for me, and I bounced into this new life I created for myself when life was unbearable for me to live."

So that is what this true story of **"Tin Can Lizzie"** is all about——parts of her life, as she tells it, and seeing it happen again to experience that **GREAT FINAL ESCAPE.** Yet the freedom that she had was because she didn't have cancer as the doctor and all others thought she had, including herself. Even though she had three strokes, she had hope in the middle of a trying, troubled world pandemic situation amidst the Coronavirus. The hospital was not a place to be during this **TIME.** So now her job was to move on and tell her story the way it was, and it was my job to recall her tales and pull everything out of my head as she revealed and poured out her life to me to record in this book of famous or shall I say "infamous" life and many tribulations of **"TIN CAN LIZZIE."**

Liz said, "So please know that someday when I am gone, maybe sooner than you think, I don't want to be remembered as the **"Classy Lady"** looking like a model. I am a successful real estate agent, but I want to be remembered as **"Tin Can- Lizzie."** One who played in the dirty streets, collected old dirty tin cans, and lived the life of my dreams." She didn't win much but said she was a leader and taught the boys she played with to go after their dreams. The dreams she had were extraordinary and exceptional. She had visions of what she wanted to become when she grew up. She said the only way to get there was to work hard and hold on to her visions and dreams.

She told me," I want to return to that life that I created for myself because only in that life is the real me." I realized that, and I was talking to a side of my sister I never really knew—she was not my sister "Liz." I am just beginning to learn to know her in such a powerful new way—a sister who loved and desperately wanted that life of **"TIN CAN!"** I could feel she was eager to return to that mysterious life where she could be all she wanted to become in a lifetime of enjoyment, leadership, and no more loneliness.

She talked to me about the chapters ahead in precious conversations in her final days. Liz said, "I don't know how I will get back to that life, but you know, sister, Dr. Rita, I will do it, and I am counting on you to get me there. As I talk more about that life, I am sure I will be able to slide back sooner or later into that life and pick up where I left off. I had to be happier than ever, as I experienced before. It will be my great **ESCAPE** on earth so they can see me and know who I am, and I could kiss and tell them all about the story myself as the **"TIN CAN QUEEN."** As our mother, Mercedes would say, "Me surprise everyone—you see!"

## A Day to Celebrate!!

### June 3, 2020

Liz, today is your special day to shine! God has blessed you as you endured many trials, still survived, and held on tight to your dreams!

Liz, you let your light shine on your Special Day as you celebrate your 80th Birthday. Not many of us are so blessed to live to be 80- what a blessing!

You were born at 5 AM on June 3, 1940, to the parents of Fred Stupavsky and Mercedes Meyer. Stupavsky. It states on your birth certificate that you were the 3rd baby born to our mother. She had two children who passed away, Louis and Richie Boy. You are now the oldest alive in our family. Then there is Dortha, Victor, me, and baby Richard.

Your life is an amazing miracle, for you have made it through so much and have lovely memories of your many successes. You were rich, poor, and blessed with having a few husbands, and you went on some nice cruise ship vacations. We have lovely memories of you and me going on many cruises together and many memories with the family, finally all together.

You, like all of us, the children of Fred and Mercedes are heroes, and we "Beat the Odds" of a life of poverty. We all survived, as my big sister led the way! You are a gifted saleslady, and you know how to achieve success! You know you are special, and you have a unique way with people in that you can get along with everyone you meet. You are a top-beat Personality Star!

You always had visions and dreams you followed and never gave up on. Keep holding on to your dreams, and you have… 20 more years to go to keep on "Dreaming" so we can celebrate your 100th birthday! I hope to get there for that celebration.

Happy Birthday, Big Sister, from all of your family!

Your life is a miracle! You survived many Trials and Tribulations and some extremely tough times, but you did it!

KEEP ON DREAMING AND ALWAYS GIVE THANKS TO OUR GOD!

From your loving sister, Dr. Rita

# Chapter 1

## EVERYONE HAS A BEGINNING

Chapter One gives you a brief description of not only my sister, Liz, but also a brief synopsis of our family background, which is the core to understanding the story of Liz and how her character fits into this family. People say your family background and upbringing determine the rest of your life, and so that was not only the case with my sister, Liz, but all of us in the family. Background and family history dictate your destiny, whether you realize it or not. Everyone must be responsible for the consequences of their choices, and my sister, Liz, indeed ran from the poor decisions she made in her whole life until now. She wanted to face reality and make restitution very late to justify her choices and make them known to others so that the truth would prevail. Was it too late in life to do this? Is it possible that such a change in her character could be understood by others when it is a **TIME** of your life when you don't have much **TIME** left, a battle that all of us must face? When we know we might meet our maker, we may want to correct what we did wrong over the years. We can't **ESCAPE** our life growing up in poverty on the inner-city streets of Cleveland, Ohio, which did have any impact on our destiny. Therefore, in retrospect, like it or not, your family background, environment, and early beginnings dictate and influence your subconsciousness and your persona, whether you know it or not. **THERE IS NO ESCAPE!**

My sister Liz was never vocal about her life story while growing up, and she never would go back and reiterate as an adult both the good experiences and the nightmares of her life. There were times when I would share stories of the "Sophia House" about when we were living in the old neighborhood, but sister Liz would completely ignore what we were talking about. My sister Dorothy and I would discuss the Sophia Street memories, but not Liz. Dorothy said that numerous times, Liz blocked everything out of her childhood. She didn't want to remember anything and didn't want us to talk about our life around her on Sophia Ave. We would bring up this person or that person and incidents of the old neighborhood, and Liz would not be able to remember. She didn't want to remember and never wanted to reveal her true identity, a name for who she was, a life she wanted to become when she was older and could dream about because it never really came to fruition.

Therefore, does It take a traumatic experience of hearing that she might have cancer again after having three strokes that she would recall such vivid memories of not only her early life as to where she got the name **"Tin Can Lizzie"** but also many traumatic episodes throughout her entire life?

Liz was born June 3, 1940, in Cleveland, Ohio's West Side, to our parents, Fred and Mercedes Meyer Magley Stupavsky. Her birth started very strangely indeed, for her birth certificate states she was born at 5 AM that morning at City Hospital, which is now Metro Hospital. Her birth certificate says that she was one of three living children and one deceased child of her mother, Mercedes Stupavsky. We do know that one live child was my half-brother, Louis, the son of my mother in her first marriage, and we know who the other deceased son was- my mother's "Richie Boy," of whom our mother talked about for years. After researching, I found out this child died at three years of age of dropsy. The mystery here is we never understood everything, and our mother's limited language is American Sign Language (ASL). But who was the other child alive? The death of my half-brother back in the year 1933 was all a mystery to us. However, in my search, I discovered more about this child and his burial place in St. Mary's Cemetery on Cleveland's west side, the same cemetery where our grandparents were buried. However, the true identity of this half-brother was always another family secret, and we never even honored this brother. Did we fully understand that we had a half-brother, and he lay in his grave until much later when I found his burial information? We didn't even think it was a brother—just my mother's "Richie Boy." That is all we knew, and that could have been anyone. Another mystery in our family's life and the lack of communication made it impossible for our mother to tell us the real story.

If Liz was the 3rd live child born to Mercedes, who was the second live child born to our mother? There was talk that Liz was a twin, but I did a lot of research, and I couldn't find any birth certificate or death notice of having such a twin. If true, where is Liz's twin, and what is the real secret of this mysterious birth? Liz herself determined that she was a twin, and her twin died at three days old, as some of my mother's relatives told her, and that our mother told her she was a twin. This possibility constantly plagued her, and she told us she could feel she had another half to her very existence. I was also told by relatives in the Meyer family that it was a big possibility. Liz said she would continue to search for this connection. I was told that on the day Liz was born in my grandmother's house, everyone was ordered out of the house for three days, and no one could enter or ask questions.

Nonetheless, the mystery and the truth of it all lies here that Liz was not born in a hospital, for there were no records in the hospital's records or microfilm files. I called Metro Hospital at the **TIME** "City Hospital." Liz was delivered not by a doctor, as stated on her birth certificate, but most probably by her maternal grandmother, Catherine Fligor Meyer, who named my sister "Liz" after her mother and named her "Catherine" for her middle name after herself. I was told that Grandma Meyer delivered all the children in the family. The family of Grandma Meyer said that Grandma Meyer delivered all of the family's children in her house, including my mother's sister, who had 12 children. My cousins told me that they called her house "The Baby Factory," where many children were delivered from the family and many unwed women. On my sister Dorothy's birth certificate, as she was born in 1942, it clearly said she was born in our grandmother's home, so indeed, Liz, being two years older, was most probably born in my grandmother's house and delivered by her.

Grandma Meyer, as we called her, was something else. She was the ruler of the family. She was my mother's mother and controlled her and our family as far as she could. She was always upset that her daughter, my mother, her second marriage, married a deaf man. She kept them apart for several years. So, to this day, what happened to the 3rd baby born to our mother, Mercedes, is a mystery. Was that another child, or was it Liz's twin? It is a mystery that only Liz or all of us can find out when we reach the Heavenly Kingdom.

Our father, Fred, and our mother, Mercedes, were deaf. Our father was born in Egbell, Czechoslovakia. He came to America when he was three years old with his mother, Katherine Stupavsky, hoping to bring him to Cleveland, Ohio, to find a cure for his deafness. We were told by our Grandmother Stupavsky that our father was deaf due to Scarlet Fever; his fever rose to 107 and burned out his vocal cords and his eardrums, and in those days, there were no cures when a person had such a high fever. Therefore, my grandmother left her country and settled in Cleveland, Ohio, on none other than Sophia Ave, where we all resided growing up; well, shall I say, "most of the **TIME**." Our grandmother immigrated from Czechoslovakia to America with my father, Fred, in 1903 and settled in Ohio mainly because of the famous hospitals we had here and that there was a school for the Deaf in Cleveland. My grandmother's fondest dream was that my father would be cured of his Deafness and be able to hear and speak again, but nothing was successful. My parents met in the DEAF Community and knew each other from the Deaf School.

My grandmother Katherine on my father's side was a wonderful woman who put my father first in finding a possible cure for his deafness. She and my father immigrated here from Czechoslovakia and left my father's older brother behind; he came to America much later and lived with his father in Chicago. He was the only one who knew my grandfather was living in Chicago. My grandmother loved my father and mother and cared deeply for her grandchildren and our family as a whole unit. The house my grandparents lived in on 9803 Sophia when they first immigrated from Europe ironically, years later, became the Klucho Grocery Store. But before it was the store, it was a saloon. The saloon was operated by none other than by my grandparents.

Both the Stupavsky and Klucho families were shocked to learn of this! My father loved the grocery store being next to our home. We know why he loved it there; that was his first home when he came to America with his grandmother. I never found this out until recently, receiving help from Jim Sigmund, a Klucho family member—a researcher and genealogist from Houston, Texas- as he searched the city and census records. Shortly after my grandfather, John Stupavsky immigrated to America, my grandparents owned and operated that saloon for about ten years. However, then my grandfather was reported in the city records as "Dead," and my grandmother, Katherine, was left a "Widow." My grandmother raised all five of her children for many years as a single, struggling parent.

We found out through the hard investigative work of Jim Sigmund that my Grandfather John left the state to marry another woman in Chicago and had another family, and he was not dead at all! When this occurred, the historical records proved that my grandmother moved from the saloon, and she bought the house next door where we lived as a family and where Victor, myself, and baby Richard were born. Later, the saloon that my grandparents operated was purchased by the Klucho family, and they fulfilled their American Dream; being immigrants from Slovakia, they owned and operated a family neighborhood grocery store.

Eventually, the house my grandmother purchased was handed down to the children, and she put our names in her Will, not my parents, because my parents were so poor. She was fearful the house would be taken away from her son, and his wife, Mercedes, and the children would be out living on the streets. My grandmother was right because so many times, my father and I had to make another appearance in court with threats of taking the house away because of back taxes that were never paid. The courts could never do anything to the children, and we lingered on. Our grandmother had extraordinary visions of caring for her son's family even when she was long gone. Our grandmother died in 1947, one year after I was born.

Both of our parents struggled to keep our family alive and all together when society, at the **TIME**, believed that all Deaf people lived under the scrutiny and false connotation of being **"DEAF AND DUMB!"** However, my father was brilliant and **DEAF**, with no speech and no hearing, and was non-educated, but he was smart and could fix anything. He would pick up "treasures" that he would find in hopes that he could sell someday for a profit. Ironically, some of these treasurers were highly-priced, even rare "antiques." But nothing was ever made of it, and many things were stolen from him, and he or the family never reaped the value of his many treasures and pieces of junk. That is why the Health Department would get after him to clean things out, for all these accumulations of his treasures and junk were a big attraction to rats. Several times, as a young child, I had to appear in our downtown court in which our father was warned to clean up or go to jail and that social services would take the children away. My parents' life was doomed, and there was always no relief in sight. This was a very tough experience for me as a young child, acting on their behalf as their interpreter, translating what was said so my dad could understand and heed the fatal warnings the judge gave him. It was a sad experience, but it inspired me to become an Interpreter for the Deaf, which is how I made my living working through college years later. As sad as it was for me, it was even more traumatic for my sisters when they helped them out. Liz should have been appearing in court to support them, but my sisters were in school during the many court hearings.

Our mother, Mercedes Meyer Magley Stupavsky, was a hero, and she was in history books. She was born in Bellevue, Ohio, and it was discovered that she was one of the first babies to survive such a tiny birth in 1909. She was born not even two pounds and was, as we were told, kept in an oven in a shoebox while she was at home to serve as an incubator. She went to a natural incubator and was the first premature baby to survive such a premature birth in an incubator in that part of Ohio. I had done much research on our mother, and my findings were astonishing. I shared those findings in PowerPoint about her famous birth experience being kept alive in an incubator. All the brothers and sisters gathered with my niece Kim at my brother Richard's house in February 2020 to watch this incredible story. It was the last **TIME** we were together and a **TIME** I will never forget. I wrote about this in the "About this Book" section. My mother's story is amazing, and hadn't been that she survived, we would not be here to tell our stories, and there would be no **"Tin Can Lizzie,"** who is the impetus and central thrust of this storyline.

The impetus of Liz's life story as she became the **"Tin Can Lizzie,"** sometimes referred to as **"Dizzy Lizzie."** She said she used **"Dizzy Lizzie"** as a cover-up for her true identity, noting that **"Tin Can"** wouldn't look very presentable on business cards. Later in life, she didn't use the Dizzy Lizzie's name came from the numerous questions that were asked of her. Liz told me she tried to call herself that name, but it always seemed like a segment of ridicule and a questioning process.

**"Tin Can Lizzie"** was amazing. As the rest of this story goes, Lizzie lived her life in the streets of the inner city, living on Sophia Ave. You hear of the **"Survival of the Fittest,"** which was unquestionable of all the Stupavsky kids, but Lizzie was the oldest and had a challenging leadership role to follow. Our family was very poor, and our parents barely had enough food to feed all of us, but somehow, they managed, and we all survived! Yes, it is a story we would like to forget, and that is what Lizzie did in her life as she moved on and forgot her past and the role she played to survive. If you talk about living an incognito life, Liz was indeed living that life.

Liz's life experiences of **"Tin Can Lizzie"** were forgotten and locked inside her heart and mind for years until she was ready to bring her out again. She wanted to pull out that hidden life that she quickly escaped, but she kept it locked inside her for most of her life. She had cervical cancer and suffered numerous radiation treatments, and until she almost heard she could have cancer again, for it was returning, she was ready to give up. But as the pendulum swung, cancer or no cancer? It was NO CANCER. She was so sure she had cancer that the whole realization of not being plagued again could have initiated a stroke right in the doctor's office. Ultimately, Liz had three strokes that one day. Liz was taken by ambulance to the nearest Specialty stroke hospital near Clearwater, Florida. Upon arriving, the doctors began quickly taking a CAT scan of her head, which showed that Liz had three minor blockages in her brain. Having a stroke was not new to her, for she had had several mini-strokes over the years. I think the odds against my sister and my family and the quest for survival were miraculous!

But it was hopeful that before Lizzie would pass away, this story of her life would be on paper and written by none other than me. Liz and I even talked about how I could get all her words, my verbal sketches of her, what I wrote down, and heard the snippets of her life on a recording. I was going to buy her a little tape recorder, but that was my idea because it was hard to write all that she was telling me in the hospital. However, I did the best I could, and between writing notes as she rapidly spoke and after our phone conversations, I would clarify what I wrote and what I remembered as her story was revealed from my newfound sister. The following few chapters are all about the life she revealed to me. I would tell her, "You are jumping around too much!" She would tell me later when she got home, and we would work out a system for her to tell me much more. Sometimes, she would sway from the sweet **TIN CAN** character to Liz being demanding and rude, saying, "Get this done for me! I am not going to tell you again! You must do it! Just make sure you write about me and the family and our family's struggles for survival in life."

Liz repeated that there were many more secrets in her life as Lizzie and that she wanted this hidden life of **Tin Can** to be known finally. I just kept telling her it was all too much too fast, and she would say that is the way it is and end with, "What do you want me to do?" I am counting on you, Rita—you can do it." She told me I was "Smart as Hell," and she couldn't understand how that happened. She then added, "Our brother, Richie, is the smartest in the family, and when it comes to working with investments, there is no better, but you are so brilliant, and you can do it and pull out my life story." Liz was a con artist she knew how to **"CON"** people to soften them up and to get what she wanted from them. She told me her story and convinced me to write her book.

Liz would say, "I will be with you all the way. We will do it together, but the story of my life as Lizzie and then of Tin Can Lizzie has to come out to be an inspiration to many others who need encouragement to follow their dreams and to make it through their **Trials and Tribulations** that life hands out to them." She told me, "I made it, and so can they; just as I tossed the next penny and took the gamble, others can do it too. Whether I would win the pennies or not, in some way, somehow, I always was a winner, and I made it through living the life I had. It was more than just tossing the pennies to see who could knock the most cans; when we were not immersed in the game, I got to talk to them about how they can reach their dreams and be all they wanted to become." She told them," Hey guys," I am going to do it, and so will you guys!" When others go through many **Trials and Tribulations,** they can make it, too, and turn those trials and troubles into a grand winner."

Enjoy as you read the next chapter of **Here Comes Tin Can Lizzie!**

# Chapter 2

## "HERE COMES TIN CAN LIZZIE"

Today, I decided to finish more of this book and needed to hear more from Liz's heart. She was in the hospital and not feeling very well at all, and she was depressed. Liz didn't want to talk, and I could barely hear her speak over the phone. Finally, she said we could talk later, and I told her I would call her when I came home from shopping. I always called my sister Liz or Lizzie, but never in my life have I ever dream she had a nickname, **"Tin Can Lizzie,"** which was her persona and her Legend. So, I was shocked when she told me that name and wanted to name the book with **Tin Can Lizzie** in the title.

I called her back later to make small talk, and I told her I recently purchased an air fryer from TV, and she asked me what kind. I told her, and then she told me she was buying the big one from the famous cook on TV, and she said it even cooks a turkey.

She said, "I want one of those so badly, but Kim said, No, I couldn't get one. But I will get one, and for this Thanksgiving, I am cooking a big turkey in my new cooker that does everything. I am going to have everyone over at my house for dinner. My lease in my Florida condo runs out in October, so I might have to have the big Thanksgiving Feast at my new home. So, tell everyone to prepare for that day and make no other plans."

On Thanksgiving 2019, our brother, Richard, and his wife, Joann, hosted the family dinner at his country club. Attendees included Rich's daughter Erica, Richard Jr. and his wife Katie, Jonathan and his wife Kristen, as well as Richard's grandchildren Liam and Carrigan, my sisters Dorothy and Liz, and Liz's daughter Kim. The dinner was enjoyable, and Kim recorded a video of everyone signing a message to their Aunt Dr. Rita.

"Our Mom and Dad would have been so proud to see those hands signing and fingerspelling for the video. I also got a chance to talk to Katie about Real Estate. We had so much in common; she was so smart! I love that lady and wish her the best in our field of Real Estate; I pray for her health. I enjoyed talking with everyone on that special Thanksgiving in 2019 at Brother Richard's Country Club. It was lovely—a nice day to remember and a **TIME** to get to know my brother's children and grandchildren better! It was a great Thanksgiving dinner that I will always remember, and I was delighted!"

Today, Liz and I talked longer than planned because the nurse came and wanted more blood from Liz. I told her I would call her back after running into the store, getting what I needed, and running out. I didn't make it out much with the Coronavirus, but I had to run and get done what I needed to do that day.

I called her back when I got home, and she said she was waiting for my call. So, I asked her if she felt more up to telling her what she wanted in her book.

She perked up so fast and said, "Book! You know I am ready to tell you more about that book you will get published, sister Rita."

I told her," I have Chapter One all completed of your beginning, and I touched on the family as you wanted me to write on, and I needed a transition to Chapter Two. I even read Chapter One to her over the phone.

Liz said, "It's great! I love it! I knew you could do it!" I was so puzzled when she told me the name of this book, and I didn't understand why she would want such a far-fetched title. I even tried to get her to make sure that was the title she wanted. I told her it was such a strange title, and people wouldn't understand why she gave it such a name.

Liz replied, "Of course, it is my name, and will be a big seller! Did you ever think I would have such an interesting, attractive, and unusual name?"

I replied, Liz, of course not! I would never even dream you would have a nickname, period!"

I began today by asking her," As far back as you can remember, what do you remember about your young life living on Sophia? You never wanted to talk about that part of you."

She said, "That early life was too painful to remember! All I remember is that I had to get out of that house! I hated that house!"

Front and back views of the Sophia House. You had to go outside to enter into the attic and the cellar which both were full of junk—and treasures that father found and was saving.

I couldn't stay in that house! The windows were permanently closed. I felt smothered and needed fresh air no matter the **TIME** of year. I needed to breathe, to forget, and to feel free! We had rats running up and down inside walls at night—we could hear them. So, Daddy made us keep the windows locked. He even nailed the windows shut because of the rats and the many burglaries in the neighborhood. I feared a rat would come out of hiding and bite me."

I asked her, "I thought you said you never remembered the rats. Did you, after all?"

She said, "Trust Me, I indeed did, but I wouldn't allow myself to remember them and surely not to admit that I did to you and sister Dorothy. I had many memories that were hidden deep inside of me. Yes, rats were coming into the house from all the junk and wood Daddy had in the yard."

"In the summer, it was so hot I had to go out and breathe the fresh air and forget who I was, and I could dream. I had no toys to play with as other children did on the street—no dolls, no skates, no bicycle to ride—none of us did. I had nothing to do but get out of that house and find something to **ESCAPE**. We all felt that same need to **"Get Out"** and be on our own and have a better life. I was very young; I don't remember how old I was exactly. I was a lot younger than the other kids playing in the streets, and I was young when I became the **"Tin Can Girl!"** I just fitted myself in the crowd. I had a lot of boldness and courage behind me, and I wanted to be accepted not where I lived but who I was! I was born to be the **Tin Can Girl** at a very young age, and finally, I stepped out into the streets and embraced my title and my secret life! Instantly, I felt the strength and courage to **OVERCOME** my **Trials and Tribulations** and all my heartaches when I took those first steps. When I was Tin Can, it was the start of being all I was born to become!"

A YOUNG TIN CAN LIZZIE JUST ABOUT THE AGE WHEN SHE FIRST BECAME **THE TIN CAN GIRL** TO ROLL OR TO PITCH THOSE PENNIES IN THE STREET OF SOPHIA WHILE PLAYING WITH THE BOYS

"Now I feel I need to **ESCAPE** again, and I want to return to the life I created for myself and be free. I know that **TIME** is near, but I am not ready yet because we must finish this book, and I must say my goodbyes. Please, sister Rita, I need you to write this book and get my story published. Please write about the hardships we all went through and about the trials and suffering our family went through. I know you know the story. I will tell you more about me. You fill in the rest of the family's story. With this knowledge, you are the only person I trust and can handle such an assignment."

Liz continued to say. "You told me and predicted I wouldn't have cancer again. You were right, and I wasn't," but I still have some health problems. So now they want to do a colonoscopy on me and figure out why I have so much diarrhea, pain, and internal bleeding."

I had to lead her back to her story—I didn't want her to stray from this burning question I was pressing on her about how and why she had this unusual name. As far as I know, I had never heard of this name, and no one else had either.

Liz said, "You are the first to hear who I am and why. I trust you. I wanted this to be a big secret to my girls, grandchildren, family, and friends."

So, Liz said, "When I was so sad and depressed, I had nothing else to do but to run out of the house. A crowd of kids always hung out by Klucho Store, expecting me to do that, as I always did. I had to do something to get my mind off that house, our hunger, our parents' deafness, and our poverty. So, I ran out and yelled, **Here Comes Tin Can Lizzie**! I am going to win those pennies today! They loved hearing me say those words and were waiting for me to yell my title! So, I would say, "**Tin Can** is back here today; let's go for it!"

"Before you knew it, an intense game would start with several boys who hung out on the street. We would take turns pitching those pennies to get those cans knocked down." She said, I always set up the cans because the other players ordered me to do so, and I didn't mind—I loved it!"

Lizzie said, "I collected tin cans, washed them out, and kept a stash of them to be ready to go. The whole idea of me trying to hit the most cans down and getting the most pennies filled my being. I was positive I would win, even when they robbed me of my pennies. Yeah, more pennies or not, I was a **WINNER**, and I learned, as the theme of this book we are writing says, "When life gets unbearable, there is always a way out!" I needed to think the darkness wasn't going to get me, but I was going to get the darkness and be an **OVERCOMER!**"

Liz said, "At one's lowest moments, when you want to end it all, you must remember and **OVERCOME** whatever you're going through. Whenever I felt my lowest, I would remember those days of being so happy, and it would snap me back and bring me to the reality that I could get through anything I was facing. I love who I was, and I crawled into the life I had created for myself—a life of escaping the old and bringing in the new, even though I was aware that this life wouldn't last long and I had to return to being myself.

But it was OK, and it got me through the pain. It was my total **ESCAPE** and gave me comfort and strength!"

AN OLDER TEENAGE **TIN CAN** AS SHE PLAYED IN THE STREETS WITH THE BOYS!

I believe it gave me peace and a fulfilled life. I would get those pennies, and someday I would be rich and help others!"

"My life on the streets filled my entire being, mind, and spirit. I forgot about everything else. I had a new identity and loved it, even if it didn't last long. You might even say that I was **"Street Smart!"** I could survive. It was an **ESCAPE**, allowing me to **DREAM** as they engulfed my being and spirit. While trying to win and pitch those pennies, I entered my new life with new parents, a new family, and a new me! Everything became new. I honestly was born again, living in a world without deaf parents, hunger, poverty, and pain."

It would be a life I wouldn't lose but be the **WINNER** and win more pennies with more success. I knew it, and even if I didn't win that day and those games, it was OK—I was still so happy! It was the drive that made me who I was in my life. So even though I was losing on the penny tosses, the boys would quit before me, and I would set up the cans and beg them for another game. When I outplayed them, and they would leave on me, I would tell them. I'll get you guys next **TIME**! Look out! I am going to beat the pants off of you!"

Liz said, "Then, I would go get the girls and play jump rope with Claire Klucho, Sandy Runyon, and some other girls." When the girls had to go inside, I still hung around the streets trying to stir up another tin can game. The girls I played with never recognized me by my **"TIN CAN"** name, which is how I wanted it. I would keep looking around and walking around the neighborhood, trying to find something to do and some action, for I didn't want to go back inside that depressing house again. Never, Never, Never!"

Lizzie said, "Before long, all the kids started calling me **"Tin Can Lizzie,"** representing the life I created for myself with the boys on the street. It was contagious, and they picked up on it very quickly."

She said, "I loved being recognized and called by that name, for it confirmed what my future would be like. I was engulfed in happiness when others would see and think of me as a **"Winner and a Somebody,"** even if I called myself by that name. It gave me hope and the strength to survive. My prize was entirely caught up in this new name and be respected! I loved that life of who I truly was. That was my Prize! I want to walk into that life again without any sadness, worries, hunger, or sickness; that is what I want to do. Yes, I will yell, **"Here Comes Tin Can Lizzie!"** and I want to start a new game."

Liz said, "I ended every big game when the boys would give up on me and end their penny tosses. I would walk by the front of the family Klucho store to ask Mr. Klucho for a few bologna slices and take the ends he gave me. Pitching and tossing those pennies did work up a hunger. Whatever bologna that was given, I shared with the boys. Then they would tell me to go to the store and get them some more meat, but Mr. Klucho would shove me out, and he would shake his finger at me and yell, "I give you, give you all that I have, you go, go!"

"The store next to our house was our very existence, and it was our life. It was back in the days of **OLD** when neighborhood stores were everywhere on the streets before the big grocery stores opened. I also played cards with the boys and the other kids that hung on the street, and it was all to win or lose a few more pennies."

Liz said, "Every game with my treasured pennies was a new challenge and a new deal to complete, even if it was just to give "pep talks" to all the boys. It was getting to the point that the boys were telling me

their problems, but theirs were nothing compared to what we had to go through in our life. However, I gave it my best "shot," and I could tell that the boys would be listening intently to what I had the boys would be listening intently to what I had to say. I thought they were all "**Crybabies**" and were **Selfish**, for they had so much more than our family had, but they still complained. They never went to bed hungry, I am sure, like we did. I would set them straight, too, at times, and I think they wanted to yell out when they saw me running out to the street, **"Here comes trouble!"** They wouldn't dare, even though I thought I heard them say that once, and did I set them straight!"

"Sometimes, as we all got older, the conversations were on sports, but I told them, "Enough of that! The only sports here are the penny tosses. So, let us see what you can do. The only thing I would do was they invited me to play baseball in the Klucho backyard, but Mrs. Klucho would come out and yell, "You gonna break a store window out!" She would take the broom and push us back to the street, where the boys would yell at me, **"Setup the cans, Miss Tin Can!"**

"Occasionally, the boys and I would go to the churchyard in the school parking lot and play baseball. When I would run out of the house and saw no one, I knew that they were up playing baseball, and I would run up the street, and when I got there, I would yell, "**HERE COMES TIN CAN LIZZIE!**" when is it my turn to throw the ball?" I went from tossing the pennies to tossing a baseball, and they didn't mind me playing, especially if they were shorthanded. I also liked that and didn't care, as long as I didn't have to bat the ball or run the bases."

As we talked, I tried to discern who my sister was, for I never saw her in this light of having this name and secret life as she poured out to me. She was someone else and not my big sister, Liz. I didn't know this person at all. I could never have a smooth conversation with her. She always picked on me and was very rude to me in our later life. This was a different person! As I said in the Preface, Liz said, "She didn't remember her past." I think she just hid it away and her many secrets as well.

When the subject came of growing up on Sophia Ave, Liz always claimed that she couldn't remember a thing and hid everything deep inside, and indeed that was not the case. She recognized these accounts of her life and our family's existence and how it was indeed. I could only think to myself, "What happened to my sister? What is going on with her?"

Today, she told me many other tidbits of discovery while listening to her as I tried to write it all down. Liz went on to say that when they finished pitching pennies, and she won nothing in the hot days of summer, she and the gang would go and raid neighbors' gardens to see if they could find ripe tomatoes, cucumbers, or something else to eat."

I asked her, "Was our sister, Dorothy, ever in these street games or hanging out times with the boys?"

She replied," Dorothy wasn't in these challenges. Indeed, that was not her way of enjoyment, or she felt she didn't need an **ESCAPE** like I did to get out of the house. She stayed home caring for Richard, our younger brother, and always helping our mother. She did most of the cooking, and our father would go to the farms and bring home several sacks full of potatoes that were kept on the back porch all the **TIME** and lasted even in the cold winter. Dorothy would make us potato pancakes, and I would help her sometimes but not always."

I then asked my sister if Dorothy or anyone else from the family knew of your existence of the *"Tin Can Lizzie."* She got mad at me and said, "No, No!" I told you—don't tell anyone! They have to read the book! They won't believe it, and they may think I made this all up, and that is undoubtedly not the case! Wait until they hear of this news. We will tell them together after the book is published! That will be so much fun, and I can't wait!"

Liz said, "I had to work hard for a Jewish family, and I had to walk to their home, which was far, and it was so dark, for it was so early in the morning. I was tired, and when I finally arrived at their house, I would sleep on their steps in the cold until they opened the door to let me in. My job was to prepare their kids for school, dress them, feed them, and clean up the house afterward. Then, I would walk in the cold in the snow or rain to go to school myself. I had to do that, and whatever small coins they gave me, I changed into pennies to play my games. We even played in the winter! When the snow was so deep, we would shovel the area in the street and pitch those pennies to see who could knock down the most cans." Then she added, "Rita, I had to work to earn those pennies to be able to toss and knock down those cans!"

Liz said, "By now, I was earning quite a reputation on the streets of being this famous **"Tin Can Girl."** I was starting to branch out to the Mt. Auburn area neighborhood, several streets over from Sophia, and before you knew it, the word got out, and I didn't have to say that I was there—they said to me. **"Here Comes Tin Can Lizzie"** as soon as they laid their eyes on me. But, most importantly, they all knew me, and even more significantly, they knew my name and reputation, even though I didn't know or remember their names right now as I was speaking. So, I became very popular with the boys all around the neighborhood. Oh, I loved being so well known by everyone of all ages wherever I would go!"

She said, "So when you ask how far I can remember when I was young, I told you the life I led as Elizabeth, Liz, Lizzie, and my biggest secret life as *"Tin Can Lizzie."* There is more to discuss about my younger days, but I will hold on for another **TIME** and move on with more new stuff. You asked me what some of the unfortunate things I can remember are. Life was just so sad, and we were thankful for whatever food we got, but I have to say we were rough and tough and all hung on the streets. No one messed with me, and better yet, I liked who I was, and I was really popular in the neighborhood!"

Liz said, "Getting pennies to play with the guys wasn't easy. I had to labor hard with the family. I worked to get those pennies and be the **"Tin Can Queen!"** How else could I support my image if I didn't have pennies? I had to prove to them that I was good to go. I remember the boys repeatedly asking me to show them how many pennies I had in my pocket. I said, "That is awful!" Oh, you know who I am! I was so mad and yelled at those guys, saying, "You guys always trusted me before—why not now? Are you trying to ruin my image? Come on now! When *"Tin Can Lizzie"* comes out for a new game and yells, **"Here Comes Tin Can Lizzie,"** you better know I am ready for a new hot game, respect, and why would I come without pennies? I was stern with them, and from that moment forward, they never questioned me again if I had the pennies to play with. I showed them that I was the **"Boss Queen,"** and they were not to mess with me. I sternly told them, "When I yell out, **"HERE COMES TIN CAN LIZZIE,"** I told them, you better be serious and watch your backs! You don't want me to check to see if you have the pennies to toss, and I could make you guys hand them over without a match!" From that day forward, the guys would wait for me to come out of the house, and then they would say, "Move over, set up the cans, because **"HERE COMES, TIN CAN LIZZIE!"** She is here! Let's get started on the next game! Then, they all yelled, "OK, Tin Lizzie," they sometimes called me and said, we are sorry, and we're ready for you!"

Liz said, "I think that incident showed the guys they couldn't mess with me and doubt my words. It showed them, and it showed me that I could *"Sell and Convince"* anyone what I wanted to sell, no matter what it was, even if it was a tin can full of car motor oil. My **"Tin Can"** experiences gave me the courage and hope to be what I wanted to become. I think that incident of the boys questioning was proof I was a born **"Salesperson,"** and I could convince anyone to listen to me and not mess with me." Therefore, no one knows this, but whenever I went into an "Open House as part of a real estate listing, I would pray and say, **"Here Comes Tin Can Lizzie,"** most of the **TIME**, I got the sale!

I was born to sell, whether convincing people to sell them something, having people invest in property, or going forth with a rental. The only problem was that sometimes I would get carried away with keeping my **"Eye on the Prize"** and forget to remind myself who I truly was!"

"Then again, sometimes I would spend the profit before I even got it. You know, I love going shopping! But I was playing out my role, and when I walked into a store, you bet the salespeople knew me, and they would yell out, "Here comes Lizzie, our favorite shopper!" They would start conversations with me and show me the latest fashion in the store." Sometimes, I would use my other name and yell, "Here comes Dizzy Lizzie," and we would all laugh in the store! But if they only really knew!" However, I always made a **"Grand Entrance!"** It was my trademark to ask any of our family members and friends. They will confirm that entrance." Dr. Rita, I still do that today when I walk into a place and say, **"I Am Here!"** It is just me and part of my nature of who I am! Please tell all my family members, friends, and business partners that when I am gone someday to the heavens, I want everyone to know and always remember that I am not just a sister, a friend, a mother, or Grandma Liz. I want to be known as "Lizzie, **The Tin Can Girl who was a Survivor!** When they read our book, they will know how much I love them, and when I am gone, they need to follow my wishes and remember me as the famous **Tin Can Lizzie!**"

In closing this amazing Chapter Two, the key to the whole story is my sister, Liz, and how she used her role as the Tin Can Girl to **OVERCOME** her many trials, tribulations, and sad days. Then I reminded her, "Whenever we had family get-togethers, you would come in late and say with your arms raised, "I am here!"

She responded, "Oh yes, that is what I said all my life, and it is a joke within the family, but I wanted to raise my arms and say, **"Here Comes Tin Can Lizzie, I am here!"** I did say it a few times, and no one even paid attention, so who would understand the real connection and true meaning of the real-life of **"Tin Can Lizzie?"** I knew my day would come when I could make the big announcement! I guess my **TIME** was not right to break the news of my name and bits of my life to everyone, but it will be soon when they read our book! So please, my dear family and friends, never let **TIME** control you, so you don't have

**TIME** to love and enjoy each other. My Family and friends think of me as who I am and that I will never leave you when I am gone someday. I will keep you in my heart, mind, and soul, so please don't forget me, and keep me in your heart forever!

"I hope everyone enjoys reading a bit of my story. **"HERE COMES TIN CAN LIZZIE!** But please know my true story of *"Tin Can Lizzie"* is more than my life, Legend, or Tribute. That name kept me alive; I was determined, strong, and a leader! It was my very being and my entire existence, and I learned to embrace it!

# Chapter 3

## SISTERHOOD

**OUR HIGHLIGHTS ARE OF THE THREE OF US TOGETHER AS WE LIVED, LAUGHED, LOVED, AND BONDED IN THE LIVES OF OUR SISTERHOOD.**

Sisters (about 1950): Dorothy and Rita, and Liz with her cross-over purse in which she kept all her pennies. She even slept with that purse! This is the earliest picture that we have of us together when we were young.

I began my phone conversation today with my sister, asking her what she wanted to discuss today. She said, "There are always stories of sisterhood, and I have plenty of them to share about my sister, Dorothy. I have some news to share about you, too, Rita, but not that much, for you didn't live with us all the **TIME** at home. You never really bugged me when you were so young. You were cute as a button, and what happened to you at a very young age was very sad. Your foster parents took good care of you and dressed you so nicely. Whenever we did see you after a long **TIME** had passed, you were so adorable!"

I quickly snapped at her and said, "Liz, what do I do to bug you now, and if so, how?"

Liz replied, "Yes, sometimes you do get on my nerves. You are always ready to talk and show me pictures, and I am just too busy to look at them, which I think I never gave you a chance until recently."

"Whereas Dorothy and I were best buddies, she bugged me half to death at times and was "bossy" to me in our younger days. I think she was tired of doing all the cleaning and cooking work in Sophia's home. I invited her to come out and play with the girls at the Klucho Store, but no way. She stayed in the house all the **TIME**. We did play together a bit, but Dorothy was always busy with household chores and family survival. But not me! I was a free **"Butterfly,"** ready to fly whenever needed."

Liz was in a positive mood in our new conversation and was on a roll. I got a kick out of talking about these things, especially when she told me, "Dr. Rita, I know you could get our story into a real live book form! You will get the help you need and make the right contacts with publishers, won't you? I know you can do it, and you love all my stories, and talking with you is so relaxing and relieving. All my life, I had these stories and secrets inside of me, and now I am getting them out to you and everyone else. You can see why you were the only person who could get my stories into a real book form, right? Now, you are not cutting out on me, are you?"

I said, "No, Liz, I am not! A deal is a deal!"

Then she shouted, "Wait a minute! What is my name?" I yelled to her, **"Tin Can Lizzie,"** of course!"

Then she said, "I think you got the big picture by now, and everyone can call me the **"Tin Can Queen"** if they like!"

She was laughing and said, "Easy! I don't have to do a thing! You are doing it when they read this book that we are writing. She laughed and laughed and said, "I can just see it now!" Kimmy and Dorothy will be the hardest ones to convince, and that is what I don't want to happen when I am gone someday."

"Well," I told her, "Liz, your life has been a miracle, dear sister, and you still have years left. We will work on this book project together t when you get home. Got it?"

She said," Now, I can hardly wait to get home when Kimmie gets me out of here so we can get down to real business. I will not let **TIME** get away from me, no way. I have to beat the clock and try to stop it ticking!"

Liz went on to talk more about Dorothy. "When we were growing up on Sophia, living in poverty, Dorothy and I were always close to each other. I can remember Dorothy and I sleeping together in one twin bed. She would sleep one way on the bed, and I would sleep the other. We learned not to kick each other, which is how we slept in the Sophia house. We learned how to get along together while in the house as well. We would lay in bed and listen to the rats running up and down our inside walls. We both were so scared and screamed out at night. It was scary!"

She was on a positive roll! She added, "We were close together in the Sophia house."

I asked her," Did Dorothy play the penny tosses with you outside with the boys?"

She replied, "Oh, no! She would look out and see me doing it, but she never did it. I asked her to try it, and she thought it was too silly of me to play in the street with the boys tossing pennies and knocking down dirty old tin cans. She wanted me to help out in the house more, but I stayed there the least amount of **TIME** so that I could be **"Miss Madame Butterfly!"** Dorothy would get mad at me, but sometimes, I think she wanted me out of her hair to have peace and do what she wanted (much better than me)."

"Our parents were deaf, and they couldn't hear the rats, but we sure did, and there was no getting away from the scratching and running noises those rats made. We couldn't get up to go to the bathroom, so we learned to hold it until morning when it was light outside. I would pull our father to the bedroom and gesture, pointing to the wall that rats were running up and down. I put it all in **"Full Motion"** the best I could do, and he would wave his hand to me like I was crazy and walk away."

I added, "Liz, I think he did that a lot, especially when I was older, and I brought my future husband, Dennis, to our house on Sophia. Dennis noted that when Mom was mad at Daddy and was signing to him, Dad would sit back in his easy chair, pull the newspaper to cover his eyes, and hide from her anger as she yelled at him with her gestures. Dennis couldn't believe how calm Daddy was and just covered his eyes. It was the same with the rats or anything else he didn't want to deal with. He would walk away or cover his eyes. I guess that is the advantage of being deaf. It wasn't that Dad didn't know you were telling him there were rats in the walls, and he didn't want to deal with it. He had to see them in the backyard by the woodpiles he saved to build a garage someday."

Liz jumped in on the conversation and said, "He didn't have a car in those days, so why did he need a garage? But later in life, when I was older, he did get a car. He had a station wagon to lug around all the kids in the back seat, and ultimately more junk— some treasured nonsense finds to cause a bigger commotion in the yard, attic, and basement."

I told her, "Liz, I remember hearing and feeling the walls shake because of those rats, too. I would close my eyes and go to sleep. When I was five years old, my foster parents took me back home to the Sophia house, and I lived there until I was ten years old. Mom and Dad had taken your twin bed away and put all of us—all three sisters in a double bed. I remember I slept between you and Dorothy. I had to "pee" one night, and I was so scared that I wouldn't get up to go to the bathroom, which was off the kitchen, and I wet the bed. I never told you and Dorothy what I did, and when you and she went to bed that night, the bed was all wet! You both were so mad at me for not telling you or Dorothy before we went to bed! I can't remember if you both took the sheets off or what. I don't think we had extra sets of sheets as most people did."

Liz said, "I am sure Dorothy washed the sheets and blankets the next morning. She wouldn't let that go as I would and be too lazy to wash the sheets and make up the beds."

Liz remembered, "When our brother Richard was born, Dorothy took care of him and would walk him in his stroller up and down the street of Sophia Ave. She was so proud of him and would show him off to the old foreign people on the street. Dorothy would walk him to the Runyan house, where Sandra's mother, Irene, would take him out of the stroller and play with him. At that **TIME**, our mother was very sick because of having a child so late in life—she had a rough **TIME**. I should have helped more in the house, but I didn't. Not me! I was out making deals with friends and seeing our plans when I got home from school."

Liz continued, "I would get up and walk up to Shaker Boulevard in the dark and sleep on the steps of the family's home where I worked until they would open the door and let me in. It was so freezing in the winter, and I couldn't wait for them to open the door. Then, I had to wake the children, dress them, cook them breakfast, pack their lunches, and get them off to school. Then, I would walk to school myself to St. Benedict's School. When I got to school, I was so tired that I would fall asleep; the nuns were always mean to me and gave me spoiled milk to drink. They would yell at me for falling asleep while in class," she concluded.

As Liz talked, I could not help but remember my **childhood**. I was thankful for the day our neighbor, Joey Klucho, wanted us to write to his nephew, Jim Sigmund, to assist me in locating our families on both our mother's and father's sides. As a researcher, I did massive investigative work to determine who I was and where my roots were. I will never forget what happened to me growing up and the day those people came and took me, or shall I say, **"Snatched Me Away!"**

Liz said, "Oh, my sister Rita, I remember you when you were taken away from us. I will never forget that day! We never knew what happened to you. I wondered why you just disappeared from us, and we thought we would never see you again for years and years. We were all so sad!"

I told my sister, "But Liz, it was the entrance to my life with my family and as a Christian. God had his hands in my life, leading me to my future so I wouldn't end badly. My basic needs were provided with a secure home, plenty of food, and clothes. I was in the fifth grade when I went back to my foster parents to go to school over on the west side, and that is where I met my husband Dennis when I was in high school. It was love at first sight! He was on the football and track team and a star at throwing the shot put."

"But Liz, it was a nightmare for me, too, recognizing having two sets of parents, one of our family and one of the foster family that I lived with. My Foster parents, Mike and Bernice, were strict with me but took good care of me. I cared for them in their later years as I did with our parents. This journey of caregiving and responsibility shaped us into the people we are today.

Liz told me, "But wait, I will never forget the day those people took you away from us, Rita. You screamed and screamed and wanted our mother. We didn't know what was happening and thought we would never see you again. Everyone on Sophia Ave ran out of their houses to see why Rita was screaming. Those people caused a neighborhood uproar, and you were the main attraction! That man and the woman just picked you up and shoved you in their big black car, and you were only three years old."

Liz said, "It was sad when they came and took you away. You were my baby sister, and you just disappeared!" You were so cute, and the lady always fixed you up so sweetly. You always wore a pretty dress. I remember you had sandals on your feet; they were red and so cute. Your hair was so pretty the way she fixed it on you. You were adorable, everyone in Sophia loved you, and you were quiet and sweet. You spoke with your big dark brown eyes. Many of the neighbors approached me and told me how much they enjoyed watching Rita as she stared at all the delivery trucks that came up to the Klucho store. They would always wave to you as if you were always sitting on the front porch steps, and then you would wave and smile back at them. They would always say, "Hello, Rita! Are you having fun today?" You would nod your head up and down and always had a huge smile."

1949: This is me at three years old, when I was taken away
from my family at the Sophia house.

"You were gone, and I had to answer questions from all the neighbors and my **Tin Can** friends. Even the girls asked me, "Where is little Rita? Did something happen to her? Is she alive? The kids that played in the street and everyone walking to the store just knew you would always be sitting on those front porch steps, enjoying the hustle-bustle and the view."

I replied to Liz, "All these years, you never told me this, and I never thought you were so bothered and sad by me being taken away. I don't know what to say to you. I am shocked that you remember all this now in such detail. Thank you for sharing this with me. I will always remember you telling me this. Thank you so very much. I am so touched, and you can't see, for you are in the hospital, but I have tears rolling down my cheeks!"

Liz said, "Rita, Rita, Rita (she would often repeat my name when she wanted me to pay attention); listen, I always wanted to tell you this, and now that I am in the hospital, I had to tell you. I loved you dearly since you were a little girl, and I was your big sister. It has been on my mind for so long, and when I got mad at you, it was because I wanted to tell you and couldn't do it. I thank you for understanding. When you left the first **TIME**, everyone was so sad that you left the front steps that you sat on every day, just looking and watching all the action in the street and all the people going to the Klucho Store."

"You have to understand, too. We didn't know what was happening and thought we would never see you again. You screamed and pounded on the window to get out. We saw your little face looking out the window as they pulled out and drove down the street. We were running after their car, waving at you, and you kept pounding until you were out of sight!"

She told me, "You were very fortunate to have foster parents, Mike and Bernice, to care for you when you were young. Dr. Rita, how old were you when you returned to us?"

I told her, "My foster parents were so very good to me, and I took care of them later in life until they passed away. But I returned to the Sophia house when I was five years old and ready for kindergarten, and I immensely enjoy sitting back on the 9805 Sophia steps, watching and enjoying the action at the store. I loved sitting on those front steps, and Mommy and Dorothy would sign and motion to me, "Must come, come house!" That was my life and how I acquired my visual language, which worked toward my advantage in my later years. I told Liz I always wanted to return to the Sophia house and sit on those steps again to see what I could recall—later in my life, I did that!"

Liz said, "Wow, I always wanted to do that! But I never got the chance as you did."

I exclaimed in a loud voice, "Liz, come on now! You hated that house; why would you want to go back there? You always ran out of that house!"

Liz said sadly, "I know, but I always think about it!" I think about those days when I was **The Tin Can Girl** almost every day. I would like to see how I would feel to see that house again. However, I don't think I could leave Florida and travel to Ohio now. But for you, Rita, I always remember the day you were "**Snatched Away**" in the neighborhood, and I will never forget it.

I reminded Liz again about the story being in the book about myself, which I started writing a while ago. I must finish it, but this story about you and our family takes precedence.

Liz said, "Oh yeah, I remember you never used your voice much when you were little. Many people asked me if my sister Rita was deaf like our parents."

I told Liz, "I stayed at the Sophia house, and I would be taken back to the foster parent's house during the summers against my will. I wanted to return to my real family; therefore, I taught myself to take the rapid transit and then take a bus to Sophia Ave. I just wanted to go home to see everyone. I was lonely, too, and missed every one. I wouldn't allow **TIME** to go by without seeing my family. My foster parents had no other children, just me."

1953, Here is Rita on her First Holy Communion Day.

Liz commented, "Our sister Dorothy did have much the same type of life as you had for a short while when she lived with our Aunt Dorothy Porter on the west side. Our aunt was from our mother's side of the Meyer family. Dorothy came back and forth but had to stay home at the Sophia house after our youngest brother, Richard, was born. I do remember Mom was very sick after her mother passed away, plus she was pregnant with our brother Richard. Dorothy had to care for Richard, and she helped out in the family, for our mother remained ill."

"Dorothy was named after our Aunt Dorothy, a relative to the Meyer side of the family. Aunt Dorothy took good care of our sister Dorothy as well. Aunt Dorothy knew of a couple who wanted to care for a child. She arranged for Bernice and Mike, who took and cared for you, Rita. I remember Dorothy making her First Holy Communion at St. Benedict's Church and getting a gorgeous First Communion dress and veil. Dorothy looked so pretty! Her Aunt Dorothy even took her to a fancy photographer to take her picture. I made my First Holy Communion a special day for me. I felt very much that God was protecting me. The church gave me my First Communion dress and veil; I remember that all right!"

I replied, "Liz, I also made my First Communion at St. Benedict's Church. My foster parents bought me my dress, and someone took pictures of you and me in the backyard at the Sophia house. I lived at the Sophia house then and stayed there until the 5th grade. Then I had to go back to live with my foster parents, and I stayed there and lived with them until I got married to Dennis in 1965."

Liz replied, "You, Dorothy, and I made our First Holy Communion at different times at St. Benedict's Church. Dorothy wore a fancy dress and veil and had her picture taken nicely, but for me, this picture was the most incredible memory of that day! Yes, we could call it **"Sisterhood;"** we made our Communion at different times in different years, but we were united and joined by Christ. Rita, you and I didn't get a professional photographer to take our pictures, but Dorothy did, and I think she deserved prime treatment for all the work she did in the house! Wouldn't you think?"

1947, Here is sister Liz in the backyard at the Sophia house on her First Holy Communion Day.

1949, Here is sister Dorothy when she made her First Holy Communion

I told Liz, "Well, Liz, it is nice that we had our joint union with Christ at our First Holy Communion, and our days were very different. Dorothy and I had someone to buy our dress and veil, and Dorothy Jane even got her picture taken in a photo studio. But later, I will go through my pictures at home, find them, hold them together, and compare how we three sisters looked on our special day. When I find them, I will let you know, and you and I could put them in our book next to each other when I talk about us three nutty Stupavsky sisters. It will be fun! You Think? Maybe we can remember the day when we made our Holy Communion. I remember when I had my Holy Communion with our brother Victor. We made it together. So, I remember that day very clearly."

Liz said, "I think it will be nice to try and find those pictures. I think I can remember that day. I was happy, but it was just a regular day. Mom, Dad, and Godmother Alice attended my ceremony at church. I remember someone donated that dress and veil. I couldn't wait to get home, remove the dress and veil, and get out and look for action in the streets."

I said, "Liz, I am talking about when the three sisters made our First Holy Communion, not you, being the **TIN CAN** girl. Is that all you ever think about? We are talking while you are in the hospital, and I am gathering notes for our book."

Liz jumped on me and said, "Listen, Rita, that was my life and the most important thing I could do for myself back then…and now, as you write my story. For me, I enjoyed the streets being **TIN CAN.** I was a rabble-rouser, still trying to pull up a game of something—pitching pennies or playing cards with the boys, jumping rope with the girls, or playing with chalk on the sidewalks. But you were better off than living in the Sophia house with all the confusion and misunderstandings due to our parents' communication barriers, heartbreak, and the stigma of them being deaf. I always think about our parents and how I wasn't helpful to them at home on Sophia."

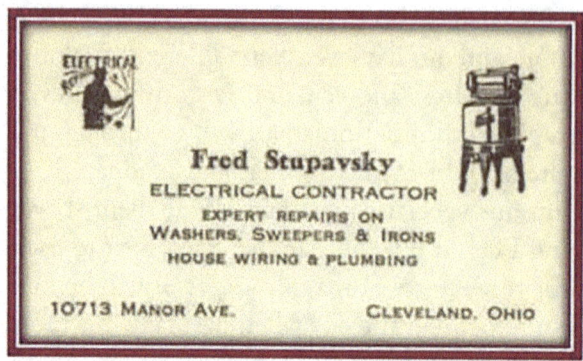

Our father's business card. Our father tried to get work so badly to take care of his family. He was good at fixing anything.

I said, "It sure did impact our lives. We couldn't **ESCAPE** our troubled, mixed-up lives, but our parents were great people, and Daddy was a hard worker, always trying to find a good job to support us. He was an excellent, self-taught electrician, but no one would hire him in the electrical field. He begged for work, and when he did work, people took advantage of him because he was deaf and didn't pay him for the good work he had done for them. Daddy worked out of his brother's house nearby, and they made business cards for him. He was a genius at fixing anything."

"Our parents were so generous to us, too. They would always give us whatever they could and put us first. When we were older, they would try to buy us little presents at Christmas **TIME**. It was because of our poverty and the deafness of our parents that we were all separated in our family, and I was taken away."

Liz said, with a chuckle, "I didn't think anyone would want me, for everyone told me I was just too ugly for another family to take me in, as you and Dorothy had been. Since I was the oldest child, I think they thought I would be okay at home to help out in the household. But not me! I didn't do a thing to help out—I was always having too much fun in the streets."

"I was happy and blessed that Alice watched over me. She lived above the Klucho Store with her parents and constantly looked out the window, watching my movements and questioning my whereabouts. Alice wasn't much older than I was—maybe about ten years older—so she was like a big sister to me!"

"I was alone in our house on Sophia when you and Dorothy were gone. It was awful and too quiet for me. I needed noise and action! I never heard voices in the house; we only used signs and body language while communicating. It was a quiet zone at all times. I would go stir-crazy and need to run and run as fast as possible, which is what I did. I started my new career as the "**Tin Can Lizzie**, which they called me for short, just "**Tin Can**.""

"Before our mother was ill and Dorothy was gone, I was out there rebelling in the streets and not helping our mother very much. I just wasn't good at it like Dorothy was. Therefore, Dorothy had to return home, and I was so happy to see and be with her again. She would bug me to stay in the house to help, but who wanted to stay there? I would run out onto the streets playing with boys. When I was supposed to stay inside, I was young and would find a way to sneak out, disappear, and look for the boys to have another game."

"Alice, my Godmother, lived upstairs above the Klucho store. She would get so mad at me all the **TIME**. She would yell at me and say, "Elizabeth, stop playing with those nasty cans! You are going to cut yourself on them, and they are dirty!" I searched for them, washed them, dried them up, and stored them. I garbage-picked them, and I got Alice so mad at me. She would watch me from the window. She sometimes found my hiding places and threw the cans in the garbage. Alice was good to me, and she was my sponsor for my Confirmation. She watched over me and ensured I would be heading in the right direction and not getting in trouble or staying out too late at night. I looked at her as a big sister, for she was very kind to me and my Godmother for my Confirmation."

Liz emphasized, "Alice was the only person who disciplined me. She didn't like me pitching those pennies in the tin cans with the boys. Liz's voice got very sad, and in a low tone, she said, "My dear Dr. Rita, I am so thankful that you could locate Alice and Sandra Runyan again. It was wonderful talking to each of them after so many years. They were in my early life, and I had never seen or talked to them in over fifty years. You located them in your quest to find people who were significant influences in our lives! I will always be grateful to you and never forget what you did for me."

"Now, I have one last request of you: Please, please, please get this book written and published quickly! That way, it can be read by so many people who knew me. If you get it done and published, they can read it before they pass away, as well as our family members- especially my girls and my grandchildren, my friends, and my business contacts, and all the people who worked for me, that did and did not like me. But they sure knew me, and they would love to hear about this wild story of the **"Real Me"** and learn about our family's hardships in growing up! I am sure everyone will think differently of me."

Liz laughed as she said all this to me, yet she said positively, "Everyone will love reading my book as they enjoy the tales and stories of the real **"Tin Can Queen!"** They will be so surprised as they never thought of me in this light of my true character and persona, proving that "Someone is not always who they appear to be in everyday life!"

I told **Tin Can,"** I like this thought of what you are saying, and it is so true. I guess none of us are as people see us in life. We never know who is behind their real faces. I agree with what you are saying! I am so proud of you for sharing these thoughts, and you sure surprised me!"

**Tin Can** said, "Then there are so many other people out there that may just pick up this book with such an attractive, catchy "hook" for a title that could save their lives somehow and in some way! They can read it, compare it to their lives, and get a meaningful and even spiritual uplift as they can apply my **ESCAPE** to something they can do in their lives. I went through some challenging **Trials and Tribulations** in my life, and I found a piece of happiness that I used to help me survive. If I could do it, so could they! It is a **"Win-Win Victory;"** it was my saving grace, and my salvation simply being **"Tin Can!"**

Liz said, "I was thinking when we talked earlier… I remember how the three of us slept together, but I don't remember you peeing on the bed. Are you sure you did that? I would have remembered, but as you and Dorothy said, I chose not to remember many things and experiences. It was probably Dorothy who washed the sheets and blankets and did what I did best—went out and found the boys! The double bed stayed on one side of the room until Mommy and Daddy saved enough money to buy bunk beds. I remember our brother Victor slept on the top bunk and Dorothy and me on the bottom twin-size bunk. It had to be way after you left us again; when you were over ten years old, you lived at your foster parents' house full **TIME**, where you went to school on the west side of town."

There were painful times as well. Liz started telling me a new story. "Dorothy and I were in St. Luke's Hospital at the same **TIME**. I had my appendix taken out, but I don't know if she got her appendix out or if it was another problem; anyway, we were in the hospital together. I remember so clearly; I was playing jump rope with Claire and the girls, and the pain was so bad on my one side I couldn't stand it anymore. One of the girls ran and motioned for Mommy to come and see for herself. I hunched down, crying in pain. I remember Mommy gesturing to Alice to come down from above the Klucho Store and see why I was crying and couldn't stand up. Alice told her parents. They drove both Dorothy and me to the hospital, for she must have been sick with something. I can't remember what it was. When I get home, I will ask her if she can remember both of us in the hospital."

Later, I asked Dorothy if it was confirmed that she and Liz were in the hospital together, and she replied, "Yes, we sure were she's telling the truth. She was in there for her appendix, and I had my tonsils taken out. I will always remember those days we were together in the same hospital room."

Liz added, "I was always sickly, for I was skinny as a rail and always pale. Later in life, I found out I was anemic. We hardly ever had good, nourishing meals in those early days and never any fruits and vegetables, and whoever heard of taking vitamins back in the day?"

I told her, "That is funny! I never heard that story of you and Dorothy in the hospital together."

She replied, "Rita, there were a lot of stories you never heard about. It was rough times in a rough "era." She reminded me I was taken away to live with foster parents; at least you always had food to eat and new clean clothes to wear!"

"But, on the other hand," I told Liz, "You think it was easy for me living with Uncle Mike and Aunt Bernice, as you called my foster parents over the years? It was not easy. They were so strict with me, and I had to do a lot in their house and cook dinner every night. They both worked, and I had a lot of chores to do. As you called him, Uncle Mike had his older mother from Bulgaria who spoke no English, and I had to watch over her while they were at work. We slept in the same bedroom, each in a twin bed. She would yell at me in Bulgarian when I turned on the light or made noises in the room. But she did love me and was always wanting a kiss from me. She smelled so bad of garlic, for she would eat it raw! To this day, I don't like garlic, and I hate the smell of garlic on anyone's breath!"

Liz laughed and laughed and said, "You are so funny, Rita! How can you remember such a thing? I thought I was the only one pulling memories out of our brains."

"Liz, you want to hear something bizarre? I told her the story that Mike's mother died in the twin bed next to me in April! We had such a blizzard on April 9th, so she laid in the bed next to my bed for three days before the funeral home could come and pick up her body. Yikes! It was something! I will never forget it! It was snowing so hard, and we had so much snow the funeral home people put her on a stretcher and carried her body out to the main road."

We laughed, and Liz said, "That must have been horrible! I would never stay in a house with a dead person—a smelly dead rat, yes, but not a real body!"

"I was always jealous of you when you were younger for having nicer new clothes, clean underwear all the time, good food, better stuff, and a better house to live in. Your foster people were older, too, but not as old as our parents; at least they could talk to you and teach you how to speak. Everyone liked it when they brought you back home to us at Christmas time. They would buy us a small, wrapped gift, usually a winter scarf, socks, or gloves, but it was nice. We were just so happy to each get a wrapped present. Aunt Bernice would give them to you, and you would hand them out to each of us."

Liz continued, "We were very poor, and how could deaf parents take care of a family?"

I replied to her, "Back in those days, people who were "Deaf" were also considered "Dumb."

Liz and I chitchatted that day, and I said to Liz, "Did you know society had deaf people labeled with the mindset that they were not capable of raising their children? I was taken away, and Dorothy was, too, but only for a short time, and then she returned. Years ago, people who were deaf were raised in state institutions and, sadly, were considered **"Mentally Retarded and Dumb Idiots."**

"I came back and forth but stayed permanently with the foster parents after I was ten years old until I got married. That is a whole other story, very painful to tell, but someday I will finish the book I started writing on my life and yours. We could both have a book out there on each of us."

Liz laughed her silly, cute little laugh and said, "We will be famous again! Just the two sisters sharing our lives with the world! You know, sister Rita, people around the **WORLD** will read our book. It will be printed in many languages. I know it; you will be so surprised and happy!"

I shared with Liz, "I started writing my own life story of my memories of not speaking, for we used American Sign Language (ASL) at home and our own "Home Signs "to communicate. We never used our voices— we would sign to each other as that was our parents' language, and we followed the rules of the house because we had no choice. Our father was strict and wanted to know what we were talking about. Therefore, we turned our voices off and kept them off until we were outside or in school. Of all the kids, I kept my voice off for longer and liked being in a peaceful world better! But we knew how to communicate our message in body language, gestures, or ASL. Our primary language was silent while I was with my family (ASL). When I lived with my foster parents, my foster father and his mother spoke Bulgarian, which was another language barrier for me to **OVERCOME**. But my foster father spoke English to his wife. No wonder it was a struggle for me in school! But I did it and worked my way through. Later in life, I went on to college to fulfill my dreams of becoming a teacher for the Deaf and all special needs children. It took me 32 years to get this Doctorate. It was a struggle, but I did it with God's Grace!"

However, when I went to school, the nuns thought that of all of us Stupavsky kids, I was the most retarded, for my language acquisition was not a spoken/verbal language but a gestural visual language. That was our first language, thus making us bilingual, with ASL as our native language. All of us siblings had a stigma hung over our heads because of our parents' deafness."

I said to Liz," Oh gosh, I remember signing to the nuns that I had to "pee" and they would walk away from me, and then I wet my pants right in the corner of the classroom. I made the sign "toilet," and I was ignored. I was always put in the corner of the classroom, for the nuns would say that Rita was the slowest and dumbest of the Stupavsky kids! My siblings and I had a stigma hung over our heads because of our parents' deafness and poverty. The nuns called my sister Dorothy from her classroom to take me home. They were so mad at me and very mean to me for wetting in the corner of the room on the floor."

Liz and I had a hearty laugh on that one, and she said," Well, at least you didn't have to go number two as I had, and even today, I can't make it to the toilet sometimes, but I don't care anymore. They are supposed to get me all better, and that is why I am here in the hospital. But I am to the point that I am used to it, and I want to get home."

Back to Liz: In her childhood, Liz was out in the streets, and she had a good command of the English Language. She knew how to use her words to her advantage and for her survival. She also had her Confirmation Godmother, Alice, next door to us, teaching her and who was always talking to her. Alice spoke to Liz all the time (by hearing the words to learn the language, one knows how to speak through their hearing). Liz also hung with the kids on the street—that is how she learned and heard the spoken word. Therefore, Liz had a good command of English, and her ASL could be very dramatic with her body language when she tried to get her points out clearly, making her bilingual, as all of us were.

Liz said, "I remember Dorothy and I had all homemade clothes given to us, made by our Grandmother Meyer, or donated from the church. We never had anything new, and I always dreamed that someday I would wear new clothes and they would be beautiful. Sister Rita, — you know I have some nice expensive clothes, which I packed in boxes for you and your daughter, Pam, when you come to Florida. You must come down to try them all on and ship them home."

I told her that with the Coronavirus and all, I would not want to fly down, and hopefully, when I come in February, our usual trip to Florida, we will go through them. She had told me a couple of times, "We will see. You will come down before you know it, and we can work on our book together."

I guess she knew more about her future than we all did.

Liz talked again about Dorothy next. "I remember that she and I took turns riding the Shaker Rapid on weekends to the Terminal Tower. We rode the old-fashioned streetcar to care for our grandmother, Meyer, who lived on the west side. The ride there was fun, especially on the streetcar on the road to the west side. I loved sitting on the streetcar and going under the dark bridges on Clark Ave in Cleveland, Ohio. Then I had to catch another bus to our grandmother's street and walk to her house. Dorothy and I did that every Friday after school. We dreaded those weekends! Going to our grandmother's house from the east to the west was a long trip. We traveled all alone, but I made friendly talk to people and wasn't shy. I had a personality way back in the day, but not Dorothy. She would never talk to strangers as I did. Dorothy kept to herself whether it was in the house, at school, or out in the community."

"Dorothy and I hated to take care of our grandmother. She was so mean to us! We would take good care of her, but she would scream and yell at us! I would have preferred to hang out on the streets keeping busy, and Dorothy would rather be at home taking care of the household, but my grandmother's children ordered us to come and take care of her on the weekends."

"Grandma was in a wheelchair, and Dorothy and I had to put her on the toilet, clean her up, and put her back in her wheelchair. Plus, we had to bathe her and dress her, and she would scream and say we hurt her by moving her body. Then, we had to lift her all by ourselves, put her into bed, and start all over in the morning to get her breakfast and the rest of her meals. We did everything for her, and she never fed us very much. Sometimes, she would send us to the corner store and buy us a couple of slices of bologna, but that was all. Our grandmother would tell us what awful caregivers we were. I was born in 1940, and she passed away in 1956. We cared for her for a long time until I was 16."

"She screamed so loudly at us that our Aunt Zita, her daughter, who lived upstairs, would come running down, wanting to know what was happening with her. Our grandmother never yelled at us in front of her daughter or when her two sons would come and visit her. She would yell at and push us away when no one was around, but Dorothy and I knew how to quickly move out of her way so she couldn't reach us. We couldn't wait until those weekends with our grandmother were over. We would return to that streetcar, connect to the Shaker Rapid, and walk to Sophia Ave."

"When I got back outside running out of the house, the boys would say to me on Monday, 'What happened to you again, **Ms. Tin Can?** We can't wait around for you! We had many games here without you!'" "They would rub it all in, and I would get furious! Hearing them say that made me dislike my grandmother even more!'"

Liz then shared, "Life was just so sad, and we were thankful for whatever we did get, but I have to say we were rough and tough and hung out on the streets. I knew how to survive in school, the community, or out on the streets, whereas Dorothy, especially you, Rita, could never make it as I did."

Liz said, "Our grandmother could be very mean, but I recall she made me a gorgeous dress once, and I went to her Catholic Church in her West Clark neighborhood. I went to the priest wearing this gorgeous dress and told him I was there to crown the Blessed Virgin Mary. He believed me, but originally, I wasn't the girl chosen to do that—a rich girl was but I got to crown the Blessed Mother after all, and it was one of the happiest days of my life while I was working hard for my grandmother. I think the gorgeous dress worked! I even forgot being **Tin Can.** I was Elizabeth, the granddaughter of one of the parishioners in the church. Grandma Meyer was delighted—not that I got to crown the Virgin Mary, but that I wore the dress she made and that I got so much attention! Yet even though I wasn't the one originally chosen. I talked my way through and convinced the priest that I was! I knew how to make a quick sale and could think fast on my feet that day. It was just one of those Lucky Days and a big win for me!"

"So, when you ask how far I can remember when I was young, I told you the life I led as Liz, Elizabeth, Lizzie, and my secret life as **Tin Can Lizzie.** I told you this several times during our conversations. There is more to talk about in my younger days, but I will hold off for another **TIME** and move on with more new stuff to my siblings, adulthood, careers, children, husbands, friends, and more of my secrets —and, of course, just more of me!"

"You asked me, Dr. Rita, what sorrowful times I could remember. Life was just so sad, and when I was out in the streets, I would be happy, laughing, and doing a lot of dreaming. I just had a good time and could forget the life inside the house. I taught myself to be **"Street Smart"** and to **"Survive"** so I could go on to my infamous legend of being the marvelous **"Tin Can Lizzie."** I was a skinny little **MITE** of a mature, grown-up woman living in *"little girl"* Shoes! But the most precious times in my life were with my wonderful sisters: Dorothy and you, sister Rita. In our younger days and later in life, you two made me rich, happy, and blessed living in a world of our **"Sisterhood!"**

## THE SISTERHOOD PHOTO PAGES TO BE TREASURED! LIZ, DOROTHY AND RITA

Sisterhood: 2009, Dorothy, Liz and Rita at Christmas time at brother Richard's house in Ohio.

Sisterhood 2009: from the left Dorothy, Liz, and Rita on one of my many trips to Florida.

Dorothy and Rita going jogging, but not Liz—she is the working real estate professional career woman!

Sisterhood: 2011, On the top left: Rita and Dorothy, with the tops of our heads cut off, and seated is Liz on one of my many trips to Florida.

Sisterhood: 2012, from the left Dorothy, Rita, and Liz. We are at a family wedding.

Sisterhood: June, 2012, from the left Dorothy, Rita and Liz at a family wedding

Sisterhood, 2014: From the left, Liz, Rita, and Dorothy waiting to board our cruise. Oh, we loved cruising!

Sisterhood 2014: Three Bathing Beauties out at sea having fun and enjoying the sunshine! Liz had to have a sun hat to match every bathing suit and every sun outfit!

Sisterhood 2015: From the left Rita, Dorothy, and Liz. Under the Caribbean palms and the purple skies, and nothing but BLUE waters behind us.

Sisterhood 2015: From the left Liz, Rita, and Dorothy—sisters looking out at the sunset on our cruise ship.

Sisterhood: February 14, 2019, Out to Dinner for Valentine's Day

From the left: Rita and sisters Dorothy and Liz at brother Richard's house in Florida.

Sisterhood: 2020 From the lef: Liza, Rita, and Dorothy in Liz's condo at Top of the World. Getting ready to go shopping, Liz's favorite thing to do. We were all so happy together,

2018 Valentine's Day Luncheon, Just the three sisters, from the Left: Dorothy, Rita and Liz

Sisterhood February, 2020: From the left Liz, Dorothy, and Rita. This was the last time three of us at' were together we were at brother Richard's home in Florida.

# Chapter 4

## LIFE MOVES ON FOR THE TIN CAN QUEEN AMIDST A TROUBLED FAMILY

**THIS CHAPTER IS DEDICATED TO THE KLUCHO FAMILY MEMBERS. THEY WERE SUCH A BIG PART OF OUR FAMILY'S LIVES GROWING ON SOPHIA. THEY WERE MORE THAN JUST OUR NEIGHBORS, AS THEY RAN THE FAMILY GROCERY STORE. THEY WERE OUR FRIENDS WHO WATCHED OUT FOR US AS**

**THE STUPAVSKY FAMILY MOVED ON IN LIFE AMIDST A TROUBLED FAMILY!**

On another phone day, while talking to Liz in the hospital, she spoke about our family- Dorothy, Victor, Rita (me), and Richie. She told bits and pieces of one topic to another and rambled on so much.

I told her, "Liz, I can't remember all these scattered bits of information you are telling me."

She said, "You can just fill in what's missing. You know more of the family history than I do."

There was so much to write about each family member, but I am only reporting what she said to me, filling in the pieces to clarify Liz's words. I promised her I would get whatever she said to me on paper and fill in her last words and some missing details. On her final day of the memorial service at the funeral home, her daughter Kim bought roses for everyone to give her, and we tied a promise on the flower.

I wrote to Liz and told her I would finish the book, and a deal is a deal, as she kept bringing it up to me. I told her to stop worrying and that I would get all her words included in her story in a readable form. I told her this many times.

She said, "I am counting on you to make this happen."

During these conversations in the hospital, I made her keep her focus every time she became distracted. I would stop and get her back on track. The first thing she talked about was her sister Dorothy.

I told her, "Maybe you should hold back on what you are saying about Dorothy until you can dedicate a full chapter just for her." However, I followed her wishes for our sister, Dorothy.

I told her, "Oh boy, I don't want to get in between you."

I knew Dorothy had loaned her a lot of money to get her out of the debt of losing one of her properties, but most of all, Dorothy gave it so she could pay her employees. Dorothy was always good-hearted and cashed some of her retirement money to help Liz. Dorothy was so considerate of Liz's workers and their families.

She also said, "When I get home from the hospital, I want to tell her my plan for paying back the money she gave me. I have a good plan, and I have to talk to her about it to set it in motion.

During this conversation, I had to tell Liz where we left off so she could refocus. She started this conversation by saying she had returned to the Sophia house while her first husband served in the Vietnam War. It was always one story after another and then on to the next. She was very young at one moment, and she would jump to another story of when she was older, talking about the troubled times she had gone through other than those our family had gone through.

I told her, "Liz if we have others read your life story, how will they understand when you jump back and forth across the milestones of your life and for all the readers?"

She was getting mad and started moving back into her Liz state again with a sharp tongue.

She yelled, "Just make it work! Please keep writing, and later, when I get home, you can fly down to Florida, and we will straighten it all out together."

From one phone conversation to the next, I would begin by reading to her what I had written in the previous discussion.

She would say, "That is enough! Don't read anymore—save the best for last. Plus, I have so many more secrets to tell. It sounds great, and I like how you are filling in the family background. Great job, Dr. Rita!

You know I am very proud of you, and you are amazing at hearing, remembering, and writing!"

It was one story to another as Tin Can Lizzie revealed all her memories and named herself. "**The Tin Can Queen**" as she transitioned back to those younger days.

She said," I would always find younger and older friends playing in the streets, and I would always find someone in the street gang to hang out with, no matter their age. I would also walk to the neighborhood stores and talk to people there. Everyone loved me, but as I got older, the name "**Tin Can**" changed back to "**Liz**."

As she spoke, I wrote down highlights of what she said, and the rest was all from memory when I wrote my notes later. She now went back to her younger days.

Liz said, "When I worked, that was how I would get the pennies to pitch with the boys on the street. Our house was an attraction in the whole neighborhood simply because of the small Klucho Grocery Store next door, and everyone came by and went to the store to shop. There was always a lot of action by the store."

"We were all excited to watch the products delivered at the store. When it came to pop deliveries, the boys were trying to steal bottles of pop when the delivery man entered the store. We loved to watch all the deliveries, and sometimes we would have to stop our penny toss because cars and delivery trucks were trying to pass through."

"A little old foreign lady lived straight across the street. She was all hunched over with a babushka over her head and face—the neighborhood was full of old, foreign, crabby ladies like this. The old lady had a broom and swept the street clean after every truck would come to the store to deliver. When we got in her way, she would take the broom and shake it at us, yelling at us in her broken-up form of English to get out of the street and to stop playing. One time, she came over and kicked the tin cans down. We laughed in her face. We were so bad! The boys shooed her back into her yard, and we continued our penny toss. These activities continued, and every day, even in the winter, we would assemble in front of the Sophia house or front of the store and play penny toss. That was the game, along with cards, in the neighborhood. It was our life and my **ESCAPE** from being in that house, and I could act out my role as the famous **Tin Can Lizzie!**"

She said," We were all getting older, and I can clearly remember those days of getting out of the Sophia House to find someone to hang out with and set up the tin cans. I never won many pitches, and you would think I would be a big winner with all the practice I had from tossing all those pennies. We would even pitch pennies against the curb to see who could get the closest when I threw or even rolled the pennies. I was happy, and it was a wonderful **ESCAPE** as I would watch that penny move to a can to be knocked down or get inside those cans."

I asked her, "So I guess you are back to that **Tin Can** age now, right?"

She shouted at me and said, "I will always be back as **The Tin Can Girl,** and you just have to make it happen for others to believe my story. It keeps going back to the days of my fondest, treasured moments. I was The Tin Can Girl even when I was older, but others didn't and couldn't see it that way. My life has been moving before my eyes so quickly lately. Please let everyone know I will always be the "**Tin Can Queen!**" I want my children to know me as "Mom, the **Tin Can Lady** or **Queen**. Most importantly, I want them to know about our life, and it was not easy to survive in our "**Troubled Family.**"

I jumped in and said, "Liz, they will not do that! They know you as Mom or Liz. You will never get them to know you as **Ms. Tin Can or Tin Can Lizzie!**"

Liz got mad and said, "Oh, please stop! They can't be that stubborn, can they?"

She asked me, "Rita, do you remember the house and how messy it was sometimes?"

I replied, "Liz, I sure do! I can remember when I never knew where our clothes were. They were always in boxes or stuffed someplace. I remember next to our living room was an old bathroom when the house was a two-family house many years ago. Well, the toilet broke in that bathroom, and Daddy didn't have the money or knowledge to repair it, and they just let it go. So, what happened? Mom and Dad put boxes of clothing in the bathroom and made it into a junk closet room. There was another junk clothes closet off the dining room, the same mess!"

Liz said, "Oh my, I remember that all right! When all of our clothes disappeared, that is where they would be hidden or stored, just waiting for them to say, **"Wash me, Wash me!"** Our dirty clothes would be in that closet, as well as some clean clothes."

I told Liz, "I remember you wore the clothes first, then handed them down to Dorothy, and then I got them. So, whenever I needed to wear something, Mommy would go into that closet to find the hand-me- down clothes from you and Dorothy. Plus, we got many donated clothes; we didn't care; we would go through boxes looking for something "cute" to wear."

Yes, we were a **"Troubled Family,"** for sure!

Liz asked me, "Rita, do you remember the old wringer washing machine in the kitchen? The back bathroom was right off the back bedroom next to the kitchen where Uncle Frank (he was not our uncle, but we called him that) used to sleep. Mom and Dad felt so sorry for him; he lived with us for years. He was deaf and had no family. We were his family. Mommy and Daddy took in many people who were deaf and had no home. I think that is where you and I got it into our blood to help the homeless people we did for so many years."

"So that was the only bathroom for all of us to use. I hated that bathroom; it smelled so bad. Dirty clothes were lying all over the floor. When we had dirty clothes for mommy to wash, we would pile them up in that bathroom, or we wore them forever before we were willing to give them up, including our underwear."

I replied, "Liz, not only do I remember the dirty clothes piled up in the bathroom, but I could also remember our Saturday night rituals. When Mommy or Dorothy would fill the bathtub with water, we took turns bathing in the same water. We all had our order: the cleaner ones went first. It was usually Mommy first, then Dorothy, and she would take our baby brother Richard in there with her to bathe him. Third, it was me, and then the dirtiest went next—you, and finally, it was Victor. You were always dirty from the dust and dirt playing on the streets. One time, Victor had to go to the bathroom, yelling at the door to "hurry up" and kicking the bottom of the door in. That kicked-in door was on there for years and years without ever getting fixed."

Liz said, "Oh, yes, I remember those Saturdays. Talk about a **"Troubled"** low-income family, which was us! Then, when we all sat down together at our meals, we all had to talk in sign language (ASL). When our dad was sitting there, he wanted us to communicate using ASL or our home signs. If we used our voices, he would sign "Stop," for he wanted to know about our lives and not talk between ourselves. One time, Dorothy and I were arguing (as we often did), and Dad was so mad at us that he told us to stop, but we didn't listen. He took his fork and lunged out toward us like he was going to stab us. We stopped so fast, and we never argued at the table again. Talk about a *"Troubled Family,"* having parents who were deaf wasn't easy for us, and Daddy not being able to get a good job didn't help us.

I replied," Liz, I was gone after I was ten, but all of you had tough times longer than I did amidst a *Troubled Family*. I could understand how you wanted to run out of the house and endured as *"Tin Can Lizzie"* as an **ESCAPE**." Life was not easy for us, but it made us strong!"

THE KLUCHO FAMILY GROCERY STORE

Liz said, "My wish and prayer is that I want my grandchildren to read about me and our family's life growing up, how tough it was, and how we all survived amidst being in a Troubled Family." I don't think they know me, so maybe they will learn more about us through this book. I hope they will come to know me for who I am and how much I had to do to make a life for myself and my daughters. I am very proud of my daughters and grandchildren. I love them very much and will always look out for them. I made many bad decisions in raising my daughters, and I regret it today. It breaks my heart because of some of the things I have done. I wish I could live all over again with my girls—it would be different! They are so kind and loving, and I hope they don't hold over my head some of the things I did in my younger years as a young and struggling mother. Let's change the topic; I want to talk about the positive influences of how I survived in my life."

Liz said, "The Klucho Family Grocery Store was a big part of my life as it was with all the neighborhood kids. We also pitched pennies into the tin cans in front of the store, and the girls and I played jump rope with the girls on the street, too. We had to be careful of cars coming and going, so later on, we jumped rope in the Klucho Store driveway. We didn't have a smooth driveway at the 9805 Sophia house—only dirt and some cinders, but Klucho's drive was smooth. The girls on the street who played jump rope were Sandra Runyan, Claire Klucho, and other neighborhood girls. Sometimes, Dorothy would come out of the house, but not that often, and she would only watch."

I had to tell Liz, "I can remember that the Klucho Grocery Store was a huge part of our family's life. I remember Dorothy knocking on the side door after store hours, asking Mr. Klucho to buy a few slices of bologna or cheese. Mr. Klucho was kind and would put the charge on our bill, which I don't think was ever paid. But Dorothy would have something to feed herself and the family. Yes, the Klucho store was our food source on many occasions."

INSIDE THE KLUCHO STORE

"I remember Dorothy telling me in those days in the store that there were cookie boxes with clear plastic covers with a handle on the top. Our Brother Victor would go into the store and purposely break the cookies, and then he would ask Mr. Klucho if we could have the broken ones. Sometimes Dorothy would say that Liz would go in and try to do the same thing, but she was more afraid of getting caught. Mr. Klucho was so kind. Most of the time, he would say, "Ok, take the cookies." "Our Brother Victor would fill up his pockets and bring the broken cookies home to us. Victor would watch who was working in the store and wait for Mr. Klucho, for he was so compassionate and generous that he would always agree. Dorothy said she thought he never really caught on to what they were doing, but maybe he did and wanted to give us the cookies. Mr. Klucho and the Klucho family were always so very kindhearted to us."

**Joseph Klucho**

I replied to Liz," I can remember the Klucho store. That was my life, too! I would sit on the Sophia house's front steps and watch the delivery trucks deliver their products. I would sit there for hours and hours just watching the kids play in the streets, people walking by going to and from the store. It was my world sitting on those front steps of the Sophia house, watching what was next door at the store. It was my own private "theater of performances." I can remember the joy it brought me to this day. Today, as I share the story of my sister **LIZ'S ESCAPE**, it's possible that it could have been mine too. I used to see it as "entertainment," but in a way, it might have been a way to escape that house, just like my sister Liz had to do. Maybe it was my "**ESCAPE**" as well, and I never realized it. I wrote all about those experiences in the book about my life. The beginning chapters are about me watching the significant action at the store and in the streets and sidewalks until I was **"Snatched Away,"** as you called in an earlier chapter. However, as I told you, my book is all "on hold" until we get your book about you and our family history completed, published, and off to the readers. But indeed, I guess in a way, watching the Klucho store goings-on was *my* **ESCAPE**, too, as well as getting out of the house and keeping my mind busy. It was how I acquired my visual solid language in the early days of my life."

Liz sharply said, "Oh, you better get my book done first, then we can write your book together when I get back home.

I gruffly told her, "Liz, I promised your book would be first! How many times do I have to tell you? But I can handle my book myself, and I will get to it; it gets all my attention right now."

Liz said, "Yes, besides me turning into the **"Tin Can Queen"** playing in the streets pitching pennies as my **"ESCAPE,"** my whole world revolved around my activities near the store and my friends there, not only for me but for everyone in our family. When you wrote about our family's history, your friend Jim, one of the Klucho grandchildren, came up with the history that our grandparents owned the store and operated a neighborhood saloon before it was the Klucho Family Grocery store! That history is so amazing! So, it was also our father's life when he came to America. That building was his home, where he lived with his father, mother, and younger siblings before our Grandfather John left the area."

"Yes, the Klucho store was a big part of all our lives, but for me. I was out playing with the boys, pitching pennies, or jumping rope with the girls. I remember those experiences as the most positive ones I had in my younger days. Please don't ask me how we got it, but when we were tired of playing jump rope, we would take colored chalk and hopscotch with the girls. It was fun, and my **ESCAPE** changed from tossing pennies to playing jump rope and chalk games. We would also draw with chalk on the sidewalks. I never could draw very well, but I would try, and we would all laugh. I just had fun, and when the girls had to go home and back to their houses, I would try to play Toss the Penny and round up some boys. I would constantly be going from the boys to the girls, switching back and forth and keeping my mind busy and active. I just never wanted to go back to the house, and Sandra's mother, Irene, was so nice to me, and she knew I would be hungry. She would offer me dinner. I was so thankful that I got to eat with my friend, Sandra."

Liz said, "Rita, do you remember the Stupavsky kids were considered on Sophia Avenue as the "Deaf People's kids?" There was another deaf family down the street. Their kids were all deaf, but we could speak and hear. Therefore, the Stupavsky kids were the center of the neighborhood attractions, with always something going on, and most of the time considered big troublemakers."

Liz said, "I was the most vocal of us kids in the family and on the street. I had a lot of personality and charisma and was well-liked by all. I was still working for the Jewish family. Their kids are all grown up, but they loved me for who I was, and I was with that family for many years. I seemed to get along well with kids; I couldn't wait to get married someday and have my children. I had my chance when I met one of the guys who hung out on the street, and we lived in marital bliss until he was drafted for the Vietnam War; later, I had to move back into the Sophia house. Shortly after that, my first husband and I ended our marriage. He was a different man after serving in the war. I was so sad."

Then, she reverted to her life in the streets.

I told her, "Liz, you just talked about your adulthood with Dorothy and your financial issues when we started this session? Now you are back in the street on Sophia when you were little."

Liz started telling me, "Then, there was our brother, Victor. He was a rabble-rouser and could do what he wanted without proper supervision. Our parents, being deaf, could not watch over all the children nor keep control, especially over Victor and, later on, our brother, Richard. Plus, our parents were older than my friends' parents. Victor was getting in trouble in the neighborhood, and eventually, the police got involved. I felt so bad for him, and I knew he was going to be taken away, just like you were, by your foster parents, but I didn't know how or when. I knew the day was coming and couldn't do anything about it. It seemed as if I was frozen in **TIME** and that I couldn't make a better move in the game of "Life of Our Family." I was his older sister and never did the job I was supposed to do. I should have guided him, but even if I had, he wouldn't have listened to me."

"To this day, I feel responsible for all the trouble Victor got into. Before long, he got into more significant problems with the police and was sent to a Juvenile Detention Home and then to two different boys' homes. I tried to make a difference in my Brother Victor's life, but I didn't think I could do it. Our parents got help from Father Wilson at the St. Augustine Deaf Church on West 14th Street in Cleveland, Ohio."

"In church, Father Wilson would also request clothing donations and food for an "anonymous" family and later bring the contributions to our house. That's how we got many clothes and food for our meals."

"Father Wilson was able to contact Father Flanagan's Boys Home in Omaha, Nebraska. The priest got our brother Victor admitted to that home, where he stayed until he graduated from high school. He wanted him to **ESCAPE** the Cleveland, Ohio, area and stay out of trouble. Boys Town was a wonderful upbringing for him and a great inspiration to do well in life, and he did!"

"After he graduated from Boys Town, Victor came home to the Sophia house, but he didn't stay very long in Ohio. He desired to make a life for himself in California, and he moved away to seek out his fortune and to spend time with his girlfriend, Marie. He wanted to find a good, secure job and probably to **"Forget and Recover"** as life moved on for him from his younger days. His life was remarkable because he had made such a turnaround from a life on the streets. I was very proud of him in his quest to do well and fulfill his American dream and how he made a life for himself. "

"Yes, our family was a **Troubled Family,** and Victor was troubled and needed recovery, and he surely got it! Victor was proof of that!"

Victor led an amazing life in his later years compared to living on Sophia and getting in trouble with the police. Liz was incredibly proud of him as she was of our brother, Richard. When he was about 21 years old, he came home to Ohio with his wife Marie to meet his family. They stayed in the Sophia house. Victor wanted to show Marie where he grew up and wanted her to meet some of the important people in his life. One of those people was Father Wilson. Victor wanted to thank Father Wilson for all that he did for him. Dorothy called and learned Father Wilson was in St. Luke's Hospital, where Victor and Marie visited him.

Victor remembered Father Wilson as a big, strong guy—a "tough priest," but that was before. Now, Father seemed a lot older and frail. Father immediately recognized Victor at their meeting, and Victor asked him how he remembered who he was. Father Wilson replied,

"I'd know that voice anywhere!" They talked briefly, and Victor told Father about his job driving police tow trucks in San Francisco. When Victor showed Father Wilson his badge as part of the Auxiliary Police force in San Francisco, and Father saw how well Victor had turned out, he cried.

IN 1967 VICTOR WORKED IN THE SHERIFF'S DEPARTMENT IN SAN MATEO COUNTY FOR THREE YEARS, AND IN 1983 WORKED IN THE COTATI POLICE DEPARTMENT AS A SERGEANT IN LAW ENFORCEMENT FOR SEVEN YEARS.

Since that day, he has lived in California and only returned for our parents' funerals and a few family gatherings."

Ironically, Victor worked as a sheriff in California for ten years—a vast difference from his life on the streets and not having the Law on his side. Then, he was the law! Victor was very influential to young juvenile offenders, and he worked with them to help them have a successful life.

After that, he and a friend became partners in a glass company; his friend was the president, and Victor was the vice president. Victor also worked as a salesman there, sometimes installing windows in tall buildings, which was his specialty. His next business endeavor was owning and operating a large towing company for ten years. After selling that business, he worked as a wildland firefighter until he was injured in 2013, after which he retired. Later, he became involved in caregiving for senior citizens. He was amazing as he reached out to help other seniors and people with various disabilities who could no longer care for themselves. I am sure our parents would have been very proud of his endeavors as he reached out to others in his lifetime.

Victor had two prior marriages. He met his first wife, Marie, when she and some friends visited Boys Town for activities, such as picnics and dances. He kept in touch with Marie over the years. Marie and her family moved to California, and after Victor graduated from high school, he traveled to California, where they were married. They had 20 beautiful years together. One of their favorite things was frequently taking their sailboat out into the San Francisco Bay on weekends.

They also had a house in Mexico, right on the Sea of Cortez, near Puerto Vallarta, which became Victor's haven after Marie died of cystic fibrosis. Victor had taken care of her during her time of being sick with her disease until she passed away. He had been her caregiver.

His second marriage of 17 years was a perpetual struggle for him. He tried to make it work, but whatever he did not help. Ultimately, they divorced.

He and his current wife, Jean, married in September 2019 after a long friendship. Victor is delighted and blessed to have Jean as his wife; we are blessed that she is in our family!

They have taken many vacations in their recreational vehicle out in the West. They are members of their Baptist church and are regular attendees. They are also involved in church and community activities.

Jean is an amazing woman, skilled in many venues, and very talented! Jean has a rich educational background, including a Bachelor of Science degree and a Master of Arts Degree in Education. She has taught various other subjects to children ages 10 through 12. Jean has been a guest speaker at California State Polytechnic University in Pomona, California. After retirement, she became a CASA (court-appointed special Advocate) for children in the foster care program and has served as president of her local charter school governance council. She has credentials for teaching English as a Secondary Language, which fits our Deaf Family Heritage as having ASL as our first language. Her expertise is a definite asset when we read aloud about Lizzie and some of the family history in **"The Trials and Tribulations of Tin Can Lizzie."**

In February 2020, Victor and his wife, Jean, flew to St Petersburg, Florida, and followed my beckoning plea to have a family reunion. I have huge news to share. They flew down, and we were all so happy to be together. It was the last time Liz, Dorothy, Victor, Rita, and Richard were together.

Liz told me, "When I get home, I want to call him and ask him why he moved out of Ohio and settled in California. Was it because of his upbringing, living a life of poverty, or was it that he just wanted a new life and needed to recover from a **Troubled Family?** I hope he and his lovely wife, Jean, have no ill feelings for me because of what happened between Dorothy and me about the loan. I know Dorothy and Victor are very close to each other, and I respect that very much, so I hope he is not bitter with me. I would tell him how much I respect and love him and Jean. Their marriage was made in heaven."

In this fragile physical state, I assured Liz that Victor had no bad feelings toward her. It was beautiful to tell them how much you respect them and how happy you are for them.

But Liz finally admitted, "It was God's will to lead Victor off to California to seek his fortune— and to settle down and be married. Today, and many years later, his current wife, Jean, takes care of Victor and ensures he is well cared for when he is sick. They make a lovely couple that God put together. I can't wait to call them, and when I get out of the hospital, I will do that. I hope he is not mad at me, for he always sticks up for Dorothy."

"Victor was out of the picture when our parents were older, but with Richard, I did not want that same behavioral outcome for Richard as my brother Victor did during his early teenage years. I knew I couldn't steer Victor in the right direction then, so how could I help Richard? I had faith that someday, I could make a difference in his life. I wanted to teach him how to survive in sales and be very successful, and surely, he was."

Then, she said, "I want you to include our baby brother Richard in the book that you are writing. Richard was something else! He was following in the path of his older brother, Victor, getting in trouble in his younger days. He was different from the little boy; Dorothy would take care of him in Sophia's house and walk up and down the sidewalks for some ladies to squeeze his cute little cheeks. I was getting older and tried to steer Richard down the right path but to no avail. He got in trouble with the police and, as a juvenile delinquent, was eventually taken from our deaf parents and sent to a reformatory. The family and I felt bad for him, and especially our parents. After those tough times, Richard made a miraculous turnaround and became very successful."

I asked Liz, "Do you remember when Richard brought his motorcycle into the Sophia house to keep it from being stolen?"

Liz said, "I sure do, and he was so proud of that stinky thing smelling up the house."

Liz and I laughed as we remembered Richie dragging that smelly motorcycle into our living room. The neighborhood was getting nasty with a lot of crime, and obviously, Richard wouldn't take any chances."

I told Liz, "I remember when our house was robbed while our parents were sleeping, and the thieves stole our parents' first black and white television and some other things. They killed our family dog so the dog would not jump on Daddy to alert him that there was trouble. Maybe it was a good thing that our dad didn't wake up, for he could have been seriously harmed. But it was unfortunate when our parents lost the **"Eyes and Ears"** of the family dog that they needed to help them survive in the life of their silent, troubled world."

After that, Richard moved back home and lived with my parents until our dad had a massive stroke. My mom, sister, and even Richard tried to care for him, but it was too hard for us all. We were so poor that Daddy had to go into a state public nursing home, and it wasn't the best one. So, Dorothy and I took Mom to the nursing home as much as possible. We both cared for our mother, and it was difficult for Dorothy, who had already moved out to Euclid, Ohio, with her daughter Lisa, to take her mom to visit her husband, Fred. I lived on the other side of town, went to college, and had two children. But between us, we tried to get there every day to see our husband, father, and grandfather. But shortly after going to the nursing home, Dad passed away from pneumonia, and it was unfortunate for all of us. Our parents had no assets, and the house was in the children's names. Mom tried to live alone in the Sophia Ave house, but it was impossible, and she was so lonely. We greatly worried about her caring for herself, her safety, and survival. We sold the house on Sophia Ave, and our mom went to a Senior Public Housing apartment where she lived independently. She loved her new housing arrangement. There was a minibus to take her shopping, and we took her for any medical help she needed. But she was so lonely, and she was always in pain with her back.

Liz went on to say, "There was something special about Richard. I knew he would succeed in life. After selling the Sophia house, he lived with me in Chesterland, Ohio. I tried to teach him what he could do to succeed in business undertakings and have associations with the business world of sales. I don't know if I taught him or gave him the inspiration and incentive to move on his own and teach himself, but he worked very hard and led a successful life."

Liz added, "Richard is among the smartest people I know with investments. He knew how to talk and sell his way through anything. He was very focused, competitive, and determined to do well, and he did! Richard, along with my daughter Gina, are very much like me. The only difference would be that they didn't make the wrong business choices in life as I did. But, if they did, they both knew how to recover quickly."

After Liz was talking about our family, I said to her, "Liz, I don't know about making this information public. Our family may have a "fit," and they may not be too happy about you telling this information about their lives if this book ever gets published."

Liz jumped on me and said, "What do you mean if the book ever gets published? Your attitude is not very clear here! And where is your faith, my sister Rita? Then, Liz sadly replied, "Too bad! It is the story of our family's life and history of living in such a poor, needy, troubled family." Then she added, "Well, if they don't like it, they can see me about it, and it is my choice to tell this, not yours, so just write it! They will be fine with what I am telling you to write."

Liz added, "It is no different than our sister Dorothy, a single parent with a wonderful daughter named Lisa to raise by herself. Mommy and Daddy helped her watch over Lisa while Dorothy worked. It was hard for her, but she handled it very well. Back then, it was much harder to be a single parent than today. Our parents adored their granddaughter, Lisa, but her life tragically ended in a car accident at the very young age of 21 years old, leaving two small children behind. Mitchell Allan was only two years old, and his mother was buried on his birthday. Neil Anthony was just a three-month-old baby at the time of his mother's death."

Dorothy and Rita took care of our mother in Ohio. Unfortunately, we lost our mother in December 1983, and in February 1984, we lost my niece, Lisa, just two months later in the same year. We had tragedies in our family, and indeed, those were some of the biggest ones. The misfortune of losing Lisa was too much for our sister Dorothy, as it was for all of us. Dorothy never overcame such a heartbreak, which is another sad story.

I quickly replied, "Liz, let us get through what we are writing now; I can't handle it anymore. I am doing all I can to write notes as we speak and then go to my computer and type the notes, filling in the missing pieces."

Liz ended our conversation by talking about our family. She made me promise to talk about them in our (Liz always called it "our") book. We made a covenant that we would do it together and get this story out and published. However, tragically, that was not the case, and here I am, struggling to write every piece of her story, feeling so disappointed, so sad, and most of all, accepting the challenge, all alone, to do this. This is not what I bargained for in our covenant together. This was one of her biggest "cons" of dropping the book responsibilities off on me to figure out, with no opportunities to ask her for clarity. She never planned on her life ending so abruptly; my heart bleeds for her. But con or not, Liz had no choice if she wanted the job done, and of course, she needed me to get the job done. I replied to her beckoning call with my heart, and she knew this, or else she would never have talked so freely with me, enlightening me of all that she did tell me and revealing some private episodes of her 80 years of life.

I kept telling Liz, "I don't think our family will believe all that you are saying to me and be puzzled about why you didn't tell them—especially your daughter, Kim."

Liz added, "Our family had gone through hell in our younger and older years. We were more than troubled and overwhelmed by what "Life" gave us. It is amazing that we all survived and can actually talk or even write about those "Trials and Tribulations" in our quest for survival! I kept so many experiences and troubles inside me, and I would never admit this to anyone, especially myself! Now, I am just ready to let all these experiences and depression days out to you that you will write all this in our book."

I told Liz, "I hope I understand everything you tell me. Plus, you are telling me to write the history of everything you said, and I am worried I am not getting this down accurately."

Liz replied, "You know the family history and can write it all up. We will go over everything when I get home, and we can sit and read our book together for hours."

I said, "OK, you know I will try my hardest. I promise you that!"

With a sad voice, Liz said, "I know you will, Dr. Rita. I know you will do the best you can. We will fix it if you don't get something right. I can't wait for the big surprise when everyone reads our book."

Liz added a closing thought. "As I moved on in life while growing older, so did our family members, carrying the troubled and even tragic memories on our backs. There was no **ESCAPE** for me and the family members. It leaves us with a stigma that hangs over our heads, no matter how hard we try to pretend or hide this darkened shadow that it didn't exist. It is there. Some days, we forget about it, but it comes back sooner or later to get us!" **TIME** always seems to **WIN OUT**! You can't **ESCAPE.**

Therefore, the time I put into this book and the accounts must be accurate for Liz and the family. If not, I would not give them the justice and honesty they deserve! We truly lived our lives in a very **Troubled Family**, and you can't blame all on our parents' deafness. But God knew our pathways and pulled us through those troubled family **TIMES**.

In closing this chapter, Liz said, "Everyone has a story to tell of their lives, and some of us are living to tell those stories and able to pass them on as our "Family Legend." Yes, our family moved on in their lives, and we survived indeed! We indeed lived in **Amidst a Troubled and Needy Family** living in poverty. I now look back and feel the pain and hardship of our struggling deaf parents and what they had to endure to survive in their challenging, complicated, and complex world. Yet, today, I am so fortunate and blessed that I had to fall back on my life of going incognito as **Tin Can Lizzie.** It was my only vice and my only salvation!"

# Chapter 5

## LOOKING OVER A TIMESPAN IN OUR FAMILY HISTORY AMIDST A TROUBLED RECOVERY

In this phone conversation again, I made Liz keep her focus. Whenever she swayed away, I would stop and get her back on track. The first thing she talked about was her sister Dorothy.

I told her, "Maybe you should hold back on what you say about Dorothy until you get home. Remember Liz, Chapter Three was about Dorothy, you, and me!"

"Oh, no! Dorothy was my life, and she will be in every chapter. Don't worry about it, sister Rita, get it all down! Dorothy and I had our share of disagreements, but our bond as sisters was unbreakable," Liz asserted, her words tinged with fondness and frustration.

I said, "Oh, boy," for I knew Dorothy had loaned her a lot of money to get her out of the debt of losing one of her property deals."

Liz continued, her voice filled with deep admiration, "It was a tumultuous time for our family. With her unwavering determination and a spirit that always saw the silver lining, Dorothy selflessly cashed in some of her hard-earned retirement money to rescue the shopping plaza. She even took over the small deli store, becoming the proud proprietor of the plaza. This bustling hub served vacationers, condos, and homeowners on the island. Dorothy, a true workhorse, toiled for 15 hours daily, managing a hot food counter and preparing all the food herself. I always yearned to repay her, but I could not."

Then, I stopped and asked her, "What do you remember of your good experiences together? "I wanted to keep our conversation positive at this point.

Liz said, "Dorothy was such a good person as she was the actual leader of the family in many ways, whereas I wanted to be but didn't put forth any effort, and I didn't know how to start. Dorothy wasn't very verbal and just did what had to be done. I was the oldest, but I probably didn't do as much to help as Dorothy did. She cared for our brother Richard when he was young. When he got older and started going to school, Dorothy didn't care for him as much. Then, she began hanging out with me and would accompany me to many places I went to. But she was so shy about going out and meeting people. I would introduce her to the crowd I hung out with, and she made a few friends."

Liz rambled on more about Dorothy, but it was mainly in pieces. She talked more about their younger life together than when they were older and repeated many of her words.

But Liz said, "Oh yes, the loan has to be part of the book, for that is part of our lives together. Dorothy has to know that I had every intention of paying back all the money she gave me, but it just didn't happen in this life. Maybe it will happen to her when I am gone. I have told you that I plan to give every cent to Dorothy. I would have told her what I had begun to do. This way, she will get her money back, and I have to work it out and need a little more time."

"Dorothy brought it up all the time, and the family members all knew of this, which made me feel terrible about this situation. I couldn't blame her—she told me she gave me all she had, and that is the kind of person she is—very kind and generous. She helped me out, and it was a lot of money. It was just one of my bad investments that were over my head. I guess I made many moves like that, which were not sensible, and it was way more than I could handle, with no **ESCAPE** from getting out of the messes. At times, I just wanted to run into the streets and get away from it all, but there was no chance—and no **ESCAPE**. There is a lot more of Dorothy, but that is all I can think of for now—or want to say right now. I can't wait to tell her about the plan to pay her back. Let's talk about something else."

Liz said, "Our parents were getting older, and our dad couldn't find a job. He was a talented and skilled electrician, but who wanted to hire a deaf man who only communicated through sign language? He had limited writing skills. Everyone knew us in the neighborhood and that we were poor. Our father was always collecting wood to build himself a garage someday, and he saved everything he could get his hands on for free."

"If I remember correctly, the city was after our dad so many times to clean up his yard, causing rats to run in the yard, into the house, and throughout the neighbors' yards. I think everyone was after our father for the junk in his yard or his kids running around unsupervised."

"Let's not talk about all that right now, but we will at another time when I finish this last procedure. You and I can properly assemble this book, even if you haven't come to Florida yet. We can continue over the phone until you come, and maybe with your daughter, Pam."

Liz spent the rest of the day talking about the rest of the family—our brothers and sisters. I guess she thought our family was fascinating.

Our mother was first married to Charlie Magley, and they had two children together, but we only knew one. It was always a mystery who she talked about all the time in sign language and was sad. Liz asked me to fill in the missing pieces about who was who and their lives.

Good times together with the Florida family in Clearwater, Florida. From the left: brother Louis Magley, sister Dorothy, Rita and sister Liz.

Our oldest half-brother, Louis Magley, was very interesting. He married his first wife, Marylou, and they had five children. The oldest children were Ricky, Kristy (Cricket), Rodell (Hot Rod), Debbie, and the baby was Linda. Our dad would spend time with my brother Louis, helping with his house projects, and Dorothy would babysit their five children a lot when they were younger. They were great kids. and both our parents adored the children. Louie and Marylou owned a tavern together and worked until late at night. They did get a divorce, and Louis stopped drinking. Louis was a lead sponsor in the AA group. He was in AA for many years up to the day he passed—far different from the life he led back in his younger days. He married his second wife, Darlene, and they had one daughter together, Laura. They eventually moved to Florida near my sister, Liz, and her daughter, Kim. Liz's daughter Gina lived on the east coast of Florida, five hours away. When Louis passed away, Darlene stayed there to watch my niece Kim's daughters, Alexis and Sophia. Eventually, Darlene came back up to Ohio and settled there. Whenever Dennis and I went to Florida to visit Liz and Dorothy over the years, we always got together with my half-brother, Louis Magley, and his wife, Darlene.

All our lives, we have heard our mother say and sign about her precious "Richie Boy," but we never understood who this child was because of the lack of communication. Amid my research, I was talking to Louis' widow, Darlene, and she told me that on my brother's deathbed, he told her of the memories he had of his brother, "Richie Boy," who died at three years old of Dropsy. It was a shocking revelation to all of us, for we had heard of him for many years but never knew he was our half-brother. I found his grave in St. Mary's Cemetery on Clark Ave in the same cemetery where our grandparents, Catherine and Louis Meyer, were buried. We never knew that he died in 1933. I found the exact location of Richie Boy's grave, which had no headstone. Before I leave this world, I plan to buy him a headstone and recognize him as a member of our family. It was just such a shame that we never paid him any homage or put flowers on his grave for so many years.

Liz said, "Rita, I appreciate you discovering all this information for the family. The research you conducted was truly amazing! I will never forget the research you shared with us on our mother and the story you created about her birth. We all loved watching the PowerPoint presentation that you designed for her. Your work was why I trusted you to write my life story in which I told you about my secret life."

"I wanted to move on to our brothers Victor and Richard, plus more on the rest of our family again."

February, 2014: A family cruise trip we will always remember! Sister Dorothy rented a travel tour bus to take us all to the port. From the left to the right: Jean and Victor, Kim, Dorothy, Liz, Rita and Dennis and their daughter, Pam.

I said, "We went on a family cruise a few years back (2014) with Victor and Jean, Dennis, Dorothy, Liz's daughter Kim, and my daughter Pam. We had a blast and toured the Caribbean Islands."

February 2014: Liz and I were true sisters. I bought matching hats for us, and we were so excited to wear them! Everywhere we went, we told everyone we were twins! We would laugh and laugh we had such a good time!

February, 2014: Liz and I in the ship's jewelry store. Liz couldn't resist, and I was her "Sidekick." Liz bought a few pieces of GOLD jewelry and things for her girls.

I became Liz's shopping buddy. We hit every shop on the ports and loved the ship's cruise stores. We were so excited to find beautiful items and extraordinary deals!

On that cruise, we met Victor's future wife, Jean. We loved her and were looking forward to the day they would be married in California. A few years later, Victor and Jean were married on September 28, 2019.

September 28, 2019. Victor and his new wife Jean, on their wedding day in Mt. Shasta, California.

Then Liz said, "Well, sometimes a Prize comes to you after many years of waiting; that is what I believe happened to Victor. He was just on the sidelines waiting for this wonderful woman, Jean, to come along to share his life. Jean is his "California Fortune of a "Golden Nugget," for she is wonderful to him. It was a long wait, but it was worth it all. I told Victor the last time I saw him in February, that Jean was his "Golden Nugget!"

Then Liz added, "Rita, I am still waiting for my true love to come along—My prince to come and get me and carry me home on his shoulders for a new existence! My day will come! I think my last try will be the best yet!"

Then there was me, and she said, "You just better be getting this book done for me! There is a lot I can say about you, my sister, but not now. We can always write what I have to say about you much later. How's that?"

I replied, "Liz, don't worry about talking about me. You said a few bits and pieces about me, which is enough. I would much rather have you talk about the other family members so I can get it all down." I told her she was moving so fast for me that I didn't think I could keep up with her.

She got impatient with me and said, "Don't worry! You worry too much! You know what I am saying, and fill in the rest! That is why nobody else can make this happen except you!"

She kept telling me, "I am just amazed how you became so smart! I can't figure it all out. Maybe it is because you are the only one fortunate enough to complete college."

I reminded her again how many years it took to get this Ph.D. My only desire was to learn as much as possible to reach out to more special populations and continue teaching teachers on teaching reading and other subjects—and all students.

I told her that she knew how to butter me up. She could convince people to do what she wanted them to do. She may think I was smart, but she was indeed "gifted" in her people skills.

Liz said, "Last but not least, let's talk again about my youngest brother, Richard. When he got older and started going to school, Dorothy didn't have to care for him as much as she did when he was younger. Dorothy made sure he would get to school, and he even joined a basketball team. Richard used sports as an outlet to keep himself out of trouble and was an excellent athlete. The family was so very proud of him. He was so skinny and probably did not have the proper nutrition as any of us did. Oh, I remember how sick he was when he had chickenpox and still has a pock scar on his forehead to this day. However, when talking to our brother, Richard, he would say he got hit in the forehead with a BB gun, and our sister Dorothy always joked about it. Both of my brothers, Victor and Richard, shot BB guns in the backyard on Sophia just for fun, not caring and being concerned about the danger of it all."

When we had a toothache, our mother would walk us to St. Luke's Hospital to the clinic dentist, who pulled our teeth out instead of filling them, even though they were second teeth.

I told Liz, "I know that our parents never took Richard or any of us kids to a doctor for treatment unless it was a major operation like you had with your appendix, and Dorothy had gotten her tonsils removed."

Liz replied," Yes, Richard went to St. Benedict's Grade School through 8th grade. St. Benedict's School and the church gave him a scholarship to Benedictine High School. They were both on East Boulevard and close to our home on Sophia. Because we were so needy, Rich was allowed to go to Benedictine High School for free, a prestigious all-boys high school back in the day. When he went to Benedictine High School, he played basketball, ran track, was part of the swim club, and played football, but because of his size, he could only play football for the Junior Varsity team. In his last year at Benedictine High School, he transferred to West Geauga High School in Chesterland, Ohio, where he moved in with me and graduated from high school."

Liz continued, "I was so proud of my baby brother, and I knew school would influence his success. He survived amidst a troubled and recovering family. He had a tough life but rose to success!" Richard is one of the finest examples of how a person can rise to success despite being from extreme poverty **Amidst a Troubled and Recovering Family."**

"Of course," Liz said, "I have a lot to say about Richard, and some of it isn't too nice, but it was remarkable how he straightened out his life and made something of it. I was very proud of him for how he came out of the darkness and into the light of success."

Liz told me, "Rita, fill in the information and background on both brothers. I know you can do it, and I don't want to repeat myself as you keep telling me that's what I am doing. My faith is in you, and you won't disappoint me! Rita, as I said in Chapter Four, Richard was something else! He was a born hustler!"

I replied, "Liz, what do you mean, a born hustler? I knew some of the things he did and was involved in, but I guess I missed some of the action by not living at home when he was in his teen years. I knew he got in trouble in his late teens, but many of our neighborhood kids did. However, their parents would keep after them and straighten them out."

Liz quickly responded, "Dr. Rita, you don't know half of it; somebody should make a movie about that kid's life growing up on Sophia! Richard was a hustler. He would play cards after school with the neighborhood's older kids and win money—most of the time! I remember when Richard was 13 years old and bought a minibike. He rented it out daily after school for 50 cents to all the neighborhood kids to go up and down the street. There were always kids standing in line to take a spin on his minibike."

I replied to Liz, "I can't believe this! You know that is funny! He started making some side money at a young age, didn't he? You must be born in the hood to think of that, right?"

Liz said, "Wait, you should see what else he did! He knew how to make money, and he was good at it! He was a natural hustler and probably one of the youngest."

Well, "I am still laughing at what you shared with me. You mean there is more?"

Liz added, "When Richard was 15 years old, in high school, he bought the first car in the neighborhood among his friends. It was a 1956 Oldsmobile, and he rented it out to all of the older kids for $25.00 a night with the stipulation that they had to double date with Richard and his girlfriend in the back seat. I told you back (to what I said earlier) Richard was something else, all right!"

I asked Liz, "How could Richard have bought a car at 15? I am sure he didn't care about having insurance or upkeep back then. It would be just gasoline money. I never remembered a car in the driveway. That is strange. It had to be an old Junker, but he kept it running and made money."

Our father, Fred Stupavsky, was born on June 22, 1897, and passed away on November 15, 1974. Our dad had a rough life and **OVERCAME** many of his obstacles in life, being **DEAF**. He was a wonderful Father to us, and we all missed him dearly.

Richard left the area after our father passed away and went to college. He worked his way through by getting a job in the college development department and shooting pool in his spare time to help pay living expenses. Some contrast, do you think? A few years later, Richard met his first wife, Mariann, in college. They were married for 19 years and had three beautiful children: Erica, Richard Jr, and Jonathan. Early in his marriage, Richard took a position selling motivational videos and recruited Liz. After a couple of years, Liz got into real estate and became immersed in selling properties. Richard went on to become a Dale Carnegie instructor.

In talking about her siblings, Liz said, "I pushed Richard to do well, and he succeeded in everything he did. Richard had career moves and advancements, which were terrific. I can remember when Richard entered the medical sales field and became the vice president of sales for a California company in a few short years. The company wanted Richard to move to California. He took the family for a summer to see if it fit. His wife, Mariann, did not want to raise their family in California, so they moved back to Lakewood, Ohio."

Liz continued, "Richard told me some information regarding his career building. He said he purchased a home shortly after returning to Ohio and quitting his job. He then started his own medical equipment business. After selling it, Richard went to work for Merrill Lynch as an investment advisor. While at Merrill Lynch, one of Richards's clients offered him the CEO position to run a chain of wireless stores in Indianapolis., Indiana. He accepted the position and recruited his son Richard Jr., an IT specialist, to join him. In 2003, Richard Jr moved to Indianapolis, and together they built a seven-store wireless chain."

Richard's new venture was named one of the top 10 new prepaid wireless company startups in 2007. He sold the company to a larger wireless company in 2008. After researching, Richard became involved in a federal tax credit service. He developed a business model and sent it to many different payroll companies with the intent of finding a venture capital company partner. After multiple offers, Richard accepted a position with Oklahoma City Payroll Company, which proved to be the hidden piece of the Golden Nugget of Richard's success.

At Liz's memorial, Richard gave a message on how Liz pushed him in sales, and she always knew he would go so far in life and be so successful. He talked about how she led him in one of her networking business ventures. Rich shared that he had lived with her and that she taught him so much about success in business and life, and he sure did! His presentation at Liz's memorial was very moving. Liz always said she is so proud of Richard, that he has been very successful and has gone far in life!

I read back to Liz about what she said about Richard, and she liked what I wrote. Then Liz said, "Richard had some rough times too, going through a divorce, and I wonder if he had any **ESCAPE** mechanisms as I did as **Tin Can Lizzie**, to keep him going. Maybe I will ask him next time we talk about how he escaped the pain, the pressure, the loneliness, and the poverty I went through. He, too, has a story to tell, as each of us in our family has miracles to share. I could have been as successful as Richie, but I loved spending money I didn't have. other people's money as well!"

2012, Joann and Richard celebrate their Honeymoon by taking a Cruise to the Western Caribbean.

Shortly after relocating to Oklahoma City, he met a lovely Christian woman, Joann. A little while later, they married in the Assembly of God Church in Oklahoma City. Joann's brother-in-law was the pastor. He married them with close family and friends present at their service. They have been happily married since 2012.

They had a lovely home in Oklahoma City. Richard continued to work for his company, and he did very well. He had 180 people reporting to him, including 18 team leads and five supervisors. Then he was able to retire.

They then changed considerably, selling their lovely home in Oklahoma City and making their new home in St. Petersburg, Florida. Our sister Dorothy also moved to St. Petersburg in a condo close to Richard's house. Richard and Joann graciously have many family "doings" at their home, and Dennis and I stayed with them (in 2019 and 2020) while in Florida. Rich and my husband Dennis are both golfers, and Rich took Dennis golfing several times.

The last time we were in Florida was in February 2020- the first time all five siblings had been together for over 30 years! Below is the first picture we took of the five of us together. We never had any photos taken when growing up in the Sophia house.

February 2020: Our last family picture together, from oldest to youngest: from the left—Liz, Dorothy, Victor, Rita, and our youngest brother Richard in his home in St. Petersburg, Florida.

Rich and Joann were gracious hosts, making us feel comfortable in their lovely home. Richard took his older brother Victor on a fishing trip with Dennis on Rich's friend Craig's boat. They caught some gorgeous fish! Victor fulfilled his dream of fishing in Florida, thanks to Richard for arranging the fishing trip.

February 2020: Out to dinner for Richard's birthday. From the left: Richard and his wife Joann, Rita and her husband Dennis. On the right: Liz, Dorothy, Victor and his wife Jean.

It was there at Rich and Joann's home that I shared the PowerPoint Presentation about our miraculous mother's history and how she survived being born at 1 1/2 pounds. This is mentioned in Chapter One. We watched this PowerPoint with all five siblings: my husband Dennis, Sisters Liz and Dorothy, Brothers Victor and Richard, sisters-in-law Joann and Jean, and Liz's daughter Kim.

Watching and reading the PowerPoint presentation was a memory we will all cherish as we took turns reading the slides for the rest of our lives. Liz thought I could write her story since I successfully researched our mother. It was a dream come true for me. While researching and writing the PowerPoint, I dreamed of going to Florida that following February to watch the PowerPoint together. My dream and hard work came to fruition. I knew Dennis and I were going to Florida because I wanted to see my family, especially Liz and her daughter Kim. Little did I know that we got a surprise visitor from Florida's east coast: Gina and her grandson Riccardo, Liz's great-grandson. It was a glorious reunion time together!

At Liz's memorial, Richard gave a message on how Liz pushed him in sales, and she always knew he would go so far in life and be so successful. He did talk about how she led him in one of her networking business ventures. Rich shared that he had lived with her and that she taught him so much about success, and he sure did! His presentation at Liz's memorial was very moving. Liz said she is so proud of Richard that he has gone so far and has been so successful.

July 1960, the younger brother Richard's creative homemade tent at 10 or 11 years old is in the Sophia backyard.

I read this to Liz, and she liked what I wrote. Then Liz said, "Richard had some rough times too when he was young growing up on Sophia. Life was a struggle for him, being very poor. He didn't have much and had all hand-me-down clothes and shoes. He was very clever and creative at a young age, just like when he made his own private "home" in the Sophia back backyard to get out of the house himself. He also had some tough **Trials and Tribulations** when he was younger and older."

After my sister Liz passed away, when I showed Richard this picture of his tent, he said, "Oh, yeah, I surely remember those days when we were very poor, and I never had any new clothes or shoes; it was tough living on Sophia! See, Sister Rita, because of those dark days, I never would go camping to this very day; I hate camping!"

Also below is a picture of brother Richard many years later at a surprise birthday party the family gave him when we were all in Florida. He is in his home in St. Petersburg, Florida, which is a far different home from where he grew up in the Sophia house. Richard came a long

2020: Now an older brother Richard many years later in his home in St. Petersburg, Florida as he is like his older sister, Liz saying, "Here I am!"

way and worked hard to enjoy his retirement. Our sister Liz was so proud of him and loved him very much!

Liz continued telling me, "Even later, when Richie was going through a divorce, he had some tough times. I wonder if he had any **ESCAPE** mechanisms, as I did as **Tin Can Lizzie**, to keep him going. Maybe I will ask him next time we talk about how he escaped the pain, the pressure, the loneliness, and the poverty I went through. He also has a story to tell, as our family members have miracles to share. I could have been as successful as Richie, but I loved spending money that I didn't have as well as other people's."

Liz would comment here and there about each of our family members, but I didn't write down every word. As I go through this rough draft, and when I remember, I will add it all in. Liz keeps telling me she wants a chapter on our lives, especially our parents' being deaf, but we never got that far in her last words. We didn't know these words were her last ones as we planned and talked about finishing this book when she got out of the hospital.

Now, I am writing every thought I can remember about what she said to me in the hospital and making clarity out of it as I am grieving. I will treasure her last and final words for the rest of my life! I am so blessed to have had these conversations with her before she was **"Snatched Away"** from our family's presence in such an untimely death! This time, she was taken, not me, and she is not returning as I did when I was **"Snatched Away"** by my foster parents, but I came back. But we will see her again someday and will rejoice as we have a grand family reunion!

Again, I am only writing what I can remember of the positives of what she said and not focusing on the negatives as she was getting upset, and I had to keep her calm.

Liz ended our phone conversation on this day, saying, "No Matter what we did living on Sophia, we were always the talk of the neighborhood between our parents being deaf, our father dodging the health department, or the police coming for someone in our family, and me running around in the streets. Victor was in trouble, and surely our brother Richard was following in his path. Look at what my brothers made out of their lives, from living in the streets to living a life of success, peace, and fulfillment! They are happily married today, and I thank God they both made it through their *Trials and Tribulations in Life!*"

Later, when talking to Richard while writing this book, Richard said, "Our upbringing, to some extent, was a blessing in disguise. We are all survivors. We all worked hard, and he said, "I am proud to be a Stupansky!"

Liz said, "I think that the secret of all our successes was to get ourselves out of the **Trials and Tribulations** we went through and worked hard to **ESCAPE** to a better life! We had to believe in ourselves and play the games of life. We had to imagine ourselves as who and what we wanted to become. We had to step out of our depression and physical state and go after our dreams and visions. We had to allow no one to get in our way as we put our faith in our Lord!"

"When I was down and depressed, in either mental or physical state, I knew what to do. I would pray and ask God to help me, and then I knew I had to help myself! I would give it some time, and then I would yell out just as I did in my younger days, **"Here Comes Tin Can Lizzie!"** I still do yell out those words today!" The words alone and my faith would give me the strength to make it whatever I was going through. I was determined to survive, and I did with God's help and my faith in myself! I did that while living in the Sophia House, and we had it hard there."

Liz said, "Of course, the talk many times was on me—how I was out late running around playing with boys in the streets. Many neighbors thought our parents didn't do a thing to put the stoppage to me. But here it is now—many years later- and I think our family was unique from their younger days to their lives today. I am very proud to be part of such a family and such a rich heritage of survival! You know, my dear sister Rita, we are all miracles, and God had his hands in our lives! Your children, Pam and Christopher, will learn more about their roots and the purpose of our survival. Our family's grandchildren and great-grandchildren will know what their ancestry is all about. Our troubled family went through a recovery process, didn't we? Since those days on Sophia Ave, your desire to do this for us has been commendable, and I will forever thank you for your excellent job! We are so grateful for all the work and dedication you gave us."

As Liz became engulfed in tears, she gently said to me again, "**Good night, my sweet sister Rita**." I replied (now **OVERCOME** in tears,) "**Goodnight, Tin Can Lizzie**, whatever you are doing in the Lord's House. Please, Liz, as you are up in the Blue Skies, help me get this book out to the world! Just as you said, it would go!"

# Chapter 6

## WHAT IS "TIN CAN LIZZIE" GOING TO TELL ME TODAY?

It was another day, and I couldn't wait to call my sister to see what she had to say to me today. I didn't want **TIME** to **ESCAPE** me, so I rushed to call her. I just never know what will pop out of her mouth next! Some of the things she is telling are shocking to me! She has me "**Spell-Bound**" for these strange episodes she talks about. Indeed, this is not my sister that I knew my whole life. You never know with sister Liz; she jumps everywhere from one person to another, from a young girl to a senior. Then, she brings up some of the same stories we discussed previously and adds more information to that story. When I call my sister **Tin Can** in the hospital, she has so much to say! I can't write it all down fast enough, and when I finish talking with her on the phone, I turn on my computer and try to write points and clarify what she said. She wants me to write this life story for her, but there is just too much to say.

I suggested that after she gets home from the hospital, I buy her a small tape recorder, and she could talk into it so we could send the tapes back and forth. No, that was not what she wanted. She said she wanted her story to be told directly to me over the phone, just as she is doing now. Therefore, I am using Liz's words but filling in information for clarity. She told me she wanted me to do precisely that, to support her saying and add more family history to each topic.

Whenever she mentioned another name, more unfamiliar experiences, or another family member, I told her I couldn't do all this so fast.

She sharply said, "Yes, you can! So far, you are doing everything right. You are so capable, and I know that I can talk so freely, and you can write it all down. You seem willing to put in the time and are so patient!"

I guess the following sentence shocked me because she asked, "You know I have a lot of secrets in my life, don't you?"

I said, "**Secrets**? No, I didn't know about any **Secrets** in your life. How would I know that?"

She said, "I'm going to tell you all of them." I have to get them all out. You know the big secret of me being "**Tin Can Lizzie**," but trust me, I have so many more secrets to share that will "**blow**" our family away and the readers, too!

I encouraged her, saying there was plenty of time. She got distraught with me. Then I said, "Liz, let me get the information you want to share correctly."

Liz said, "You got to get it all down now! Oh, I have all the confidence and faith in the world in you!"

Liz was very demanding, and I just kept wondering how I would do this and get this all straight. Now, I have to worry about what these hidden secrets are. I thought to myself, "What can they be?" I also asked myself, "What have I gotten myself into? I don't want to be in a big family blow-up!"

She told me, "Well, Sister Rita, you know one big secret of how and why I became **Tin Can Lizzie**." I want everyone to know that story and how it can help them, as it helped me. I can't wait for the family to learn what has been in my heart for years to tell them. Now, I am finally telling them through you."

I told her, "Yes, you told me all of this. Liz, your purpose in wanting your book published is not only for the family but also for struggling people who need help and encouragement."

She said, "My name alone, as it is in the title of this book, will make this book a big hit! People are suffering all over the world, and they give up! But they don't have to—they can **ESCAPE** as I did, make it all right, and reflect on the good times and who they want to become. That is why there is so much suicide in our world—people don't know how to handle the **Trials and Tribulations** in their lives. I thought about it myself in my younger days and surely in my older years, especially when all the bill collectors were trying to get money from me. I was trying to run from them and forget it all! The people must do what I did, **ESCAPE** in a make-believe world, and make it their best. We must clear our minds to handle it much better when facing reality and decide what to do next. It is a lift that our human bodies experience and heals us. I have been healed so many times, both mentally and physically."

I said, "Let's change the topic to when you were **Tin Can** and a younger, happier Liz." What about when you were very sad? Did you have many sad times? I am sure you did!"

She said, "I want to tell you everything, for there is so much to tell you. I have a lifetime to tell you. I am trusting you to get this story out. I am sure someone will come along and help you. Again, she told me, "Think about a book with this title. It must attract a huge audience. It will be a big hit! When reading the stories alone in this book, they too can be encouraged to "*Keep up the fight*" for whatever **Trials and Tribulations** they are going through!"

I asked her, "What if the family doesn't like what I wrote?"

Liz snapped at me and said, "Too Bad! It is what I am telling you to write: "**TIME** is of the essence. Whatever **TIME** we have left is precious, and the minutes and the seconds are few. We have to be strong and ask God to give us direction and lead us to the answers to know how to fix things and live in Peace!"

I could hear a tear in her voice, and she softly said, "Please know I love my two sisters very much! I am much closer to Dorothy because she lives near me in Florida."

I told her, "Liz, you talked about Dorothy in your younger days and about me, too."

But Liz said, "Rita, my memories of you and Dorothy are strong in our younger and later days. I was always around Dorothy in Florida and only saw you when you visited us. Yes, we talked on the phone, but I was always with Dorothy. We had some great times together and some not-so-great."

"As you know, she gave me some of her retirement savings, as I told you, so I could save one of my shopping plazas that were going under. I will never be able to thank her enough for what she did for me, but our relationship will never be the same. How can I give her back all that money she loaned to me? I can't, and it always comes between us, no matter how I try to convince her that somehow, she will get back her money. It was the downside of our relationship for many years. I have another plan for how she can get her money back. I will tell her when I get home from the hospital."

Liz said, "But with Dorothy, she was always on the serious side and very depressed because of losing her only daughter, Lisa. I stayed with Dorothy a few times in her new place in St. Petersburg, but she was so picky that we often didn't get along. However, Dorothy is one of the best-hearted people I know, and she would give you anything but is sad. I wish I could make it all better for her with a magic wand, but I can't! I feel so bad for her and try to help. I can't make right what I did in the past, but I have a plan—you will all see!"

She quickly changed the subject to the other sister, me!

She said, "Rita, I have always respected you for what you did with your life and how you became a published writer and got your doctorate. You truly dedicated your life to your family and the deaf people in the "Deaf Community" and how you and Dennis worked in your Deaf Ministry. I love how you can do sign language; when you sign, it is so beautiful! When I got home, I never told anyone I wanted to work with young, deaf teenage kids and teach them how to dance and succeed. Rita, I will do that as soon as I get home. When you and Pam come to Florida for what I want to give you, you will have to teach me more Sign Language. You have accomplished everything I wanted to bring about but never got the chance to. But, for sure, I will be dancing with young deaf people when I get home—just like you can dance!"

I laughed and laughed and said, "Liz, when we went on the cruises, I begged you to get up and shake that body around, but no, you would not. You gave me so many excuses."

Liz was laughing her cute laugh again and said, "I just enjoyed watching you shake and shake and bounce up and down! Dorothy and I made a lot of videos of your performances. I loved how everyone clapped for you! It was so much fun!"

"When we cruised with you, Dorothy and I enjoyed how you danced on the cruise dining room floor. You are talented in many ways and know how to make moves on the dance floor. So, look out, sister. When I get home, I will get well and dance just like you!"

"You can do everything that I never could do, so in that sense, you fulfilled my dreams. Then, on the February Florida trip, I learned that you could write, do sign language, dance, and sing. I never heard you sing before, and you shocked me! You also always said the prayers in the family, and the Holy Spirit led you."

"On your last day in Florida, you stayed an extra day, and that was the day I wanted to spend just with you, but we never got together that last day. I was so sad, and that was the last time we saw each other for now. I was waiting all day for us to go to Richard's so I could see and talk to you. That was when I first thought you could write my story."

I told Liz, "Don't remind me of the day we were supposed to spend that Monday with Victor, Jean, and Dorothy. I waited and waited for you that day to come to Richard's, and by the time the three of you were ready to come, it was too late. Dennis wanted to get on the road for our trip back to North Carolina early the next morning. I waited for your call for the whole day!"

In this conversation, I told Liz, "You were always so kind and generous to us when we came to Florida to stay with you over the years. You made us feel so comfortable and accommodating for my family. Pam said you were the best! She had a blast with you as you would drag her along on your business ventures and go shopping, too!" Pam said it was the best time of her life when she was with her Auntie Lizzie!" I always have to laugh—you always told Dennis that he is your favorite brother-in-law, and he is, for he is your only brother-in-law! You always said to him that he was the best cruise director and that you would hire him to be your private escort."

Liz replied, "Sure, Dennis is my favorite brother-in-law. No one has to know he is my only brother-in-law."

I told Liz, "Oh, you are too kind to your baby sister and so special to my family, especially my daughter, Pam."

Liz then jumped in, saying, "Let's start talking about other things you will write."

"Do you know I was the top saleslady and traveled to different cities, pushing my motor oil company's networking in my younger years? I was so lonely—so very lonely. I would stay in hotels and cry and cry as I felt I had no one to turn to. Sometimes, I wanted to **ESCAPE** and become "**Tin Can**," but it wasn't possible at my age. There was no street to run into and call the boys over to toss the pennies to forget how lonely I was all grown up and so alone."

"The stakes were much higher now, and I had a harder role in life in which I made many mistakes. I grew from my mistakes, but the growth only lasted a while. When I would get on my feet again, I would make the same mistakes and get in another jam. I was always successful and popular but always getting in jams. It made no sense to me, for I was going from one direction to the next. I was always thinking of the big dream of how success and riches would come my way, and at times, they did. When things were going down badly for me, I would try to become "**Tin Can**," then I made my name more sophisticated and called myself "**Dizzy Lizzy**." Do you know I even had business cards printed saying, "Let **Dizzy Lizzy** put your house up for sale?" But it wasn't the same. I had nothing to cover up the loneliness or the triumphs I had as "**Tin Can**," and now there is no possible **ESCAPE**." Then she said, "I thought to myself, "**Dizzy Lizzy**" won't make it, either. I tried, but no relief, no comfort, and **No ESCAPE!** I was in limbo, or shall I call it "**Chaos?**"

Then I said, "Liz, you are being so hard on yourself! I guess we all do that in our lives and our families. Please, you are making me so sad. Let's cheer up and make the rest of our writing together a victory! I am sad enough that you are stuck in that hospital all alone with no visitors due to COVID, and you are waiting for that last procedure. You know your brother Richard and Joann tried to see you but were turned away, for the hospital was on another "lockdown" due to the Coronavirus.

Liz said, "Oh, yes, I know they tried to come to see me. I would have been so happy because I don't get to see them very often. When we are together, Richard is always very nice to me, and if we go out, he and Joann always treat us to a meal. Richard is so very generous, that is for sure, and I appreciate him and love him. I surely know that he loves his golf!"

Then I added, "Well, Lizzie, he's retired and loves that golf game! I know because I am married to an avid golfer, and he loves it like I love reaching out to people and writing, just as you do when you help someone."

Liz said, "I think he is the smartest guy I know with finances. He has helped me with some of my insurance papers and life insurance policies. I want the insurance money to go to any of my children or grandchildren who need help and not have any of it used to pay any debts after I am gone!"

I said, "Liz, your girls love you so much, and they do so much for you in different ways. They would do anything for you—you know that!"

Liz added, "I think the best thing we can discuss today is my girls. Oh, I love my two girls and was happiest when I was with them. Also, I was with my sister Dorothy and you, Rita. When my girls were growing up, I wasn't there for them much at all, for I was always working, trying to support them and being successful in so many careers. I was good at everything I tried to sell because I worked hard to succeed, but my girls suffered."

"I would be lost without both of my daughters, each in a different way."

Liz began talking about her oldest daughter, Kimmie. She said, "She is so dear to my heart. Kim does everything for me in a way no one else could do. She is my caregiver, my friend, and my companion. We have such a special relationship—we constantly yell and fight, and I can't do that with anyone else. We yell, fight, move on, and return to loving each other again. She puts me first, even before her health concerns and plans. Kim was so busy taking care of everything, her family, and I didn't have time to tell her some of the things I am telling you now. I wasn't ready to tell my story and all of my secrets, but I am now, and that is with you. But that's OK. She will be so surprised and happy when we read our book together. I can't wait until that day comes!"

"Kim is so special, and she has health problems. I worry about her, yet she is always there when I need her. Kim never fails, and I know I make a pest of myself, but Kim still puts up with me! My heart bleeds for her because she has gone through so many health issues herself, and here she is, there for me—to run me to my doctor appointments and bring dinner to me. She is so special, and our relationship is to be treasured! Kim is so caring and would help and do anything for anyone. I have helped many people in my life, too, but nothing like Kim—she cares and gives her life to me and others. She does have a temper now, but so do I, so we just let out our "steam" and move on."

"Kim's son Derek went through a terrible boating accident, and now he has quadriplegia as a result of the accident. She was, as everyone was, very devastated, but she was always there for me. I have given help or outreach to others over the years, and I got it all back to me by my Kim in my life by helping me. Kim went through a horrible time having cancer, and she suffered. Liz's voice shook as she said, "I was heartbroken for her because of what she went through—she worried about her children—Derek, Alexis, and our Sophia (the name of the street on which we grew up)."

"Kim had leukemia and required a bone marrow transplant. I only wanted and wished to do something to help her and be a bone marrow match, and I couldn't. I prayed and prayed and asked God for a miracle. God answered our pleas: my daughter Gina was a 98% match!"

"Gina unselfishly donated her bone marrow, which ultimately saved Kim's life. I completely stand in awe of what Gina did for my Kim! Gina was my heroine! She did what I could not do without any provocation or fear. I always knew Gina was "me" in every sense of our lives. She gave part of her life for her sister to have life, and if I could have, I would have done that. To me, Gina is such a special person in this world! She's an amazing daughter, and I wish I could have helped her and her three girls more than I did. I had chances but was always too busy working on a business sale or deal. I robbed them of knowing their mother and their grandmother better. It was a loss of **TIME**, and I am sorry for being so selfish today."

"Regina is just like me in some ways—she thinks and talks like me in business, but she knows how to handle her finances, which is not like me. Gina is very wise in building a successful career for herself and handling it so her business can thrive—unlike me, who had a taste of "Success" and then constantly made stupid mistakes and poor choices."

"My daughter Regina (Gina) lives far from me, far from her sister Kim in Florida. I can't say enough about her. She is a successful businesswoman, and she is so bright! It is sad to say that today, I am guilty of working every day and not spending quality time with my girls. Gina walks in my shoes; she knows how to handle her **Trials and Tribulations.** Gina is very forgiving, and she doesn't hold a grudge. She thinks, talks, and acts like me. As she gets older, she even looks like me! Everything that I achieved was noteworthy, even though I lost a lot. Yes, I had success, but nothing like the achievements Gina has. She is brilliant at handling business ventures I didn't know how to handle. I can't believe I looked at her today and saw me—better yet, Gina was me! When I am gone, she will live on and be everything I tried to be and failed. Gina will handle her wins and successes much better than I did, and my daughter will know how to play the game of life. She will know when to take a chance—toss or discard the token. She is brilliant! Rita, when I am gone someday, please know that you will always be with me, primarily through my daughters and grandchildren. Please look over them and help bring them always closer to you, our family, and with God! I know you have helped Kim in the past, but please help Gina, too."

In this dialogue, I told Liz, "Both Kim and Gina know how much you love them. I know you lived closer to Kim, so you were with her more— and her children, Derek, Alexis, and Sophia. You sent me pictures of Gina's girls and said you were proud of your grandchildren. You would always brag about their many accomplishments to me and others."

Liz said, "What I guess bothers me the most about Gina was in her younger days when we lived back in Ohio. I should have helped her much more than what I did or was willing to face. My problems began when I married my second husband, the girl's father. Like all marriages, we had good and bad days in our relationship. But it seemed like the bad took over the good, and my two girls suffered. My second husband was married before, and he had two children, whom I adored very much, and I would do anything for them. It was a full house with my two girls and the two children from my second husband."

Liz said, "My second husband was a roofer, and when the weather was bad, he didn't make much money. I was the one who got into so many professions at that time, working day and night to try to take care of the family. I was the main provider to support the household."

I told Liz, "Yes, Liz, you were so good and generous to everyone. You always took in people that needed help and needed a home. You were a mother to many."

However, as I have heard from my sister Liz, some people she took in weren't always helping in the household. They would take advantage of living there and were not friendly to the girls.

Liz explained, "I was so busy I didn't see this immediately. Eventually, I did, but the damage was already done. I feel terrible today, and those memories haunt me. My husband would also help in the household, and he loved his four children. However, he was out of the house a lot."

Liz said several times, "I always loved him for the life we had together when we were first married and for his love for his children. He was a good person and father to his children, but things didn't work out for him and me."

Liz and her husband lived in Chesterland, Ohio, and there was always a house full of people in her home, including our brother Richard. She worked so hard in many professions and part-time jobs. Liz started selling Avon, ladies' wigs, Fuller Brush, jewelry, and you name it, and she did it! She was a prize saleslady and began a networking business selling motor oil. She ran seminars and would fly to many cities, but she said that is when loneliness and depression set in severely. She missed her children but had to earn money to keep the house and provide for a growing family. She would call the girls as much as she could.

1970: Liz and Mary, on Mary's wedding day

She took in a young girl, Mary, who was wonderful to her girls and was like their "big sister." Liz loved Mary and "watched "over her as if she were her daughter. Liz has helped so many others and given them a home, too.

After my sister passed away, the funeral staff home posted her obituary on their site in an area where there were messages of condolences and favorite memories could be posted to Liz's family. Mary wrote the following message there on July 3, 2020. Here is the message exactly as Mary wrote it:

"To my 2nd mother, Liz…as I write these words to you, so many beautiful memories are going through my mind. From when you took me in at nine years old to the last phone call right before your 80th birthday. I have so many memories of you. One of my favorite memories was the wedding you gave me. I felt like the most beautiful princess on earth that day. We celebrated holidays, birthdays, and so much more together. We were a big family, as you would say. Thank you for the love, knowledge, and strength you gave me, along with such an awesome family! You are a piece of my Rock! I love you, Liz, Always and forever!"

Below is the funeral Home Link for Sylvan Abbey Memorial Park, Clearwater, Florida. Put this in your browser, and it will take you directly to Elizabeth C. Seither's Memorial Page. The Funeral Home permitted me to use this picture, message, and link to Liz's Memorial Page. https://www.dignitymemorial.com/obituaries/clearwater-fl/elizabeth- seither-9245702

Liz was able to buy a gorgeous home in the upper suburban neighborhood of Walton Hills, Ohio—nothing like the Sophia house or other houses she had rented. It was a magnificent place with a built-in swimming pool. Liz worked day and night to pay for her purchased home and keep up with the mortgage payments.

Liz said, "I had a lot of trouble in my marriage, and I was so depressed! I didn't know how I would provide for my family. I tried to work and care for my girls but didn't know what to do. It was one of the lowest times of my life."

Liz and her husband were having marital problems. Liz completely lost it, and Dorothy said that is how she ended up in a state psychiatric hospital.

I knew she was in the hospital, and Dorothy and I were trying to help her, but we didn't know what to do or how to help her. She was locked up, and I couldn't even get to a nurse's desk to see how she was doing or if I could come to visit her.

I will never forget Dorothy calling me one night saying, "Oh Rita, I just went to see Liz to try and find out if I could get her out of that awful place. There was a lady with a spaghetti mop on her head running around screaming, and patients were running up and down the halls screaming and crying out all kinds of things. I was so scared! Can you imagine how our sister felt? I was so upset, and Liz cried. She wanted to get out of there and back home to her girls. I needed to get her out of there, but I didn't know how. I went home to make phone calls to see if I could get help to get her out."

Then I told Liz how I remember that awful time. I got a call from a lawyer two days later to get her out of that crazy nuthouse and to go pick her up. I think Liz's girlfriend or one of our uncles contacted a lawyer who gave the lawyer my contact information. The lawyer called me and told me Liz would be allowed to get out because she had no other mental history. He said for me or someone else to pick her up. My sister Dorothy was working, so I told the lawyer I would pick her up.

I hurried up as fast as I could to go pick her up. I had no idea where I was driving and just wanted to get there and get back to take care of my two children, Pam and Chris. I had to ask a neighbor to help watch my children. Then I hopped into my car to look for where my sister was. I finally found it. I had to park far away from the entrance. Then, it started snowing hard. I had no boots, and my feet were frozen. I found my way in, and when I saw her, I didn't recognize her because she looked awful! When she saw me, she hugged me and hugged me and said, "Get me out of here!"

She said she couldn't sleep—afraid she would be killed by one of the other patients or medical help. She said she felt she was on death's door with no **ESCAPE**. On the way home, I got into a white-out snowstorm, and my little car was all over the roads. I dropped her off at her home, where she wanted me to take her, and I made sure she got into the house OK. She was so glad to be home, but her two girls were not there. Where were they? We didn't know. Later, we learned that Social Services had come in and taken the girls away. They put them in a foster home where they stayed for a short time; this was the first time we heard about it. Liz was panicky, and I had to get home to my kids. It was a bad day, and I told her that when I got home, I would call Dorothy, and she could help make phone calls to find out where the girls were.

Gina was so scared in the foster home, and Kim told me she would hide under a table at the foster home. She was so frightened that she cried for her mommy and stayed near her older sister, Kim. Gina told me she remembers sitting on the front steps just waiting for her mommy to come and take her home, but it didn't happen. I am sure the girls will remember those days for the rest of their lives. But things got better, and Liz got well, and eventually, Liz's daughters were brought back home with their mother. Our parents cared for the girls during that recouping time and cared for Dorothy's daughter, Lisa, while Dorothy worked.

It was a hard time for Liz and the family. After my sister passed away, Regina told me she remembered how difficult that was for her. Both girls will never forget that awful experience.

Liz said, "There were many times that the girls suffered because of my poor decisions when I left them in the care of others, and I realized later I should not have done that. It was another of many mistakes I made raising my two girls in our lives. All those memories haunt me to this very day, and I can't forgive myself; so, if it bothers me so much, it has to haunt my girls as well. They know I am very sorry. Sometimes, I couldn't help what I had to do, but other times, it was just reckless thinking."

"It was a terrible time, as many times were. I tried and wished I could be **Tin Can** again with a possible **ESCAPE**, even if it meant for a short period. I didn't know what to do and just let the darkness hover over my head that kept me in bondage. I prayed and prayed the whole time I was in a psychiatric facility and prayed that God would grant me my prayer to take care of my girls. The girls remembered that they were in that foster home, but I never wanted them to know what had happened to me and why I was in that terrible place. I made Dorothy, and you promised you would never tell the girls, but eventually, not so long ago, that news came out, and it was heartbreaking, and they asked me many questions."

When Liz started working again, she handled several jobs at once. She was back selling Avon, Fuller Brush, and jewelry, and then she started selling wigs and having wig parties. Liz tried opening a wig boutique, but that didn't last long. In talking to Dorothy, she reminded me of when my sister Liz bought a nice family restaurant across from Geauga Lake Amusement Park. She was so happy, and Kim and Gina were waitresses in that place. Liz figured it would be a "Gold Mine" because of the location and being on the main road. The restaurant was always packed because it was the center of attraction, with the amusement park across the street. Everyone worked hard, and Liz and the girls worked many hours. I remember them telling me about it, but I never went there to eat dinner. It would have been a good investment, but Liz and the girls couldn't handle it all, and it was a lot of pressure for everyone involved. There was always so much that had to be done, and a single mom and two girls couldn't handle it or have the expertise to know how to handle it. Liz just did things and didn't think of what had to be done, and it was another lousy purchase that shouldn't happened. But Liz tried and soon discovered that coming across that business deal didn't work out for her and the girls!

Liz was amazing, but the pressure was back on. It wasn't too long before she started getting overwhelmed with depression again, and the dark shadows hung over her continually.

Liz applied for a divorce from her second husband. It was a hard time in her life, but she survived. She was very lonely, and shortly after she married her third husband, he came to live in the Walton Hills household. He was a great guy and a hard worker and helped out with the household and the girls. Liz wanted to tell me what happened in that marriage. Liz told me she wanted us to write a chapter on each of her husbands.

However, I told her, "Wait! I can't write one chapter on each of your husbands!" We both laughed, and it cheered her up.

This third husband was good to Liz, provided help in the household, and was very good to the girls. That marriage didn't last very long because Liz's life was too hectic for him. She was always into something. Living with Liz was difficult, and he had never been married. As I recall, Liz had a house full of people, plus her two daughters. She scared this great, hardworking guy away, which was way more than he could handle. She then got a divorce from him; it wasn't even two years before they had been married. I don't know who wanted the divorce—the husband or Liz.

Life was too much for Liz, and she worried so much about her girls, Kim and Gina.

Lizzie said, "I recall putting the Walton Hills home up for sale, and I will never forget it. The house sold very fast, and I packed everything up and made plans to move to Florida to be our new home. I knew I had to tell my family, and it was sad, but I had to do it to make a new life for myself and my girls."

I will never forget the day Liz and the girls left for Florida. We were at a family wedding with my mother Mercedes, Dorothy, her daughter Lisa, my husband Dennis, and myself. We said our goodbyes, and I was heartbroken. Liz and the girls moved away to Florida to fulfill Liz's dream of real estate sales and to have a better life for her girls. My children and I were sad because we spent our holidays together in Liz's big house. All the kids would open up many presents, and now it was all over.

Liz said, "The girls and I moved to Broward County, Florida, in the Pembroke Pines area. We were excited to get a new start in life. However, a hurricane came, and we left that area to visit my friend, Josie, in the Indian Rocks Beach area near Clearwater Beach. I heard about home sales in Florida and put my attention and strength into learning the real estate business."

"While the girls stayed at Josie's place, I took off for the day, returned to pick them up, and told them I rented a house in Island Estates on Clearwater Beach! Therefore, the girls and I went to the Pembroke Pines area and packed up and left that area; plus, I never really liked that area, and my lease was up. That is how we got to Clearwater. I knew it was the best place for the girls and real estate sales, and I was right!"

The topic quickly changed, and Liz said, "After we got settled in Clearwater Beach, Dorothy and I took a vacation. Oh, we had lots of fun together! Dorothy and I went to Greece and had the time of our lives!

Liz being escorted out of the trolley to go up the mountain in a cable car.

After settling in Clearwater Beach, Dorothy and I took a vacation. Oh, we had lots of fun together! Dorothy and I went to Greece, and we had many great experiences! I bought several mink jackets and one full-length coat. I wore the long mink coat to get home on the plane, and Dorothy wore a mink jacket. She also had a mink jacket in her suitcase and another in her garment bag. I had two more mink jackets in my suitcases. All those jackets were inside out and folded so they couldn't be visible. Oh, we wondered how we would make it home to the States! This trip was before she loaned me her money to save the shopping plaza. We had so much fun together on that trip buying authentic gold jewelry.

We met several Greek men on that trip, but then again, they thought we were rich, and we thought they were not only rich but also romantic! They swept us off our feet!"

Hearing about this Greek trip interested me, and I wanted to learn more about it. Therefore, I asked Dorothy much later, and she told me more details about that Greece trip. Dorothy intended to go sightseeing in Greece, and Liz only planned to go shopping!!!!

Dorothy said, "Liz and I went to a nightclub and saw the Greek dancers with broken plates on their heads while they danced, which was very interesting! Our cab driver asked if we wanted to go to a private casino, and we said, "Yes." A person had to be a member to get into the casino, and the cab driver was a member. To go up the mountain, you had to take a cable car. That was so scary for me, but it was a fun experience to remember about our trip.

Dorothy said, "I will never forget that trip we took together. I was so mad at our sister! I couldn't get her out of the mink coat stores. She was buying and buying mink coats for her daughters and herself. She went from one mink coat store to another, shopping and searching for the best deals. She had to try almost every mink coat, including animal furs. Liz had so much fun but also aggravated the store owners and me. But the problem was we didn't have that much time to do all this shopping, and Liz didn't have enough money to buy everything she wanted. Liz was "on the buy" for mink coats and 24K gold jewelry."

Liz wore this full-length black MINK coat while going home on the plane.

While mink coat shopping, Liz found the shop she wanted to deal with after visiting it two or three times. She started bargaining with the owner, and he was getting so irritated that he grabbed her by the arm and kicked her out of the shop as he yelled, "Don't ever come back!"

Liz in the **MINK** coat store in Greece, she just couldn't decide which ones she want to buy.

Dorothy said, "Now she had a problem because that's the shop where she had picked out everything she wanted to purchase. But Liz, being Liz, returned to the same shop the next day and started to bargain again. Anyway, Liz made all her purchases with my charge card."

I asked Dorothy, "Did you buy a mink coat, too, or just Liz?"

Dorothy replied, "Yes, I bought one, and they sent it home to me in the United States in my correct size. But your sister bought several, and she wore the full-back diamond mink coat just as she said on the plane going home, and I wore one. Her thing was to buy mink coats and authentic gold jewelry, and she spent all of her money."

"The last day, right before we left to go home, she bought the gold jewelry in a shop at the hotel where we had stayed. When she was wheeling and dealing with the store owner, I kept yelling at her and saying, "Liz, we have to leave! We will miss our plane! Well, we did make our plane, but not by much. But the worst thing was when we were sitting on the plane, they passed customs sheets to claim all your purchases, and we freaked out."

I asked Dorothy, "What happened, and why were you freaking out? Didn't Liz think she had to claim those purchases of mink coats and all that jewelry? I never heard of this story at all. I remember that you and Liz went on that trip. I remember seeing Liz wearing the mink coats when we were in Florida, and I thought how silly that was, for in Florida, it is hot, and any kind of coat is unnecessary, especially a warm fur coat."

Dorothy replied, "Are you kidding? Liz didn't think of that until they passed out the claim papers. I was so nervous, and I didn't know what to do. I said to your sister, "Liz, now you did it! How will you get by with this one with all the purchases you made, especially all the jewelry you just bought?"

Liz with all of her luggage at the airport coming home from

"Liz was fearless and told me to wait. Then she went to the restroom on the plane. When she returned, she told me, "The Jewelry problem is taken care of! Don't worry about it! I have it all under control."

Dorothy asked her, "Liz, what did you do?"

Liz told her, "I stuffed the jewelry in my latex underwear and wore the rest! I didn't know I had to claim my purchases because I had never traveled internationally."

Dorothy said she almost died!

So, when it was time to get off the plane at LaGuardia Airport in New York City, Liz told me, "Dorothy, whatever you do when we go through customs, just keep walking! I will catch up with you, and I will find you. Don't stop and wait for me or look back; whatever you do, act like you don't even know me."

Dorothy said she was so mad at Liz! She didn't talk to her for the rest of the time going home, including going through the New York airport to get on the next plane to come home. It was indeed a trip she will never forget! It wasn't that Liz was trying to be dishonest; neither one knew that was what you had to do to claim most of your purchases.

Now, this was after the fact, and what would they do with those purchases? Liz would have to leave them there.

Dorothy and Liz's trip to Greece was the talk of the family for years. Who could ever forget the story of the infamous Liz and her mink coats?

**TIME** did move on, and we missed the family in Florida so much. Soon after that big Greek trip, Dennis and I made a yearly trip to Clearwater, Florida, to see my sisters and nieces. **TIME** passed quickly, and one year went into the next, like a rush of the tropical winds in the Florida sunshine. We usually stayed with Liz in either one of her condos or one of her houses on the island. She was always welcoming to us and showed us a great time! Then, my sisters and I would go shopping and hit the "Flea Markets," which we loved to do for many years.

When talking to Liz in the hospital, I told Liz, "You know, every time I went to Florida, you were always part of that trip. I never made a trip without seeing you and being with you. Most trips were with Dennis and the kids or just Pam and me. We had a small recreational vehicle, and one year, we even took my foster parents with us before they passed away. We traveled in the recreational vehicle (RV) and stayed with Liz, her girls, and sometimes one of her husbands or live-ins."

2014: Oh, how we loved to cruise! On the left is myself, and sisters Dorothy and Liz. We were going on board that Carnival Cruise Ship, Paradise. Our favorite thing to do was to get dressed up and dine out and shop in all the ports!

Liz said, "Oh, I remember those trips we had with you, and then we went off on one of the several cruises you planned for us. We had a great time, didn't we? We loved to eat those fancy dinners, and when we stopped at the ports, you know how much I love to shop!"

I replied, "Oh yes, February was when we always came to Florida. We are all looking forward to February 2021 to do something special together."

She said, "Yes, you are right, but now this Coronavirus changed everything for everyone during these times. But hopefully, by next February, when you and Dennis come down, the virus will be just a bad memory for all of us. Our world will be getting back to a new normal. Maybe even Victor and Jean could fly down again, do you think?"

I replied, "Dennis and I have come down every February to see everyone for years, and maybe we can even go on a cruise again, sail to "Never-Never Land," and enjoy each other. The boys can have their golf games, and they will be happy, and the girls can go out and do our favorite thing—shopping!"

Liz started talking about all four of her husbands, and I stopped her and said, "We are on a good roll now, so let's hold off on the husbands."

"Oh, yes, I just want to get to a chapter about our parents being deaf and what a struggle it was."

I added, "We had American Sign Language (ASL) as our first language with a combination of "HOME SIGNS," which is how we had to communicate at home and in that life."

Liz said, "I want a chapter on how these two marvelous deaf people struggled to stay alive and how our dad did any job to help feed us. People took advantage of our father and would have him work and not pay him. I want one or more chapters just on our parents, and then, I want a chapter on each of my husbands and live-in partners, but those stories will blow the readers away!"

I told her, "We will have **TIME** for those stories later, but let us continue with what **TIME** we have right now."

But Liz yelled at me and said, "Rita, are you sure we will have enough **TIME**? We never can be sure. The clock could be blowing away fast, like in a tropical windstorm. We can't take a chance; we must use our **TIME** wisely. You had better promise to give me the **TIME** and write all four chapters on each of my four husbands! Each husband had a different wild story to tell, and I don't know how I survived those marriages and live-in partners, but I indeed did. There were survival stories to tell my daughters, grandchildren, other family members, friends, and whoever reads our book. Rita, that is why it is essential to get this book out. People think they have problems, but it is nothing like our family, and I have endured. Life was tough for us, but by the grace of God, we survived as our readers can as well!"

Liz was doing well in real estate, and she and her girls moved from their condo into a lovely house in Island Estates in Florida. We always figured perhaps that house was jinxed or possessed, for its address was 666—the sign of the beast as in the Holy Bible. While living in that home, the girls could even tell you some spooky stories that no one needed to hear in their busy lives on the island. But Gina told me that her mom rented that house, and later, her mom bought it and changed the address number from 666 to 668. We lived there for about six years. Then, Mom sold it, and we moved back into a condo on the island.

Liz and the girls lived in a few condos and homes on the Island near Clearwater Beach. Another house that Liz had was exquisite, with the Gulf Bay water in her backyard. It was a lovely place with an expansive boat dock.

Gina told me she and her sister, Kim, attended Clearwater Middle School. She was in the sixth grade, and like most young girls, she would have occasional problems with her girlfriends. One time, they were mean to her. Gina was so upset that she went to her mommy and cried. Mom was so understanding and wise. Gina said her Mom gave her two choices:

1. Suggest the family move away and go to a different school and

2. Face the challenge and stand up for herself as Liz did when she was young in her Tin Can Lizzie days. Gina said that her mommy could always help her make the right choices.

1980: Liz's wedding day with her fourth husband. It was a glorious wedding celebration having her daughters as her bridesmaids. On the left is Kim, the gorgeous bride Liz, and daughter, Gina.

Liz always said, "I taught my girls not to run away from their problems and emotions but to do as I did. I faced them with courage so I could **OVERCOME** them. I had to do what I could and became **Tin Can Lizzie to survive!** Even today, when I am overwhelmed with stress and problems, I remember my Tin Can days and how strong I was! I taught my girls that when they are going through hard times, they must find a way of **"ESCAPE"** as well. I encouraged them to face their **"Trials and Tribulations."** One can find perspective and move forward. The results may not always be what is wanted or planned on, but with faith, they can **OVERCOME!"**

It wasn't long afterward, within a short period of **TIME**, Liz fell in love again. She found her fourth husband, and they had a lovely big wedding with her daughters, Kimmy and Gina, as her bridesmaids. Everything at the wedding was so beautiful. They had a gorgeous cake, the girls had fresh flowers as bouquets, and the place was full of fresh flowers. The groom looked so handsome, and he and Lizzie made a gorgeous, happy couple for the whole island to see! It was a beautiful wedding with the happy couple exchanging their marital vows.

Liz said, "Rita, let's make sure we write a whole chapter on this marriage to J.P. (as she called him, short for his full name). You must remember that I was never a bridesmaid—only a bride, and there I was, a bride again! I thought I was so lucky; you think, my sister? The girls loved him, but so did everyone else on the island. He was friendly, popular, well-liked, and well-known in a short time. Everyone knew him! He was such a charmer, and the ladies were after him being so good-looking!"

This husband was a French Canadian, and he thought Liz had a lot of money, and she thought he had a lot of money. As the story goes, he thought she was a millionaire and was living "high off the hog," as they say. Each of them had nothing. He moved into the house and continued with his "business ventures." However, since neither had money, they only survived by living daily. But you would never know, for Liz was doing very well in her real estate business. They had a good time and met various distinguished

1984-85: Sister Liz wearing her white mink coat from Greece at the boat show parade party that they gave on the island.

and popular business professionals. They gave exclusive parties for the holidays. The happy couple would lead the yearly boat parade, and Liz would wear one of the mink coats she bought in Greece.

This husband was a dreamer. He spoke French and was very charming and romantic. He had a nickname, "Frenchie," which we all called him. He was well-known on the island, supportive of Liz, and good for the girls. He planned to add stone driveways for mansions on the Island and in the area. Shortly after, he took money from the homeowners who never got their driveways done. Liz quickly learned that of all her husbands, this one was a prominent con artist, and he was swindling people out of much money. Their marriage would have lasted much longer, except Frenchie was caught and put in jail. Liz had no idea how slick he was, and he had a bad reputation in their area. Liz wanted nothing more to do with him after she learned what he had been doing.

He was also a gambler and loved the dog races. I remember visiting my dear sister Liz one time while in Florida. He took me to the Greyhound races, which was a unique experience. However, he was kind and respectful to the girls, which was so crucial to Liz that her girls were protected. But once in jail, that was the end of that marriage, and Liz went for a fourth divorce.

Liz was very lonely again after the divorce from her French Lover ("Frenchie or Pierre," as we called him). Yet, **TIME** continued to pass. She diligently closed sales and did well. She was driving an expensive Cadillac in no **TIME**, as it was her pride to take clients around to see properties in her fancy car.

In another conversation, Liz said while in the hospital, "Rita, you have so many talents and gifts, more than I ever could have."

I sharply said to Liz, "You know that is not true. You have a big heart and reach out to others like I do."

"I remember visiting you and the family one Christmas, and you just couldn't wait to show my husband Dennis and me your latest venture. You closed a property deal in a community in the heart of Clearwater, Florida. You said that one of your property real estate deals was going under. It was a home mainly for people with disabilities and seniors. You felt so sad for them to be without a home."

It was an Assisted Care Living Facility (ACLF). You felt so sad for them, for their facility was going into foreclosure, and the residents would have no home. What did you do? You bought the house for all the people in it. They would have been out on the streets or transferred to other state facilities if you hadn't bought that big house. I will never forget that Christmas when you, Dorothy, Gina, Kim, and I handed out lots of gifts you purchased. You had Dorothy wrap all the gifts for each person and all the staff at the house. You bought housecoats, pajamas, slippers, blankets, and toiletries. It was a holiday visit I will never forget. We took pictures of you handing out the gifts to everyone. Liz, you were so proud, and we were also proud of you. You held onto the home for quite some time until you decided to sell it to someone else. You did not fear caring for them and always kissing and hugging them. They got from you the love they seldom had from their own families if they had one."

Liz said, "Oh, I loved visiting those poor people and caring for them there. They needed me. We had a lot of fun, and they loved me to pieces, especially when I brought them things. They all called me "Miss Lizzie." I would bring them big bulk food items. They would watch for my car to pull in the driveway and come running out to help me take stuff out of the car."

"I would bring Dorothy, Kim, and Gina; they also loved going there. I did have a big heart for those people and the others in the community, and the real estate agents respected me for what I did. Then, I finally sold the house to a couple who moved into the place and cared for all those people. I returned to visit the residents; they all wanted me to be with them again. The residents said it wasn't the same as when I owned the home. It was a special time when I could reach out to others and make life much more bearable for them and be happy—and it did not take much to make those people happy. They all went through tough times in their lives as I did, so I knew their pain, heartache, and the tribulations they were going through. I wanted to improve their lives and give them a nice place to live."

I replied, "You were so generous, and Christmas was your favorite time. I remember when we would go to your house at Christmas in Ohio. You and their Aunt Dorothy had many gifts for my children, Pam and Christopher."

Liz said, "Yes, I loved Christmas! I wanted everyone to be happy and enjoy the season's holiday festivities. I would purchase presents for everyone! I bought gifts for my family first and surely overdid it! I also bought gifts for my employees at the real estate office, many of my customers, and even strangers I invited to my house for Christmas dinner. Christmas was my favorite time of year, mainly because growing up on Sophia wasn't much of a Christmas for us. I could tell you some real stories of what we did for Christmas back in the day, including stealing a Christmas tree one year. So, I made it special for all!"

I replied to Liz," I remember that year! I still lived in the Sophia house, and we had no Christmas tree. I remember Dorothy saying she would argue with our dad, begging him to buy us a tree. But it was a head shake, and Daddy would sign, *"Me broke, no money."* But you were so determined that we would have a Christmas tree that year. Therefore, You, Victor, and one of Victor's friends went up to the corner of East 102nd Street and Sophia and waited for the man to close the Christmas tree lot on Christmas Eve. I knew what you were planning, and I was worried you would get caught by the police and we would have no Christmas at all. But all of you jumped the fence he put around the left-over trees and took the biggest one. It probably had not sold, for it was so big."

"You, Victor, and his friend dragged that tree all the way home. I couldn't believe it when you pulled it through the front door. I was in shock! Then, all of a sudden, Victor took off the wrapping around the tree, and when the branches flared out, we were all in awe! The tree was huge, and we had to figure out what we would do with it. Soon, Daddy came into the living room, and he just stood there shaking his head. He was so mad, for he figured we didn't pay for that tree. Daddy kept tapping his head and pointing at Victor as if it were all Victor's idea. Daddy was mad for a while as he yelled his shrieking guttural sounds. Then he walked away. We were left to figure out what to do with this huge tree. We wanted to decorate the tree, but we couldn't get it to stand up. Victor shoved the tree into the corner, leaning against the wall, hoping it would hold it up. We didn't know what to do. Then suddenly, our Daddy came back into the living room and brought a stand for our tree, which he made out of the wood in the backyard."

Liz said," I will never forget that year. Dorothy complained so much that we had no tree, so I had to think of a way to get one. I remember Victor was blamed for stealing that tree, but it was all my idea, and I orchestrated the plan. I figured, "Why not? We needed one; they would only throw those trees in the garbage truck. But it was so much fun! I remember Richard and your eyes lighting up when you saw that tree. I will never forget how surprised and happy you both were. We had no tree lights to put on, but that was ok—we had fun decorating it. We made all our decorations and hung our old socks on the tree. I remember Dorothy popping popcorn, and we made a garland, but we only wrapped it around the front of the tree, for we didn't have enough. I remember Victor's idea to fluff up the bottom of the tree with toilet paper like it was standing in the snow. We didn't put on much toilet paper; we knew we would need it in the bathroom!"

I told her, "Oh, Liz, it was such a joy setting up that huge Christmas tree; we spent most of the night making decorations. We laughed and laughed as we decorated our stolen tree. We wanted to make a star for the top, but we didn't have the proper paper; if we had made a star, we would have been afraid to attach it for fear the tree would fall over. Looking back, it was amazing that Victor, you, and the others didn't get caught taking the tree. We didn't have any gifts to go under the tree, so we just put our favorite items and pretended they were new. Oh, those were the days!"

Later, when my sister passed away when talking about the group home with Kimmie, she said, "Mom loved her residents, and most of the time, she called them her "tenants." They were all government-assigned; some were good in health, and some were not. Many of her tenants had mental and physical disabilities. They were everything to Mom, and she loved them all very much, and they loved Mom. I would take two residents shopping every two weeks at Albertson's Grocery Store. The residents would guard the grocery carts like hawks. The tenants loved going shopping with her; they would end up with four grocery carts of food. She would often call me because there wasn't enough room for the groceries in Mom's big car. She would have her boys load them in my car. She also would call them "her boys" because they adored her and were so generous to them. They were so appreciative that Mom would buy them their favorite foods, and when their birthdays came around, WOW! Mom gave them grand birthday parties and invited our family members there."

She also said, "Oh, Christmas! My mom bought out Walmart for them and spent all her money buying nice, useful gifts for her tenants. Mom had a heart of gold and would love to buy things for them, even if it wasn't their birthdays or Christmas. Mom loved to make them happy, but really, they were making mom happy!"

My Sister Liz by her navy-blue fancy Lincoln. She was known all over the island with her big fancy cars.

I told Kim, "Wow, thank you for sharing the group home story! It reminded me about our Christmas on Sophia, for your mom surely did love Christmas!"

In another conversation with Kim after my sister passed away. Kim and I were talking about Mom and her cars.

Kim said, "Mommy had several Cadillacs over the years, which she loved. Everyone who knew my mom knew she would be taking clients around in a fancy car. First, she had Cadillacs. They were always an off—white, pearly shade, or creamy-colored vehicle. Then she had a big Lincoln that she eventually sold to buy her Mercedes. She had to earn a lot of money in sales to buy that Mercedes. Marketing real estate for her was easy; she was natural and gifted at selling anything!

Kim said, "Aunt Rita, I did find a picture of my sharp-looking mom in front of one of her other cars. She was so classy, as was her fancy car! I think it was a navy-blue fancy, higher-model Lincoln. It, too, had all the bells and whistles a vehicle could have! She liked that car as well. She had so much pride in that Lincoln! Here is my mom's picture with her showpiece, a high-model expensive car."

Kim said," I don't think she was in love with it, as she was with her white and gold-trimmed Mercedes. Yet, she sold that Lincoln after many hard-working sales, working late hours at

Liz's gorgeous white Mercedes with gold trim. She absolutely loved that car!

night to buy the car of her dreams, and that was the white Mercedes with the gold trim."

"Oh, Aunt Rita, "Mom's favorite car in the world was her white Mercedes, which she took pride in! Whenever she pulled into Island Estates or Clearwater Beach, everyone knew it was Elizabeth Seither, the realtor. They would all say," **Here Comes Lizzy Today,"** as she pulled her gorgeous car into her private parking spot for all to see and admire. She owned the Islands Estates Real office, and it seemed she owned the whole island. Everyone knew her and knew that her trademark was her good sales abilities and her fancy cars! Everyone loved her to pieces! She had everyone working for her in her sales office on the island. And what did Liz do? She drove the clients around in her fancy cars to make another sale. They would see her coming and say," **Here Comes Lizzy!** Where is she taking us today to find us a home?"

LIZ'S LOGO: NEED A HOME TO BUY OR RENT? HOW ABOUT A BEACH HOUSE WITH A GOOD OCEAN VIEW GETAWAY? GIVE LIZZIE A CALL!

SHE'S WAITING FOR YOU!

Liz's Real Estate Executive business card. The card was fancy, like Liz's and her cars. Liz loved her classy, big cars. She was so well-known on the island. Everyone loved her to pieces!

I responded to Kim, "It is almost like it was for mom to be back on the streets of Sophia when she ran out of the house, and the boys would say, **"HERE COMES TIN CAN LIZZIE!** Your mom loved that, as she heard them say those words! Plus, it was an incentive to push her to get more real estate sales, and it reminded her of the olden days when she got into the big action on the streets of Sophia to toss the pennies or to make a deal." She passed out her business cards to everyone.

Kim said, "Aunt Rita, her clients were picked up with class! She was so proud to take clients to her real estate openings in that car. She loved it and took her clients for joy rides in it, too, as she showed them the beautiful Clearwater Beach area."

Kim replied, "Aunt Rita, here are pictures of her white Mercedes trimmed in gold and one of mom standing by the car of her dreams! That white Mercedes was the talk of Clearwater and the real estate profession. She was always **"On Top of the World,"** selling real estate left and right." We do have a picture of her by the car. I will treasure that picture of Mom and that white Mercedes she loved so much! Aunt Rita, you must put that in the book that you are writing."

Kim said, "Yes, Mom's fanciest car was her white Mercedes, and everything was trimmed in gold. Oh my, it was so gorgeous! As I think back, the door handles, the wheel rims, the grill grate, and the trim were all shiny gold. It was so fancy, just like Mom wanted it to be, and she loved it so much! She took care of that car like it was her baby! Mom used to say all the time that she wanted to be buried in that Mercedes!"

Kim asked, "Aunt Rita, do you remember that white Mercedes of hers?"

Liz standing with her white and gold trimmed business suit on the side of her white and gold trimmed Mercedes.

I replied to Kim, "Yes, I do remember it, but for some odd reason, I remember it being all a light shade of gold. I guess that is what she wanted me to think of her car. She used to pick up Uncle Dennis and me at the Tampa Airport in that car, and the first thing I would say to her was, "Me love, me love—love your car!" That is how your Grandma Deaf would express herself when she loves something. Her name was "Mercedes" as well; maybe that is why mommy loved having a Mercedes; it was a piece of grandma. Uncle Dennis and I would hear all the stories of who she chauffeured around in that car in her real estate sales in the Clearwater area until we arrived at her house on the island."

I replied to Kim," Yes, your mom could sell anything! She was a gifted salesperson and very respected. She worked hard until the Lord called her home and took her out of that hospital room. I miss her so much as I write this story."

Kim replied, "Aunt Rita, you must put in your book that real estate was one of the biggest things she loved! I always knew she was not going down at the end of her life without losing her last deal, precisely what she did! She didn't drive much in the last two years, so I needed time to take her around to do business. She had something that came up with real estate, even if it was a rental property that we worked on for weeks at times, to make one $700 commission, and I was always there for Mom. Sometimes, she didn't answer all the right questions, but people loved her! They loved her love and respect for them, in real estate, and for others. Clients knew they could use another realtor, but they wanted "Lizzy" to find them a home to buy or rent! My Mother made her last deal go through even after she has gone, and I announced it at her memorial!"

**TIME** was passing, and before long, the girls were grown up and on their own. Kim had one son, Derek, married Peter and had two girls— Alexis and Sophia. Regina had a career as a visual display artist when she met her husband, Johnny. Much later, she opened her own design company in 2014 and is very successful as a home designer in a high-end interior new home design business. Regina and Johnny had three girls—Bennett, Brie, and Brice.

2002: GRANDMA LIZ WITH HER GRANDDAUGHTERS
ENJOYING THEIR TIME TOGETHER!

From the left: Brie, Grandma Liz, Brice, and Bennett

Liz continued to work in real estate. She lived alone since the girls had lives of their own. **TIME** passed by her too quickly, and she was looking for a close companion. She met Michael. Liz adored him, and he adored her. Liz moved into his gorgeous house on the island with a built-in swimming pool. He, too, was significant to Liz and the girls, but their relationship didn't work out. Michael wanted Liz to stop working in real estate and travel and continue to live in his home together. However, my sister did not want to stop working while staying out late at night in her real estate business.

Liz had expensive taste and was way too far in debt. Years before, Michael did try to bail her out of some of her financial jams, but it was impossible to make any headway. Numerous other problems were going on, so their lives together and living arrangements quickly stopped.

Michael always wanted Liz to stop working and go traveling with him. He was a great guy and so good to Liz and the girls.

Liz was selling well but would spend as much as she made. She continued to be in deep debt, and Michael continued to help her out several times, but Liz was out working all the time. They were good together, and Liz did care for him. I am unsure why those two broke it off; I can only assume that Liz refused to stop selling real estate and did not follow his wishes to travel. I wasn't sure, but shortly after they broke it off, Michael married someone else later on. Liz took that news hard and was always sorry they were no longer together.

Shortly after breaking it off with Michael, Liz was diagnosed with cervical cancer. She rented a beach house, and her second husband's son, Mark, lived with her. At that time, I took a leave of absence from my work within Cleveland Schools and went to Florida with my husband, Dennis, to help Dorothy and Kim care for Liz. The radiation of all those treatments had destroyed the linings of her bladder and colon, and she suffered from severe internal bleeding and diarrhea. She regained her strength. But she was lonely, so she continued to do what she knew best: selling real estate to get herself out of debt.

Liz had her own real estate office on Island Estates in Florida and another in Indian Rock Shores in Florida. Liz's story of selling real estate was published in a few real estate magazine articles featuring her success She moved from the big beach house to Indian Rock Shores, where she had a condo where my husband Dennis and I would visit her. My daughter Pamela had an extraordinary relationship with her Aunt Liz and stayed there with her on Pam's vacation. I took my sisters on another cruise with my daughter Pam and my niece Kim during that time.

We went on several cruises, and we had so much fun! Those were enjoyable and memorable days, and Dennis would get mad at the sisters because they had so many suitcases! Of course, Liz had to have a hat for every outfit. Liz and I spent a lot of money in the picture studio, where she ordered several big canvas paintings and many pictures. Liz and I had the same passionate, fiery fixations—we loved getting pictures taken and collecting them. Here is a studio picture taken on one of our cruises as we all got dressed up for the dinners, and I always danced away at those dinners!

2016 at the cruise photo studio. Just the four ladies went on this trip with my husband, Dennis. From the bottom left: Liz and Rita and on the upper left: Dorothy and Rita's daughter Pam.

**TIME** was constantly moving forward, and Liz searched for another male friend. Her last live-in partner was Ernie, whom she met on the Internet. He was several years older than Liz and madly in love with her at first sight. Ernie adored Liz, and on their first date, he asked her to go on a cruise with him to Hawaii, and of course, she accepted. It was a 24-day cruise, and it was fabulous! They had a lovely cabin with a balcony. She accepted the invitation because she loved cruising. Ernie came to live with her in her latest condo at Top of the World in Clearwater, Florida. He was very sickly, but they got along well and were good companions. Liz took care of him, and he was so kind to her. He adored my sister and said many sweet nothings to her daily, which she loved and needed.

When Hurricane Irma hit Florida in 2017, Liz was kind and generous. She wanted everyone to be safe and welcomed everyone to stay with her. She didn't have to evacuate, and she had electrical power. Dorothy and Kim were there, and she also had her granddaughter Amber (her granddaughter from her second marriage) come with her entire family. Amber had done all of Liz's real estate paperwork and designs for several years and did beautiful work. Everyone stayed for about 4 or 5 days until the hurricane blew over and power was restored in the surrounding areas.

During the blast of Hurricane Irma, Ernie got sick, and they had to call 911; he was rushed to the hospital. Later, the doctor called Liz and said Ernie had a stroke. Ernie never returned to the condo. However, while Ernie was in the hospital, Liz fell while showering at her condo.

Therefore, 911 was called again—the same 911 ambulance medical people came to take Liz to the hospital. She had broken her collar bone and fractured her arm, and she was taken to the same rehab nursing home Ernie was at, but she didn't stay there very long. Liz hated that rehab center, but Ernie was so happy to see her and spend time with her.

Kim was Liz's spokesperson and was always with her through everything she went through. She was her power of attorney and made important medical and financial decisions for her. She arranged for Liz to be in the same rehab nursing home as Ernie. Liz hated it, and she said she would rather die than ever go back to a nursing home again. Kim always listened to Liz, and she agreed to have her sent home. Ernie remained in the rehab center for a short time. Then he got sick and was hospitalized and contracted MRSA, and he passed away. Liz was sorrowful; she cared for him while staying with her the best she could.

Kim helped her, ran around for her, and made her meals. Kim was excellent to her mother, and my sister Liz called her "*My Angel*." Liz stayed in Kim's condo for a while, but the stairs were too much for her to climb.

As **TIME** went by, Liz was starting to feel stronger. Kim searched and found her Mom a lovely little one-bedroom apartment on Mexican Way in **Top of the World**. Liz loved it there, and her apartment had no steps for her to climb, for she was on the first floor. After her lease, Kim thought Liz could live with her old-time Asian friend, Mona. They found another condo in the same development but on Irish Lane, and they lived together. That condo was the last one Liz lived in before she passed away. That was the place she wanted so anxiously to return to so she could say a proper goodbye to everyone—and for me to go to Florida and write her life story. Liz had the main bedroom with a big back room; her office was where she had her computer and worked from home. Liz never gave up her real estate work and rental properties; even in the hospital waiting for that colonoscopy procedure, she had a SALE! Kim helped her take care of things and ran around for her and the paperwork. We were so proud of her for having made that last sale.

As **TIME moved on**… Gina's oldest daughter, Bennett, married and had a son, Ricardo, born in January 2019. My sister Liz adored her great-grandson and loved him very much.

**TIME** was moving so swiftly, and finally, the family planned a trip together in February 2020. We had a family reunion. Our brother Victor and his lovely wife Jean came from Weed, California. My niece Gina came in from the East Coast of Florida and blessed us by bringing her grandson, Ricardo. It was beautiful that Liz spent time with her great- grandson, whom she just adored. We had such a grand time together, and I shared the PowerPoint I created for my research about my mother and her extraordinary and miraculous birth.

February 2020: From the left, Great Grandma Liz, Grandma Gina, and Great-Grandson, Ricardo gathers at the family Reunion at Uncle Richie's house in Florida.

Right after the family reunion, after Liz was back home in her condo, **TIME** started to take a sharp turn for her. She had a terrible fall in the bathroom and was hospitalized for that fall, but still, she was not regaining her health. She had severe bruises all over her face and body. We were apprehensive about her. Liz was determined to make it to her 80th birthday, and she did on June 3rd, 2020! She was so happy that day! Kim planned a small "family and friends" gathering for her. I designed the cake and contributed since I was unable to attend.

**TIME** did not give Liz or me any favors, and the hands never got stuck. It can never go back or slow down, the clock keeps ticking away.

Soon, the clock started ticking ahead, and it was after that time that Liz believed her cancer was coming back and that history was repeating itself. Thinking that she had cancer could have caused her to have a minor stroke and be hospitalized. However, while Liz was in the hospital, the doctors decided they would help her with her other health needs. They wanted a colonoscopy ordered.

During this hospital stay, I received the gift of **TIME**, for Liz had the opportunity to share her most profound stories and some of her **Deepest-Seated Secrets**. She requested that I write a book on snippets of her and our family's lives.

**TIME** was a gift, allowing us more seconds to keep ticking. But **TIME** was turning into a big gush of tropical, cold wind, and it felt like a race with Liz and me going against the clock's ticking. It was a wonderful time meeting my newfound sister, **Tin Can Lizzie,** and learning about this lady I never knew before, whom I called my **"Big sister Liz"** for years. In our evening conversation in the hospital, Liz closed with a fitting thought.

With a serious and sad tone, Liz said, "Sister Rita, Please tell my girls and grandchildren that I will be with them and guide them through tough **TIMES**. Both of my girls are so special, and I love them dearly! I love each one differently because they have unique qualities and talents. I am sorry I never spent much time with my girls and grandchildren. I was always trying to close my next sale. That seemed to come first in my life, which was wrong, and I am hurting so badly because of what and how I did things. I can't go back in **TIME** and get another chance at this late stage of the game, but when I leave the hospital, I will spend more time with them and love them even more."

"In my last days, I will be different for the grandchildren, and I will be on top of all they do in their lives and their many successes. I will keep **TIME** for them and not let it run away without being in touch with them. I want them to know that when they need me, as their mothers need me, I will be there helping them get through whatever is challenging them in life. Rita, please tell them I will always be with them and the rest of my family until we meet again."

"Rita, please make sure you write all this in the book, but when I get home, I will tell everyone myself."

By now, I was tired while listening to Liz and making sense of what she had already said, and I had to write the notes on my computer.

I told Liz, "I can't believe how much we covered in one day with two phone calls. I am very proud of you, and I promise I will complete everything as you requested. I will fill in the rest and provide more information on our family members. You will love our book, my dear sister, Liz!"

Liz said, "I guess that is all for now. I thought we had a good day together writing **OUR** story. My girls will be so proud of me for what I said from my heart. I know the family will be proud of you, sister Rita, for writing this book about myself and **OUR** family. I can't wait to surprise them when we read this story together after the book gets published! It will be our family **LEGEND** of how we all survived in a world that was not made for struggling kids like us with deaf parents and who were so poor!"

She agreed that we covered a lot today for **OUR** book (I love how she calls it "**Our Book**"), but Liz said there was so much more to cover. Listen, Rita, please don't forget to call me early in the hospital. Tomorrow will be another new day to learn more about the "**Trials and Tribulations of Tin Can Lizzie.** "I thank you with all my heart, but please just get it done, for our **CLOCKS ARE TICKING,** and **TIME** is of the essence!"

She was so tired, and so was I, and she closed this long day of conversations with each other. She closed with another lovely goodnight, "I love you, my sister Rita, I love you, good night!"

When I write this footage (these accounts of Liz's life), as the camera keeps rolling over and around the life of the **"Tin Can Queen,"** I can genuinely say again, "Good night, my sister **Tin Can,**" wherever you are and whatever you are doing!

# Chapter 7

## THEN, THEY WERE FRIENDS

I couldn't wait to call my sister today to find out if the colonoscopy had been scheduled yet and see how Lizzie was holding up. When I called her, I could tell by her voice that she was very depressed, and I asked her if she was up to talking today.

Liz said, "Yes, I have to be, and all night, when I wasn't feeling well, I was so hungry, thirsty, and weak. I thought about the conversations we had yesterday about my girls. I miss them so much. I have so much more to say about them and how much I love them. Can you tell me what you wrote about Kim and Gina yesterday? I have so much to say about them!"

I could tell she was crying when I started reading some of what I wrote to the girls. Liz told me, "OK, you better stop reading, or we will never get through what I want to say today. It all sounds great; I have much more to say about them."

I added, "Liz, we can talk about them when you get home—how's that? But right now, I don't want you crying and upset. You need your energy and strength for the procedure."

Liz said," My dear sister, I am so thankful you gave me this **TIME.** It keeps my mind busy and helps the day go faster until the staff comes and gets me for that procedure—that I don't care about or want! I look forward to our talks; it is another **ESCAPE** for me as we discuss this book. My mind is so busy, and I feel so peaceful! So now I know, if I forget some of these things I am telling you about, everyone I know I will have a backup, now that it is also in writing."

"Okay, I mentioned my friends to you several times, but I thought I would like to touch on them. Maybe you can provide some background and clarity. You said you have been doing that as you are writing."

I told her, "Yep, I will do my best if you feel up to talking. So, do you want to talk a little about your friends today?"

Liz made it a point to say numerous times that she was always very lonely in our phone conversations. The only things I could write about were what she spoke about and who she spoke about. She was lonely and had many spurts of depression in her marriages, live-in relationships, family, and businesses.

She made it clear that her closest friend was her friend Sammy B in her younger years, late teens, and early twenties.

Liz said, "I truly loved him and never had anyone I could be so honest and happy with. I was never intimidated by him. I also got him in the networking oil business and trained him to be a leader, just as I trained our brother, Richard, and many others. I knew my friend Sammy would go far as a leader. We never had a serious relationship, ever to be married. He was not that kind of partner to me. He was the closest friend that I ever had, and there was never any intimacy, only a true friendship. He always stood by me and was there when I needed a shoulder to cry on. When I heard he passed away, I was in shock for several days because of losing my long-time friend."

"Sammy was in the group of twenty guys that hung out together, with my second husband being one of those guys. Frank Gaglione was another one of the guys that hung around in that group from my past. Rita, when I get home, I want to call Frank and his wife, Carol, and tell them you and I are writing this book, and I want them both to be featured. Will you do that for me?"

I replied, "Liz, when you get home, you can call them yourself; they will love to hear from you. But I will remind you when we work together to expand our book."

Liz said, "Out of that group of guys, there are only two guys left: Frank and one of the guys who lives in St. Petersburg, Florida, close to our brother Richie and our sister Dorothy. I want them to get together and meet. I would be so happy! Maybe you can get them to do that for me. My second husband, Rich, moved to Florida with his third wife and mother.

Frank and his lovely wife, Carol, were Godparents to Rich's two children, Mark and Lauren, from his first marriage before he married my sister. When Rich first married my sister, Liz, it was fine, but the marriage didn't work out well. Carol stays in touch with Kim in these later years, especially when her son, Derek, got in a boating accident. How awful that was!

After Liz had passed, I talked to Carol and Frank. Frank told me how close this group was, and he was heartbroken that Liz was no longer alive. He said she was one of the "guys" and got along with the whole group that hung out together—just like she hung out with the boys she played Penny Toss with within the streets. She had a lot of personality, charisma, and a unique way of dealing with people. Frank talked about Liz and Rich's marriage, and he said that Rich had a lot of faults, but everyone did. Frank did say that he didn't respect him regarding how that marriage went, but he was still one of them. Frank was a long-time great buddy to Liz and her second husband, Rich, and his late brother Jerry, a professional football player. Frank said they had so much fun and had some great times when the guys met, but now only two are left. Frank said it is all so sad that a group of friends that were together for so many years is gone. He said that he misses his friends and their wives.

When I called Frank, he and his wife Carol were in shock, for they deeply admired Liz for many years. They saw her last when they were in Florida at Liz's second husband Rich's funeral. By this time, Rich had already remarried again for the third time. But Liz was at his funeral and supported their children, Gina and Kim, and Mark and Lauren from his first marriage. She loved those four children so much, and Mark, her X-stepson, lived with her and helped take care of her at the beach house she rented.

About 1950: Liz and her best friends from the left: Claire, Jackie, Sandra, and Liz.

Liz jumped to her younger days, living on Sophia again and the friends she grew up with in her more youthful days. Even her friends in Sophia were getting older now.

Liz talked about Sandra Runyan, whose mother, Irene, and our mother were so close. Mrs. Runyan helped our mother raise her children, cook meals, and survive poverty. The only other friends she talked about back then in the early days were Joey and his sister Claire Klucho, who was the same age as Liz.

Liz said, "I was back writing to Sandra and getting emails from Joe Klucho. After so many years, it was wonderful to be in touch with them again. But Sandra would call me, and I appreciated that so very much! We both talked and wondered where **TIME** went. I told her it seemed like yesterday when we lived on Sophia Ave as best friends and neighbors."

Liz talked about many memories and her faithful friends while growing up.

Liz remembered, "I will never forget when Sandra and I were maybe no more than ten years old. We would go into the back bedroom, off the kitchen, and jump high on the bed. It was so much fun our mom didn't hear our giggles due to her being deaf. We laughed so hard and said how it tickled our stomachs. We were friends for so many years, from our younger days to when we were older. After I married my first husband, my new bride, Sandra, showed me how to make toasted cheese sandwiches. We never had them while growing up at home. It didn't take much to make me happy, and I was thrilled! Everything was so simple back in those days."

"I loved Sandra's mom, Irene, and Sandra loved our mom. Mrs. Runyan was always very nice and invited me to her house even after marriage. When we were older, Sandra and I always talked on the phone; I don't know what happened; we drifted apart. Just within this last year, you found Sandra and her husband, Len, for me, and I was so happy we were in touch again. I wish I could have seen and hugged her, but talking on the phone was a blessing."

I asked Liz, "if she remembered the names of the boys she played Penny Toss with."

She said, "Not at this moment, for I am tired, but the next time we talk, I will remember all their names and let you know."

The only other long-time friend she talked about was her friend Donna, but that wasn't until high school when they started the girls club, "East End Neighborhood Girls' Club." I was so proud of that club and how Donna and I reached out to many girls who needed support."

I asked Liz, "What is that Girls' Club? Tell me how all that happened. Did you not hang out in the streets anymore?"

Liz was talking again and said, "Well, I was getting older and too old to pitch pennies. Some of the same boys I hung out with got involved with their schools and sports, and I didn't see them around much anymore. I had found another crowd I hung out with, Donna and a few other older girls. We were so proud of the girls' club we started. We all saved our money from whatever jobs we could get and bought red and blue blazers with a created emblem. We were tough, and no one would mess with us, but we also did good things in the Woodland

Community. We took in other girls who needed support from living in the tough streets in poverty and the projects, and we would help those girls with their problems."

"However, it wasn't that I didn't have my problems," she said. "I had plenty, but all of us did in the neighborhood. Our parents were deaf, and we were destitute, with little chances in life except what we did for ourselves. However, who we are today is due to our upbringing by our parents, who were deaf. But we turned those sad times into good times and had many good times! We loved reaching out to other girls that needed friendship and support."

"Let me tell you, Donna was a tough one, and no one in the eastside tough neighborhoods would ever mess with her. But I knew how to handle those rough and tough kids as well... but not like Donna! She would get in physical fights with anyone who would "double cross" her, and they would be sorry. Even today, she is a tough but good person; you know that Rita, right?"

I said, "I know that, and she has been your friend through some of your darkest times for so many years since high school. Both her and Bill, her late husband."

Then Liz said, "Oh, we got into big battles over the years, big time, but we always became friends again. I think Donna was my girlfriend for the longest in my life. When she married Bill, they both were my friends. We were all very heartbroken when Bill passed away. He was such a great guy, easy-going, and funny. Donna and I were lasting friends through all of our lives."

Liz asked, "Rita, do you remember her husband, Bill?"

I replied, "Of course I do. He was a wonderful man, and Donna and Bill adored each other. I remember them staying with you in the Island Estates condo, and when Dennis and I came to stay with you, we slept in your bedroom in the downstairs garage. We all had a lot of fun together."

Liz said, "Donna and Bill did everything together. It was such a perfect marriage, and when he was sick, Donna and their daughter Tina did everything for him. They even had him flown into the Cleveland Clinic for better and more technical medical assistance. We did go half on the island condo together, but, as you know me, that didn't go very well.

They helped me out of losing that place. They were both excellent people. Later, Donna and Bill moved to Florida, and I found property on the beach for them to rent.

As you know, after Bill passed away, Donna permanently came to live in Florida from Ohio. Donna and Dorothy are very close friends today and do many things together. I feel bad because initially, she was my friend since we were in the Girls Club together. We still see each other often, and the three of us have good times together, sometimes with Kim. But now, she and our sister Dorothy hang out together frequently, and I don't get to see them much."

I told Liz, "Yes, I know Donna, and you were friends for a long time before and after she moved to Florida."

Liz replied, "Oh yes, I had a lot of good friends who helped me in the real estate business when I had my own offices. I had the Island Estates Real Estate Office for many years, and I lost that. But then I had another office in Indian Rock Shores for a long time. Several office workers put up with a lot from me, but they were wonderful!"

Liz said, "You know my sweet sister, Rita, I have had so many friends, some so good and true to me, and some backstabbers who took advantage of me and were not nice. But the greatest friend I ever had in my later years was, guess who? My dog Faith! I adored that dog, and you know what they say: "Man's best friend is their dog, and surely that was my Faith! So, as I talk about friends now for our book, I want to come back and talk about Faith."

## MOM'S BEST FRIEND, FAITH

Later, I asked Kim about her Mom and Faith. Kim told me, "Aunt Rita, when you write Mom's book, and in the chapter, you say you are featuring Mom's friends, please can't forget the greatest friend Mom had in her last days: our dog, Faith. That dog meant everything to Mom! "

I replied to Kim, "Oh yes, Kim's mom talked about Faith when she and I talked in the hospital in her last days. But I didn't think much of it at the time."

Kim said, "When I left Moffitt Cancer Hospital, Mom took good care of Faith. Later, when I went on little road trips to see my son Derek and sister Regina, mom always begged me to give her Faith while I was gone."

"Aunt Rita, I don't know if you remember the story of when mom was on the elevator with Faith when she was living in Americus in the Top of the World, and mom passed out in the elevator and was bleeding. Faith licked Mom's blood off her face so she could breathe. Faith squeaked and cried until help came for Mommy, and 911 was called. Faith was so scared, and so was Mommy; Faith wanted to ride in the ambulance with Mommy. She was adequately cared for by tenants in the Top of the World until I came to get Faith while Mom went to the hospital.

Faith saved her life that day, and from that moment on, Faith and Mom had a unique and special relationship."

I said to Kim, "Oh, yes, I remember when Aunt Dorothy called me and told me mom passed out in the elevator at Top of the World, and she went on to tell me how Faith saved her life and that our sister, Liz is back in the hospital again."

Kim said, "Faith was Mom's bodyguard and never left her side. They were indeed "inseparable" and as closely connected as any human and animal could ever become. When Mom ate a meal, Faith ate with her, and Mom treated her like a royal queen. Whatever Mom did, Faith did it with her, for she was her outstanding "watchdog and overseer.""

"Mom and I had to agree that I wasn't giving up Faith, but only having joint custody with Mom for Faith. That little dog was so good for Mom; it gave her a reason to get up, walk, and move around as she walked Faith. Mom would call me and tell me it was time for Faith to get groomed, and if I didn't have time, Mom would give her a bath, condition, and blow-dry her hair. She would clean her ears and eyes so carefully every day for the sweet little girl. Faith just loved the royal treatment my mom would give to her! Faith would always lay on mom's

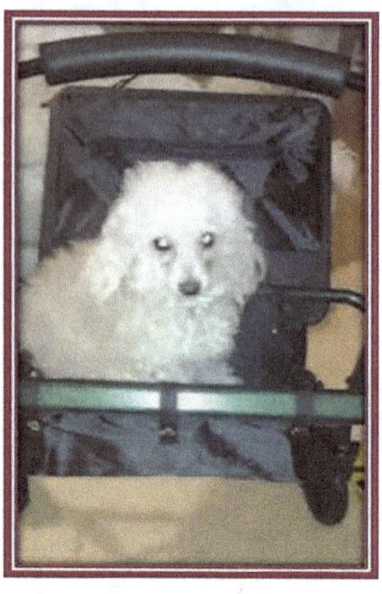

Grocery Store time! Mom sneaks Faith in with her at the store. Well, she is her therapy dog and her bodyguard and overseer!

Faith going with Mom for all of her therapy sessions. She was with her all the time.

On the top left: Kim and Gina and MOM sitting holding Faith's brother Buddy. He would jump on Mom's lap as soon as he came in the door, and Faith would lose her soft lap seat sitting with MOM.

Faith guarding Liz's money box and her valuables. No one better mess with her master!

lap and weasel her way right up to get all the kisses mom would give her. Faith was everything to Mom, and she was always her best friend."

Kim said, "Not only was Faith Mommy's best friend, but Buddy was also. When Buddy visited Mom, he jumped up on Mom's lap. Faith's seat was taken away by her big brother, Buddy, again; Buddy was only a visitor. Faith was mom's best friend, and mom's best friend was Faith, not her brother, but she loved him too when he visited."

"When mom passed, Faith took it very hard. She kept looking for Mommy when I would bring her to Mommy's condo after she passed. People say dogs cry when they lose their caregivers, which was the case for Faith. After mom passed, Faith would pace back and forth, run from her bedroom to all of her mom's condo rooms, and keep looking for her. Mom left her suddenly as Mom left us all. **TIME** gave us all no justice and blew in like a sudden windstorm with no warnings and no "**GOODBYES!**" Faith spoke to Mom's picture and would give her lots of nudges with her head to get Mom to play with her. It was only a picture, but Faith could feel and remember her magical and loving hugs and kisses from her beloved master. Faith would still give her picture more tender hugs and lots of kisses. Faith sensed something was wrong, and her caretaker would not be coming **HOME** with her again. She longed for her hugs and touches again and wanted to be reunited with her. Faith missed her so badly, and so did all of us!"

Here is a picture of Faith. She misses s her master so much. Faith sits in royalty just as her Majesty is sitting in royalty in heaven. She's waiting for her master to come back home.

Kim said, "Aunt Rita, when I hold Mom's pictures up to Faith, she kisses them and tries to lick them. I say to her, **"Here's Grandma!"** It is so sad! She wants to grab Mom's photos moans. and cries for her second mother and caretaker. Now, I tuck a picture of Mommy in Faith's little bed, and she cuddles up on it and lays next to it. Therefore, in closing this chapter, writing about a few of Mom's friends she had in her life, I would be upset if you did not include another survivor who is lost without Mom and her dog, Faith. Thank you, Aunt Rita, for writing this story on our little dog Faith, who had a wonderful relationship with my Mom! I wonder if Faith knows Mommy is in Heaven, her new home."

Going back to Liz in the Hospital, Liz said, "Rita, I also have another person I want you to include in our book—Carol. She is a fairly new friend who is so good to Kim and me. She does so much for her and watches over her like her guardian angel."

"She would take Kim to many of her doctor appointments and for her treatments at Moffitt Cancer Center. Do you know she was even both of my granddaughters' Confirmation sponsors when they got confirmed? Carol was only a phone call away, and Kim knew when she couldn't come to help me out, she would ask Carol and be at my place in a snap! She is the greatest, and I also know her brother as well. They are both great people, for sure!"

I replied to Liz, "I know Carol has done a lot for Kim recently, and I was so excited that she came to your 80th Birthday Celebration. Kim took pictures of both of you. She looked radiant. And so did you!"

Liz said, "Didn't she look gorgeous? I love that lady and know she will always look after Kim and her girls if I cannot. She would do anything for them and has come to my condo whenever I need her."

I told Liz, "When I come to Florida, I want to meet her and her brother. I want to thank them for how much they do for Kim, the girls, and you too."

Liz said, "Please do that for me. I would appreciate that very much."

I told her, "Don't worry, I will, but now you have to rest and get ready for that procedure whenever they come for you. You need to rest."

She said, "Don't worry about that procedure for me. I don't care about it. Kim wants me to go through it so they can find out what is wrong with me. I don't want to disappoint her, but it is tough to hold on like this."

I told her, "Liz, as Kim said, you waited this long—you might as well wait a little while longer. Give it a little more **TIME**, and you will soon be home. Just hang in there, my sister. Please, I don't want you to worry anymore."

She said, "Don't worry, Rita, I will be fine!"

I replied, "Liz, you sound so tired, and I can barely hear you. I think we did enough today. I will call you later, and I hope they get that procedure done! You can't go on without food and water with your health conditions and being a diabetic. I feel so bad for you, and I could cry!"

Liz replied, "Don't cry, or you will make me cry again. Until tomorrow... give me a call. I have a lot more to tell you and a lot more secrets. Just remember I love you and thank you for all you do for me. Dr. Rita, working with you is a good distraction and keeps my mind busy while **TIME** passes by." I am so happy you can remember all of this and fill in the gaps. You, indeed, are amazing! I can't wait for my family and friends to read all about the **Trials and Tribulations of Tin Can Lizzie!** It couldn't happen without your patience, skills, and persistence!"

Then I closed with, "You better go, Liz, and get some rest, my dear sister. Remember, you will be back home soon, and we will work together when you arrive. I love being close to you in this book-writing experience! I have talked to you more these days while you were in the hospital than I ever did in our lives together! Be strong, brave, and positive; please know prayers are going to the heavens for you. Your family loves you! I will never forget this precious **TIME** we spent together writing about your **Tin Can Lizzie experience**s! I Love you! I will talk with you tomorrow."

Liz said, "I love you **MORE**, my sister, Dr. Rita! Don't forget to call me later! I will be waiting. We have a lot more work to do together! I will always remember what you are doing for our family and me! I can't wait to talk to you more about our story tomorrow. I will hold on to that thought until we can talk again!" I am so weak, but you gave me the strength and the **TIME** to make it through these dark hours waiting in the hospital. I thank you, thank you, and thank you. I know you will keep your promise to me to finish our book and to get it published. I love you, Dr. Rita!"

Rita replied to her sister," I love you too, my dear sister **TIN CAN**. I am so proud of you for **OVERCOMING** dark times in your life. But you survived as we all did through our Lord Jesus Christ, who constantly took care of us! I will treasure those beautiful times we had in these days while you were in the hospital! I will talk to you tomorrow. Please stay strong and brave, and I will speak to you tomorrow morning. Hold on, Liz, hold on! I will be praying for you."

# Chapter 8

## WHAT HAPPENED TO TIN CAN? TODAY IS HER BIG DAY!

### June 29, 2020

I guess the day started like any other day in the hot summer of June 2020 during the Coronavirus pandemic, but it was a day I will never forget for the rest of my life. My sister Liz was in the hospital, and she waited over four days to get a simple colonoscopy. The procedure was postponed to the next day. She had no food and no water for that whole time. I called the hospital on Sunday, June 28, and my sister was so upset! She was hungry and fragile and tired. She wanted to get out of the hospital and go back home. We were all pleased but tense about this procedure, but we all knew and believed she would get through this procedure and get to come home. Today is her big day!

I said to Liz, "How are you, honey? Are you OK? Did they say when they are going to do the procedure?"

Liz replied to me," Rita? Is this Rita?

I said, "Yes, Liz, it's me. I'm just calling to see how you are doing and what is going on."

She said, "They still didn't do the procedure. What is wrong with this hospital? I was so upset, and I cried all night. Now they are saying that the air conditioning is not working. The floor doctor was nasty when I asked when they were taking me."

He said, "What do you want me to do? Should I buy the AC part for you?"

Liz added, "I couldn't believe how he talked to me. I have never been treated like this before in a hospital."

She was so upset that she couldn't talk any longer. The poor woman started to cry again, and I didn't want her to be upset again.

I prayed with her as always and said, "Liz, please don't cry. You will be all right!"

She said," Thank you, my sister, and I love you. I better go now. I have to find out what the hell is going on! Kim keeps calling the floor personnel and asking, too. Kim is so good to me. I love her so much!"

I told her I would call her later. However, Kim texted the family, saying no phone calls and that she needed to rest.

I knew she was weak from not eating or drinking, and I was just so upset for her. She cried hysterically, "**PLEASE, I WANT TO GO HOME!**"

Little did I know that Sunday would be the last day I would ever talk to her. Everyone was anxious for her to get that colonoscopy done so the doctors could find out why she was having colon issues. I couldn't wait for her to get home to dictate more pages in our book and to go over what I have done so far together. I wanted to know more secrets that she wanted to tell me. I wanted to learn more about my sister, whom I never knew. She revealed so much to me! We talked more in those five days on the phone while she was in the hospital than we ever did in our whole lives.

February 2020: The Last Hug, as the two sisters bid each other farewell, hoping to see each other again soon. This was the last **TIME** I saw my sister, and that memory will linger forever.

I kept holding on to the image of the last time we saw each other and hugged. It was when I was in Florida in February 2020 at my brother Richard's house. I couldn't get that image of her and me hugging together out of my head at all.

I was praying, "Dear Jesus, let that not be the last time we see each other, please, dear Lord. Liz and I have so much work to do in our book, and I promised her I would finish it. I can't do it myself; we need to do it together, and I must confirm what she said so far from what I have in my notes. I started writing a few chapters I read to her, and she loved it. We need to do so much more together. There is so much more work, and I need her, and I don't want her to leave this world. Please, Lord, I beg you to take care of her."

Those were the last words I heard my sister say. I went to sleep that Sunday night, just praying that everything would go well for her, whether she had the procedure or not. Since she was so weak from not eating or drinking for so long, she would be strong enough to make it through the process. I wanted her to go home and live and have more **TIME** and get this done at another time when she wasn't so weak.

When I woke up that morning, I first checked my texts; I knew Kim would have an update on Mom. I have been in the habit of doing that ever since Liz had a stroke in the doctor's office last week.

On June 29, 2020, Kim wrote, "Good morning, Family."

She wrote, "From what I understand from the nurses, Mom had a restless night, but she's sleeping soundly right now. They're taking her down from 10:00 AM to 10:15 AM for her colonoscopy at 11:30 AM. Mom has a hard time waking up whenever she is under anesthesia, but this situation might give her a good time to sleep afterward. Hopefully, she will be coming home tomorrow."

We all started responding to Kim, wishing her well and asking her to keep us updated, and we prayed for her!

My brother Richie wrote, "Well, that is good news. I hope the results of that test are better than expected."

We all were genuinely concerned about how my sister would do because she was so weak from not eating while waiting for the procedure. I know we were all glued to our phones to hear any word from Kim. Finally, at 12:45 PM, we had an update from Kim. She said that her mom just had her colonoscopy, and she does have damage to her colon from the radiation treatments she had when she had cervical cancer thirteen years ago. The chain of events from that time forward was not very good and left us in shock!

Kim's texts and testimonies summed up the events of that horrible day as Kim and Gina talked to each other via FaceTime. This was a day from hell for all of us. Kim said that when she spoke to Mom, she was very nervous that morning and told us that she had assured her mother that she would be fine. Mom told Kim she was starving, exhausted, and so weak. She said to Kim that she just wanted to go home. Mom told Kim they were taking her to the procedure room at 10:30 AM for the 11:30 AM colonoscopy procedure.

At approximately noon, Kim told us that the doctor had called her and everything had gone well after the colonoscopy. Depending on how Mom woke up from the anesthesia, she could most likely bring her home. Kim texted us the good news. I was so happy, and I prayed Mom would wake up soon. However, things began to shift dramatically after that message.

About 15-20 minutes later, Kim texted us, and the same doctor said mom had suffered a massive stroke and her blood pressure was 70/30. Kim told us that the doctor said mom was bleeding profusely and she was being taken to ICU. I was so upset since earlier I heard that Kim could bring her home today, and now she is bleeding badly, and her vitals do not look good.

The same doctor called back again ten minutes later and said that Mom didn't have a massive stroke. He told Kim that Mom is better and responsive to verbal commands. Kim said he assured her that her mom was improving and her mental faculties were intact. She was alert, but her blood pressure was shallow. He said they were giving her blood. First, my sister had a stroke, and then she didn't have a stroke. It seemed so contradictory and so unsettling to all of us. What was my sister's actual condition?

Later, Kim called the floor nurse, who told her that her mom might not make it through the night. She said that Kim needed to get to the hospital right away, for it was life-threatening. However, Gina lived too far away and would not be able to make it in that short amount of time. We all knew that my sister was holding on to when her daughter, Kim, could get to the hospital. The nurse said they are still "unsure" about what went wrong. Due to the COVID-19 virus, no visitors were allowed in the hospital; however, the nurse was kind. She let Kim come in through another entrance. The nurse told Kim that she had never seen anything like that. The doctor who performed the procedure said she had a stroke and was "remarkably responsive." then, the same doctor said she didn't have a stroke. Finally, the floor nurse noted that it was not making any sense!

The nurse was very concerned that Regina wouldn't make it in **TIME**, for the nurse remarked that Liz would be lucky to make it another hour. **TIME** was running out for her mom.

Liz was put in the ICU at 6:15 PM, and she wasn't doing well. Kim was allowed to see her, and thank God she could get in by her side, which was a miracle. Things just went way down for sister Liz, and then she was put on life support. **TIME** was not holding out for my sister. Our amazing Kim called each family member on FaceTime so they could say "goodbye" to Liz. When Kim contacted me, I couldn't believe it to see Liz with the tube down her throat. She wanted to get this procedure done so she could go home. I was shocked! Is this my sister? It can't be! There must be some mistake! Is this the one who implored me to finish our book? To see her now was "mind-blowing!" Is this the one who begged me to finish our book?

Seeing her now was so shocking I yelled again, "There must be some mistake!" I had to ask myself, "Is this a bad dream, a nightmare?" But no, it wasn't, to hear Kim say, "Aunt Rita, this is a Goodbye call, for mom doesn't have much **TIME** left!" This message was way more than I could comprehend and the biggest shock of my life! Hearing this message was not the news I wanted or expected to attend, and I will never forget it for the rest of my life!"

I said to Kim, "Goodbye? What do you mean goodbye?" Kim said," The nurse told me Mom has only one hour left."

I was so shocked! How can this be? I only got a second on the phone because we got cut off. It will be an image in my mind that I will never forget as I could see her eyes open and her lips trying to talk to me. But I told her, "**Tin Can Lizzie**, you hang in there. You know I love you. I will finish your story!" I will! I saw a twinkle in her eyes, and then we got disconnected. This scenario was not like how you would picture someone dying and not how you think your goodbyes would be!

That was the last **TIME** I saw my sister alive; only for a few seconds, but I saw her! I thanked my niece, Kim, for allowing us to say a final goodbye in my sister's last moments of her **TIME** on this earth. I couldn't believe it! How could a simple procedure go so wrong? Liz was too weak for that colonoscopy and waited too long before she had it done. She came so close to death so many times, but our good Lord was always with her. She still attempted to make an **"ESCAPE"** before the valley of the shadow of death came for her. I was praying that she could make another **FINAL ESCAPE** and get better from this awful procedure; I asked the Lord for some more time as I was on my knees. Gina called and asked me to pray in a group text to the family, and I did.

Kim and Gina FaceTime each other while they were with their mom. They said Mom's eyes were open, and she was holding the side of the bed with her right hand until Kim took her hand, and Mom gently squeezed it. Gina said it was like Mom knew something was wrong as she lay there in bed in the ICU. I wondered if Liz thought this would be her last day on earth. Or did she think there was still time for a quick **ESCAPE**, to run out of that hospital room as she ran out of the house on Sophia when she was younger?

Gina said that mom's eyes were very glossy, and Kim asked for a cool washrag to wash her eyes and prop her head up to be more comfortable. Kim said one of the physician assistants (PA) came into the ICU room and started to look at her vitals and bleeding issues on mom's right arm. It all seemed like it wasn't going very well for my sister. But thank God Kim was there, and Gina was on the phone with FaceTime.

Another nurse came into the room and asked if Kim would like a prayer for her mom's Last Rights, and Kim accepted. A priest was called. Gina said another woman came into the room and dimmed the lights. She had two small batteries—lit candles and a handmade, crocheted blanket.

She asked if Kim would like to put it on her. Then she asked Kim if she would like the priest to speak to her on the phone. Gina said that the

**TIME** of death was drawing closer as she watched on FaceTime with Kim right there.

Then Gina sadly said, "Her eyes closed, and she passed away." Gina was able to share that moment with her sister while on FaceTime. Thank God Kim could come into the room to be with her mother and include her sister, Gina, on FaceTime. Shortly after, the physician's assistant came closer to the bed, and they knew their mom was gone. **HER TIME RAN OUT**! There was no turning back. There indeed was no "**ESCAPE**" for Lizzie this time.

### The Physician Assistant (PA)pronounced Mom's TIME of death. @ 8:37 PM on June 29, 2020.

A few minutes after the phone rang, I knew the news. "Yes," Gina told me, "**MOM IS GONE!**"

I was screaming and yelling, **"NO! NO!** It can't be! We all need more **TIME**, and I needed more **TIME**!

Gina was crying and said, "How could this be, Auntie Ree-Ree?" (what she always called me), "How could this happen? She died from a colonoscopy! It is not fair! "Then Gina said, "I have to go and make phone calls; this is so heartbreaking!"

Liz and I had too much to do yet, and I realized that Liz passed away with no **ESCAPE** this time. She was now with her mother and father, her niece Lisa, and many others who went before her.

Liz came close to death so many times, but she was always able to make an "**ESCAPE!**" However, this **TIME**, she had no saving grace, and God did not answer our beckoning calls to give her more **TIME**. God just picked her up and "**SNATCHED**" her into the heavenly kingdom, for He wanted her home!

I screamed and screamed, "She can't go now! We just started on her book, and I was rolling along, making great progress. I had several rough draft chapters done, along with other introductory Insights. Where do I go from here?"

I want my sister back; I do! I will never see her again; that is all I was thinking! With this book's excitement, I thought of all we will be missing in our lives, sharing her life of **Tin Can** with the family. Then I thought of no more visits to Florida to see and visit Liz. There are no more cruises or anything with her, for there is no more **"Tin Can!"** **What happened to Tin Can?** I must find her again. I have to keep searching for her, and I know her spirit will pop up or she will appear in my dreams. I know she will when I least expect it; tonight, as I write this chapter, she is here—I know she is!

*Gina asked me to say another prayer on a group text, and I did as I was down on my knees before God. Was I praying, "Lord, what are we going to do? Lord, give us the strength to get through these **TIMES** ahead.*

*I continued praying by myself, wanting to ask God for more **TIME**, but **TIME** was gone and instantly vanished with **TIN CAN LIZZIE'S** fast **FINAL ESCAPE** into the Heavens.*

## TODAY, ON JUNE 20, 2020, MY SISTER LIZ PASSED AWAY!

## SHE WAS "SNATCHED AWAY" AND TAKEN INTO THE HEAVENS!

Dear Lord, help us all get through this appalling big shock! It will be a day and a memory my family will never forget!

I screamed and cried out to God, "Please, please, how am I going to do this? I have to write her story, and how can I do it with her gone? What do I do now? I don't know if I was directly yelling at our Lord or Liz. I don't know. How she died is not right! A person goes into a hospital for a procedure that needs to be done to help you feel better, not die!! I told Liz, "I am so sorry that all this happened to you when you had so many goals before you would meet your maker."

I yelled to Liz, "We had a covenant together, and I promised I would stick with our story! Liz, how can this happen? You were planning to come home to see your family, and you and I were going to finish our (as you called it) book."

I knew more about her these days over the phone than I did in a lifetime. But she said there was so much more to tell. I couldn't wait to write it and read what I had written to her. Whenever I read her what I wrote over the phone, I would ask her how she liked it, and she would say, "It is just right! I love it, and you too, Dr. Rita, for making this book possible!"

She was given one hour more to live at 4:15 PM, but she stayed alive four more hours as we all prayed and asked for more **TIME** with the family on a group text. We feel she was holding on to give Kim enough time to get to the hospital to see her and hold her hand one last time. The nurse on duty that evening did a gracious thing. She allowed Kim to come in to be with her mother for her last remaining minutes on this earth. Liz would have held on for Gina to get there, but it was impossible. However, Gina was with her and Kim on FaceTime. Kim Face Timed me as she did to all members of the family. I only got to see her for a quick minute, and I will never forget the look she gave me as she hung onto the side of the bed with the tube down her throat. Her eyes were wide open, never missing a second to be with us. Then, I lost the connection. I begged Kim to let me see her some more, but she said she had more phone calls, for her mom's time was so short. I said goodbye to my **Tin Can** and told her again how much I loved her. How did **TIME ESCAPE** us? We were planning an excellent ending, not like this!

The time of death was 8:37 PM, as it was pronounced by a physician's assistant on the ICU floor. It will be a day I will never forget for the rest of my life, as I can hear my niece Gina say to me repeatedly, "Auntie Ree Ree (as Gina called me), **She's Gone!**"

The wonder and mystery of Liz's death is how this can happen. Did she die of a colonoscopy—a procedure that so many people go through, and it is not life-threatening? Was it a sign of the times since she was hospitalized during the worldwide pandemic? What happened? How did she get snatched away with no notice and no warnings? Sure, people pass away unexpectedly in different ways, but we never dreamed she would die this way.

Now, we have to live with the reality of her death and how she died. She will live in the echoes of our hearts, minds, and spirits forever! Our family will miss her dearly, and Kim will have a hard time adjusting to life without her because she is so used to doing everything with her, and she was with her every day as her daughter, friend, and caregiver.

I will miss her, and now I have a job to do! I have to put what she told me into a book form. I have to get it all on paper. She talked so fast, and it was so hard to write everything down. The weight is hefty on my shoulders. Liz would keep talking to me until she had no more breath in the conversations we had together in the hospital. She told me that there were many secrets in her life, we will never find out that she has never told anyone, and she was going to tell me to be written in her book. She only told me two; the first one was how she became **Tin Can Lizzie**, and the second was how hysterical she was when she was in the mental institution. But she said she must talk about so many more of her secrets.

Maybe the family and her friends could share more information with me over **TIME;** I'm not sure. But somehow, I asked God in our family prayer for more **TIME.** Perhaps this is His way of revealing more about Liz's book, which will be compiled from the words of her family and friends. Today is the day my sister, **"TIN CAN LIZZIE,"** made her **"FINAL ESCAPE."** I want my sister back—I do! I thought about everything that would be missing in our lives, along with the excitement of this book, while she shared her life of **TIN CAN** with the family. Then I thought of no more visits to Florida to see her, no more cruises, or anything with her, because there is no more **"TIN CAN!"** **What happened to Tin Can? I must find her again;** I have to. I don't know how to do it, but I must try! I have to keep searching for her, and I know she will appear; I know she will when I least expect it. As I write this chapter, she is here. I know she is! I am struggling to write this chapter, and she keeps pushing and gnawing at my mind to write and be the writer she told me I was!

Readers, please note: Please know how much I struggled with writing this chapter. I didn't know how I would get through writing it. I started it so many times, and I had to stop. I was just too overwhelmed. There was so much to write, and my fingers would freeze on the keyboard.

I was continually procrastinating, but after much prayer to our Lord and asking Liz for some inspiration and strength. I made it through! I have to keep my promise to her, and I will get this book published! Then, I completed this first rough draft of Chapter Eight, which was all about the day I lost my big sister! I wrote about the terrible events she had experienced being in the hospital waiting for a simple procedure. Today was supposed to be *"HER BIG DAY WHEN SHE COULD COME HOME!"* Little did we all know that it was her big day and *"THE DAY SHE WENT HOME—HER HEAVENLY HOME! IT WAS* HER FINAL ESCAPE** was far different than Liz, her daughters, or all of us expected and planned on when it was **TIME** to go to her heavenly home.

**THE ROUGH DRAFT IS DONE!** It was such a relief! As I relived that terrible June night all over again. I could breathe again! But this time, Peace, love, and a strong determination to get her story out engulfed my entire being! I wasn't alone. **Tin Can** was right there with me as if holding my hand! I was shaking, and then I felt peace and calmness. I looked out the window, smiling with a sense of accomplishment. Suddenly, there was one bright light shining over my window. It was **Tin Can** smiling down on me! This **TIME**, she was a dynamic, gorgeous angel. She was there for a few seconds, and then she quickly disappeared and escaped back into the heavens! I know it confirmed her pure "**Delight and Gratitude**" that I was writing her story! This light around her was such a dynamic, bright pillar. Then, quickly, it moved upward toward the heavens. Then, I asked myself, whatever happened to **Tin Can Lizzie?** We will never know, for she escaped again, vanished from my window. **Tin Can Lizzie** was happy and proud of me and the whole family who submitted stories, which was her dying wish, and she pleaded with me to get this book published. She wants to encourage others in this world who have had a rough life like she did. However, for now, we must know that we are happy for her to live in God's Kingdom. She will bounce around like a gorgeous angel or a butterfly, and we will see her again when we least expect it!

# Chapter 9

## WHAT DO I DO NOW?
## DEEP WITHIN THE CLOUDS

Well, this is the day after the shocking news of my sister Liz passing from a colonoscopy. I was still in shock, as we all were. When I got the news from Gina last evening, saying **"She's Gone,"** I was experiencing trauma and needed someone to talk to who would understand the same grief I was feeling. That night, I called my brothers, Richard and Victor, to see how they were holding up, for I was "out of it" and still in disbelief. I seemed to be walking around in a **"Deep Cloud"** myself, oblivious to the world around me. The family seemed very much shocked, as I was!

My husband Dennis didn't understand the deep grief that I was experiencing, for he didn't realize or know all the details of what Liz had revealed to me. She had asked me to write a story about her life and the history of our family as we grew up with deaf parents and lived in poverty. She told me secrets that she had deep within her soul and had never told anyone else of her experiences growing up on Sophia Street and in her later years. Dennis knew I was talking on the phone to her so often while she was in the hospital, yet he didn't know that Liz and I were conversing about the book she wanted me to write and get published. Lizzie gave me explicit instructions on what to write. She told me some of the **"Secrets"** she had in her life, and sadly, Lizzie didn't get the opportunity to tell me all her "secrets." Her biggest **"Secret"** was her in her true-life role as **TIN CAN LIZZIE.**

**TIME** was her thief, silently stealing her deep-seated **"Secrets"** away. **TIME** won the race, leaving Lizzie and many more **"Secrets"** behind.

She expressed deep and sincere grief about our family history and what they experienced in the **Trials and Tribulations** in all of their lives, as well as her life.

The following day, I didn't know what to do. I made a few phone calls to other family members and friends to give them the sad information that my sister was **"Gone."** I was a mess and very upset. I wanted to help but couldn't while in Ohio and not Florida. I knew Kim and Gina were trying to make funeral arrangements, and they did their best as they looked for a funeral home. I thanked Kim again for making Facetime conversations to say **"Goodbye"** to Liz on that dreadful June 29, 2020, evening. On Wednesday, July 1, Gina and Kim went to various funeral homes to see where they could have a memorial for our sister and their mother. In mid-afternoon that same day, my sister Dorothy called me and told me they had found a lovely funeral home. They set up the memorial for my sister, Liz, on July 5, 2020.

My two nieces, Kim and Gina, knew this funeral home was the perfect place, and a lovely luncheon would be served. The staff shared that we could only have about 10 minutes to view my sister in the cold room due to the virus. The thought alone was chilling, and I couldn't imagine what kind of room this would be! She would not be out for public viewing, and it would include only direct family members.

I wasn't planning to go to the memorial service, but my sister Dorothy called me and told me I would never forgive myself for not making plans to fly to Florida to say **"Goodbye"** to my sister. She said she would pick me up from the airport, and I could stay with her in her condo. I told her I would have to think and pray about it. My mind was so confused, and I feared going to Florida because Coronavirus was rampant there. I gave it more thought and prayer and decided to check with the airlines online for flight information. I booked a Friday, July 3rd flight that left Cleveland at 6:00 AM, which was so early with a layover in Baltimore, MA. I pulled together some everyday clothes and something unique that Liz had given me a while back. I will wear them to the memorial service. Dorothy told me to pack everything in a small suitcase and then put that one in a giant bag to bring home some of Liz's stuff she had boxed for Pam and me a few weeks earlier. Dorothy said she had seen those packed boxes in the bedroom, waiting for me to go through when I arrived.

I woke up early that morning, and Dennis took me to the airport. Upon arriving, I checked in my suitcase and had my carry-on with my computer and medications. I made it through security, for it was tight due to the virus, and I boarded the plane to go to Baltimore. I had all three seats on the plane. It was a lovely day, and soon, the sun was out shining. I stared out the window, thinking about everything Liz had told me these last five days and what she wanted me to do. My mind kept me remembering every word of the covenant we made several times, but now I have to write this book myself… how can I do that? Why did she leave me like this? However, I had made the promise to her that I would write it. There were many points and stories I wanted to go over to get more clarity with her, but now she has already passed away.

I had no idea how to do this, but strength from our Lord and lots of help from Liz in the heavens deep within the cloud will lead me. I needed to write with clarity, merit, and honor. Soon, the plane landed, and I had a short layover in Baltimore. The gate to Tampa was easy to locate, and I was very proud of myself; I felt Liz was also proud of me. It was strange to see everyone with masks, but it was mandatory at the airport and on the plane. I boarded the plane heading to Tampa and asked myself, "How did I get here?" I was still in distress and couldn't believe I was doing this for my sister…or was I selfish and doing it for me? I had to say "**Goodbye**, "and I just kept dwelling on the fact that the Lord had taken her home, and I had to think about this book that she wanted me to write about her and our family. Plus, I will miss her so much!

I still can't believe I am on a plane heading toward Tampa, Florida. Liz wanted me to come and spend some time there a few weeks ago. She was so kind—the most inviting she ever was! She said she had clothes for my daughter Pam and me, and they were all packed and ready in boxes for me to go through in her bedroom. I recall very vividly that I told her there was no way possible that I could come to Florida. I couldn't even think to get on a plane where the coronavirus was at its worst and in high numbers, worse than at home in Ohio. I told her I would love to come, but there wasn't a way I would not take such a chance with my health conditions. I could hear the sadness in her voice, and I told her I would try later when COVID-19 was over.

She responded that she understood how I felt, was keeping those boxes of clothes and other stuff for when I did come, and that our names would be on the boxes. She told me to hurry up here and we could go through her packed boxes. I told her I was sorry again, but she said, "We will see. You might be down here sooner than you think." So, I was wrong, and she was right.

So, here I am on a plane heading toward Liz's home in **"TOP OF THE WORLD,"** where she lived, just as she said I would be doing. I left so early in the morning and was anxious to see everyone! I was trying to envision how her memorial would go, and I wondered how I was ever going to make it through the service. Since the evening she passed, I couldn't control my emotions and tears that were constantly flowing. I will never forget Gina's words, **"SHE IS GONE!"** Her  absence would be deeply felt. How will I comprehend the truth that she is really **"GONE?"**

The plane was not crowded as I walked further to find a seat. On this plane, I could only think about my sister—I will miss her—and how I would ever get the book completed and published. I couldn't stop thinking of all that she revealed to me and how she was so excited to share this information she had hidden within her mind, soul, and every fiber of her being for some 80 years. She always told me how she wanted her "going home celebration" to be and that she wanted me to give her eulogy; she said she wanted beautiful, dreamy music to be played at her service, and she wanted it to be happy, not sad. She especially wanted dream songs to be played, for she was quite a dreamer! I was shaking. I could feel her presence closely ever since the plane landed in Baltimore. I didn't know how her service would be, but I knew that her girls, Kim and Gina, would take care of everything, and they did!

Finally, I found three seats together (you couldn't have a person in the middle seat during the COVID-19) and sat down. Looking out the window, I never realized I was right on the plane's wing side again as I was coming from Cleveland to Baltimore. As the plane went up in the skies, I could feel her spirit while looking out the window. I kept staring out the window while the plane headed toward the Blue Skies and the white and fluffy clouds. I thought I saw her shadow while looking out between the fluffy clouds. I was stunned and wondered if my mind was playing tricks on me. I kept looking out the window when the plane was high in the skies, and the clouds kept closing on me. I felt her spirit telling me to keep looking out the window and into the clouds, and I did.

I didn't understand what was happening, but I saw the clouds moving closer to the window over the plane's wing. I couldn't believe my eyes, and I felt her spirit with me as I always did on my trips to Florida. She was out there! I never went to Florida without going to see her, and now, can it be possible that she is coming to see me? I said and asked her, "Liz, are you out there? I am here and on my way to your condo. I am so sad that I am coming to Florida for your memorial to say my "Goodbyes!" Where are you out in those gorgeous Blue Skies?" I gave her back her favorite saying, "**I AM HERE**," as she did to us when she arrived late to our family gatherings or when we were waiting for her to come so we could go shopping or out to dinner.

I kept staring out the plane's window into the clear, beautiful, bright Blue Skies and white clouds. Then, as I looked out, this time, it was her! I saw her shadow sitting on the edge of the wing. Liz's spirit was traveling with me to Florida to go to her condo again!

Liz's spirit was on the tip of the wing deep within the clouds, waving and talking to me within the echoes of my mind.

Also, I want everyone to recognize how our family survived the **Trials and Tribulations** they experienced. It was a struggle for all of us; this way, they could get to know our family and me better! If our family survived, so can they! This was such a powerful message to me! I hurried up, took out my laptop, and started typing everything you are reading now. She was amidst gorgeous fluffy white clouds and smiling down at me.

I was so apprehensive about taking this trip all alone. But when I left Baltimore and on my way to Tampa, I wasn't alone anymore. Liz's Spirit was following me and leading the way! It was a beautiful sight, and the fluffy white clouds encompassed the plane's wing. I kept typing away while looking up at the clouds.

But then suddenly, dark black clouds covered the fluffy white ones. It happened so fast I couldn't believe my eyes! It was scary to see.

I felt Liz telling me, "Rita, watch out. Many people might give you a hard time with my words, even our family members. Please be strong, and don't let anything stop the progress of getting our story of me and our family to fruition. If one publisher rejects our story, go to another, but watch out for those black clouds that can be doubtful of this story."

"This book must go out to the family and others worldwide who may need to read my story to help them in their lives! This story also must go out to everyone I know and who knows my family. I want them to know who I am and understand my life and many struggles. Additionally, I want everyone to recognize and understand how our family persevered through the Trials and Tribulations they experienced. It was a struggle for all of us; this way, they could get to know our family and me better! Even though some of us are in the **"HEAVENLY"** clouds in the skies. **"WE SURVIVED!"** The only way others could understand us is by reading this book. That is the only way it can happen!"

"She said in my mind that some people have **TRIALS AND TRIBULATIONS,** as we all did growing up on Sophia and even more later in life. Hopefully, they can find proper perspectives and move forward. It may not be what they wanted or planned, yet there is a time they have to **"Let Go"** and **"Let God"** take control of their problems. They need to rise above what they are going through and do what is necessary for peace and life. It would be their only **FINAL ESCAPE."**

My mind and spirit were engulfed by all her words and what she wanted me to know and act upon. I thought, was this a final directive to continue with this book? What was going on? I could feel in my spirit that Liz clearly emphasized that she was following these funeral proceedings and knew what she wanted me to do. I looked out the window again, and the gorgeous clouds appeared once more, fluffy white against the Blue Skies. What a strange phenomenon, but it happened—believe it or not! It's okay to doubt my words about this remarkable experience, but please don't doubt what Lizzie told me or our family's history!

Then, as I continued looking out of the plane's window, I told Liz as I talked and even signed to her, right there sitting in my seat on the plane, "Liz, every time I came to Florida before, you were always there waiting for us to arrive. We would get together, have fun, and do our favorite thing: **"GO SHOPPING!"** Well, this is the first trip you traveled almost the whole way with me! I whispered to myself, thank you, my big sister, **Tin Can,** for giving me the strength to get on a plane to be with you one last time."

I could feel Liz reply, "Dear sister Rita, I will always be with you and the family until we meet again!"

The next thing I heard was the pilot's voice saying, "Folks, we hope you enjoyed your flight from Baltimore to Tampa, Florida. We are landing in beautiful, sunny Tampa in about ten minutes. There is nothing but sunny Blue Skies above. Enjoy the sunny Blue Skies when you land for your Tampa trip. Please prepare for landing." I didn't want this glorious trip to end. This trip I feared taking was a blessing and a miracle I will never forget!

I had to close my computer because the plane was ready to land, and Liz was still trailing me. I quickly saved what I had scribbled on my laptop and stuffed it in my travel bag. I wanted to remember this experience and write about it in this book. I felt sad to leave Liz, for she was with me every mile of the way, through the clouds and the echoes of our spirits joining together. It may seem strange to you as a reader, but that is how it happened. It is a miracle that she traveled with me on my way to Florida for her memorial and to help clean up her stuff at her condo. I looked out the window; it was just bright and sunny Florida, welcoming and inviting me to the sunshine state. There were Blue Skies and no clouds. I think my sister Liz was so happy I was coming with her; the gorgeous Blue Skies and the bright sun shining were proof of everything.

The plane landed, and of course, I had no idea what I had to do next or where to pick up my baggage. I just followed the crowd, and they were entering a tram that took us to the airport's ground level. I followed the crowd to the baggage area, taking on a dimension of **Tin Can** myself as I talked to people as we walked along. I was very friendly, especially after my wonderful experience with my sister. Everyone I was talking to told me what their plans were or asked me where I was headed. I was sad, but I told them with a genuine smile and responded to my plans. I told them, "I will meet my sister in Clearwater!" They replied, "I hope you and your sister have a great time together on your short vacation." Another lady asked, "Oh, are you going near Clearwater Beach?" I replied, "Yes, my sister Liz lived there on the island for years, and now she lives on the **Top of The World,** a senior living place. She loves it there, for it is heavenly, peaceful, and quiet. All her neighbors are just special **"Angels"**; they are delighted to live in that community." The lovely couple said goodbye. I hope you have a great time while you are there in Clearwater. That place sounds like an excellent senior development. I will check into it on this trip, for we might like to make our home there."

I couldn't resist telling the sweet couple, "You will just love it there, in this **"HEAVENLY"** piece of the world that represents all countries. There are lots of activities for seniors. It is a 55-year- old residential community. Each section represents a certain country. My sister Liz lived on Americus, Mexican Way, and now resides in the Irish Lane section. She has a condo on the ground level, and it is easy for her to go in and out."

The couple thanked me again, and I saw the wife write down the name of the complex on paper. We said our goodbyes, and they both wished me a beautiful experience while visiting my sister.

I finally arrived at the luggage carousel, and there it was, my luggage already making a trip around again; that gave me time to find someone nice to help me get my luggage to the carousel. I asked a young, nice-looking man if he would lift my heavy suitcase (two pieces of luggage in one) onto the carousel, and I quickly pushed it right outside. When I reached the waiting area, I called Dorothy on my cell to tell her Liz's favorite, saying, **"I am here!"** While waiting for Dorothy to pick me up, I took the **TIME** and looked into the heavenly Blue Skies to tell my sister, **"I am here!"** The pilot was correct; there were only Blue Skies above the heavens looking down at me; soon afterward, sister Dorothy and her girlfriend Donna (Liz's friend for so many years) came by to pick me up in the long line of cars picking up their passengers.

I was surprised to see Donna. She got out of the car to help me put my luggage in the back of Dorothy's car, and off we went. We stopped at a restaurant to get a snack and then headed past Clearwater Beach to the **TOP OF THE WORLD** complex to Liz's home.

I was shaking as I exited the car and walked to her condo. Dorothy and Donna were ahead of me, and I snapped a picture as I hesitated and felt shaky about entering Liz's home. I knew she wouldn't be waiting for me this time to welcome me with her open arms to greet and hug me, so instead, I did Liz's

Here we are at Liz's Condo, and I didn't have the heart or strength to walk in. I stayed back to stop and pray to ask our Lord and my sister for strength to walk in her condo without her.

favorite thing and yelled out to her, **"I am here!"**— as she always did to us when we were expecting to go somewhere together. As we entered the condo, I could feel her presence.

Donna was waving to me to go into the bedroom, and sure enough, right in the corner were all the boxes Liz had packed for Pam and me to go through. When Liz called me two weeks prior, she had reminded me the boxes would be waiting for me, and sure enough, they were luring me to open with our names on them. I felt her so near to me as I looked in the spaces in her room to see all the boxes of what she wanted to give to us before she passed away. Yes, she wasn't well and had health issues, but she thought she would be able to go through this stuff with me and, hopefully, with Pam. It was very heartbreaking!

I just stared at the boxes, knowing going through them would be a big job. I just needed time to think about all of this and had to go through everything. I couldn't take all she packed for Pam and me because I did consider sending it home, but it would have cost a fortune!

After Liz's memorial service, Dorothy helped me go through the clothes and other items to see what I might want to take home for Pam and me. It was a difficult chore, but it had to be done. We worked for a few days to clean up her room and go through the boxes she had put away for us. It was a tough, sad, and challenging chore for us to do, but we had to get it

Here are all the boxes we transported from Liz's condo.

done. Kim was looking for Liz's roommate, Mona, to find a smaller place to live, for she didn't need two bedrooms alone. Liz had Pam and my names on everything, including little jewelry cases with She still attemptedthought we would like.

  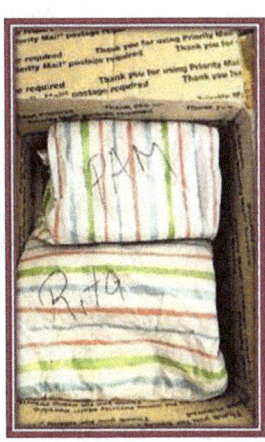

Here are the clothes that we laid out to sort, and the jewelry cases that Liz wrapped up with our names on them for Pam and me.

We laid everything on the bed as we took the items out of the boxes she had packed for us. Her bed was full of clothes as we sorted them. First, I was looking at each piece and then tried on some of my options. Whatever I didn't decide to send home, we packed up and donated to various charities.

We just put everything in boxes and went to Dorothy's condo to repack things correctly to be mailed to my home in Ohio.

It was a tremendous job, even though we condensed everything as much as possible. The next day, we took eight big boxes to the post office. We returned to Liz's condo after dropping everything off and ensuring her bedroom was cleaned.

We left her bedroom spotless, and it was my last view of an experience I will always remember!

Kimmy was there the night before and left extra pictures of Liz, Dorothy, and me on the bed for us to see. It was such a confirmation from my sister that she was watching us from high above **IN THE CLOUDS**, right up in the heavens! It was another sad day, but I knew Liz was there with us, peering out between the clouds to observe and supervise us while we packed up her things. Liz was waiting for us. How did she know I was coming to pack her things and bring them home for my daughter, Pam, and me? I can never believe her death when people say it was just her time to leave this world and go into the heavenly clouds. I will never accept that theory! But it did seem that Liz thought her **TIME** was close to leaving this world. There were too many signs Liz had left behind that she knew she didn't have long. She experienced an unfortunate death and another sad episode in **The Trials and Tribulations of Tin Can Lizzie**. My sister Liz loved living at the **TOP OF THE WORLD'S SENIOR DEVELOPMENT**. Therefore, as I close this chapter, I cannot resist saying, "Liz is now living **ON TOP OF THE WORLD** with all of her gold and splendor with her "**Wings of an Angel,**" enjoying the full view way up in the clouds and the beautiful BLUE colorful skies! Yes, Liz is enjoying her **FINAL ESCAPE**!

This chapter is a very unique experience. I went up into the clouds on a plane, **my sister's spirit** was there. It is a good reminder that when we look up high **INTO THE CLOUDS**, she wants us to know that we can see her sitting on one big fluffy cloud, just gazing down at us.

Liz as we see her as she looks up in the **Heavenly Skies and Clouds**, with her wings of an **ANGEL!**

# Chapter 10

## THE DAY OF LIZ'S MEMORIAL

### July 5, 2020

O n this day, thoughts about how Liz's memorial service would turn out were racing through my being. It will be a special time to remember all the beautiful memories of Liz's final Goodbye Celebration.

I was staying at Dorothy's condo. I didn't sleep much but got up early and started writing about my feelings that day. I was so overwhelmed, and there was so much going on with funeral arrangements. Kim and Gina were in charge, and they mainly wanted to do everything as their mom would have liked it to be done. They had a tough time getting to any service location because of the rampant virus. We were blessed that this particular funeral home was so accommodating; all the funeral homes had such strict restrictions. Dorothy and I were in suspense and didn't know what to expect when we heard Liz would be in the "cold room." I couldn't imagine anything like that due to the virus. Our whole world is changing; what used to be our usual way of handling and attending a funeral is just so different.

Dorothy was ready about the same time I was, and of course, being Stupavsky/Stupansky members, we wanted to take a picture to remember this day.

Sister Dorothy standing in her condo wearing a dress Liz gave her as she was embracing the picture of her daughter, Lisa.

Me with an outfit that Liz gave to me a few years ago.

Shortly after taking pictures, our brother Richard took us to the funeral home. Richard's wife, Joann, was in Oklahoma to visit her dad in a nursing home, so she was not with us; it was only the three of us. We talked on the ride to the funeral home, saying we had no idea what would happen and how. We spoke of the tragedy of our sister's death and how it was so unexpected to Liz and all of us. Before we left the car, I reminded Dorothy and Richard to wear their masks because the virus was widespread, especially in Florida, where many seniors are. I was told that we had to comply with the protocol and rules regarding the virus.

As we walked in, we were greeted by the funeral home staff. The three of us were in **AWE** of this beautiful place. I could feel the spirit of **Tin Can Lizzie's** spirit as it raced through my mind and entire being. We looked around and waited in the reception room to be called to view Liz in her casket. I knew she was with the Lord and other family members waiting for her in heaven. The reception room was a table full of roses Kim had purchased, with cards, pens, and ribbons. Kim and Gina asked us to pick up a rose, write a goodbye message to Liz, and tie the card to the flower.

We all gathered outside the cold room to have a picture taken of us holding a rose and our last message to Liz. Liz 's viewing area was ready for us to view her one final time.

On the left: Kim, Gina, Richard, Dorothy, family friend Donna, and Rita posing for a picture before we entered the **"Cold Room."**

We were only allowed 10 to 15 minutes for viewing, and it was just for immediate family and a few close friends. There were about 10 of us. Kim's daughters Alexis and Sophia, Liz's step-granddaughter Amber, and family friend Carol also went into the cold room to say goodbye. We each took turns walking to the casket to present our message and the rose. Individually, we said what we wanted to tell her and took a few minutes by her side.

Liz's remains were in a wooden—type casket, which was positioned up high on a pedestal. She looked beautiful and was all in her natural state with no makeup. Her beautiful long hair was so pretty. She had the white dress on that she wore for her 80th birthday gathering, which she had told me she wanted to wear after she passed away. She said it was her wedding dress, as she would be married into the union of Christ Jesus.

Regarding her 80th birthday celebration, it had been planned by Kim. It was a small, warm family gathering. Even though I wasn't there, I designed and contributed the cake to the party; I wrote a special card for her, which Kim read aloud at the party. Liz loved the message on the card attached to this book's Preface. Kim's daughter made a video of her mother as she read my card. Liz's expressions on the video were so touching as I watched. Liz laughed when I mentioned she had several husbands. She chuckled with a big smile and said, "True, so true!" Liz was so happy she made it to her 80th birthday on June 3, 2020. Liz said

Liz was so happy that she made it to her 80th birthday on June 3, 2020

on the video that I hit it just right! Liz had told me that her celebration was one of the happiest days of her life.

Being in the **Cold Room**, I reminded myself that it was only her physical body, not the new person, as she was in the arms of Christ Jesus. It was the last time we were together in Florida, but we will always be together in my mind and spirit as this angel, **"Tin Can Lizzie."** The vision of her lying in that coffin will be a memory that will be hovering over me for the rest of my life until we see each other again. She looked so gorgeous! I gently laid my pink rose and note on her heart with the message, **"My Tin Can**, I will keep the promise I made to you; I love you. Your sister, Rita."

Lord, please help me finish the book she wanted me to write. In Jesus's name, I pray.

Before we left the **Cold Room**, Kim and Gina asked me to say our final group family prayer, standing in front of Liz's casket. I don't remember what I said, and I didn't know if I could get through it, but I did! I asked God to lead me in the spirit to say the right words. I hope I did.

Each place setting was set up so beautifully, just as the **Tin Can Queen** would have loved, with her poker chips and hankies on the table.

We then gathered in the reception room and saw the beautiful display of all the food and flowers on the table. Due to the coronavirus, Kim could only invite 20 people. If it hadn't been for COVID, there would have been so many people who would have given their last respects to her and attended her "going home service." However, with the virus, everything had to be done according to the Florida Health Department's rules.

Kim and Gina came the night before, and they set up several round tables so beautifully with pink tablecloths, glitter, a box of tissues, candles, Liz's real estate business cards, and sparkles of stars and make-believe diamonds (just as she liked). As she told her daughters, Liz wished to give everyone a beautiful white linen handkerchief and a bright yellow/ gold poker chip for her memorial service.

This table presentation's incredible feature was that Kim and Gina did what their mom wanted. Liz had purchased handkerchiefs and poker chips many years ago. The hankies were beautiful. Every time Liz moved, the girls tried to throw away the poker chips because they were just more clutter that Kim had to pack. Liz replied, "Oh no, don't you dare! Those poker chips are very special to me, and I want them to be given out at my funeral someday with my handkerchiefs. I have been saving them for so many years. Make a nice display. I am counting on you!" They were saved, used, and displayed, just like Mama wanted.

She wanted everyone to remember her when they might be going through some of the ***Trials and Tribulations*** in their lives.

There was a reason why Liz wanted those poker chips saved: because of the relationship of her early life pitching pennies in the streets of Sophia. Little did Kim and Gina know about how their mother threw pennies on the streets of Sophia Ave in her very young years. I

An exquisite luncheon was planned for the guests to break bread together, in Liz's honor!

told them the day before about what she said to me in her last days in the hospital about who she was and that she had many secrets.

She finally reached a higher level and wanted everyone to have a poker chip to take home and remember her always. She told the girls, "That will be for the people who come to her funeral—they can take home a little piece of me always to have and as a good luck piece when they "down and out "as I was so many times! "This was Liz's extension to go on forever in her legacy as **"Tin Can Lizzie."**

Elizabeth C. Seither

Liz's Memorial Card

Her holy memorial cards had been designed by Kim and placed on each table; she had taken a picture of Mom's beautiful hands for the card, with her rosary wrapped around her fingers right before passing away in the hospital.

The layout of the luncheon was exquisite! It was full of fresh pink flowers. Liz would have been pleased and proud of her daughters, Kim and Gina.

Charming pictures of Liz in front of the room and fresh flowers sent by her friends.

This is where, in regular times, the casket would be set up. But, again, due to the coronavirus, there was no casket display or public viewing. We were blessed to always have this funeral home with a short viewing and a small gathering with social distancing. The front of the room was set up beautifully to give her tribute and honor!

We give you tribute, our love, and our honor, my sister! This was the display at the Front of the main room. This setup was gorgeous and so memorable!

The family took turns having their pictures taken with their mom and sister, for this was the only day we had to say our **"Goodbyes"** and give our mom and sister tribute. This memorial was a significant culmination of my sister's life and death, how she came into this world, and how she returned to her heavenly home. Yes, it is a memorial event and a memory of our lives that we will treasure forever!

Kim and Gina joining in love and in a joint union with their mother for the last time. They loved their Mother so much!

Siblings Dorothy, Richard, Rita, and Liz (in Spirit!)

Amber, her step-granddaughter from Liz's second husband, put together a video of all the pictures she could gather. It was so wonderful when I watched to see my sister Liz at different stages of her life.

Some people started to fix their plates from the luncheon display while John, a long-time close friend, and a lawyer, told how he knew Liz in business and what a perfectionist she was. The theme of this message was that Liz expected everyone's best, whatever they did in life in their professional and personal world. On a comical note, he told some personal stories. Amber's video was still playing, with Liz's pictures on the wall in the celebration room. John then asked everyone to go around to introduce themselves and share stories of their most memorable association with Liz. Liz's friends, co-workers, and family shared some of the fondest memories of Liz. One person said he had no family, and she made him feel he was part of a family. Liz was exceptional in doing that; she would pull strangers in to live with her and provide for them until they could get on their feet again. Helen and Cindy (her real estate workers for years) worked with Liz and knew her well, and so did Glenn, who did everything for her and was her handyman. As we went around the table, others shared how much they loved Liz, what she meant, and how they knew her. I could feel **Tin Can's spirit** hovering over that room in a way that was so **POWERFUL AND STRONG** that I will never forget. She filled my being with the desire to tell the story to the guests as she talked to me about her new existence. I hesitated to tell the guests the story of **"Tin Can,"** for it would be hard for them to understand without knowing the family background. I did tell Gina the night before about the book, and I read one of the chapters in the story to her. She was shocked, and she loved the story. Gina told me, "You must tell Kimmy and everyone else at the memorial what you wrote!"

Dorothy, Richard, and I were sitting at the table in front of the room where Liz's pictures were displayed. The one big center picture was taken on a cruise together. She loved that photo deck on those cruises and spent a lot of money on all of her photographs, as I did. In that sense, Liz and I are just alike. Someday, I want to go on another cruise and relive some of our memories and experiences. I need to do that and reconnect with her spirit on the Blue Water and heavenly Blue Skies.

Of the family, it was Kim, then her girls Alexis and Sophia, Gina, and Dorothy shared their stories of the beautiful **TIMES** they had together from when they were younger until they were older. Kim and Gina's stories were sad as they expressed how much they would miss their mother. Kim shared that she was her Mom's caregiver, and they were together every day.

I wanted to do what Gina asked me to do: share some of her mom's real story. I was very hesitant to reveal Tin Can's existence. I did my best and came out with how the *Trials and Tribulations of Tin Can Lizzie* all came to reality.

It was my turn next. I boldly stood before the guests and began my summarized message. I told everyone how Liz asked me on a recording on my home phone to write a book about her. I called her as soon as I could on the hospital phone, and we talked in her last days about what she told me about her life. She had already named this book **"The Trials and Tribulations of Tin Can Lizzie."** She was on a roll in that hospital room, and I couldn't write fast enough about everything she wanted in her book. We talked more during those times than we ever spoke in the last few years, and of course, she had to get in the previous words and told me to "Be quiet and write!"

I discovered that I genuinely didn't know my sister! The Liz on the phone was different. She told me that someday she wanted to return to the happiest days of her life as **"Tin Can Lizzie."** I told everyone that she had said when the time came, it would be her **FINAL ESCAPE**, and she would be greeted in the Heavenly Gates of Heaven. She told me my Dad, Mom, and niece Lisa would be waiting for her, and she would say her favorite saying— **"I am here!"** Of course, I told Liz she wasn't going anywhere, and she would still be around, but little did I know those many hours on the phone together were the final conversations we would ever have. I was heartbroken when Gina told me, **"She's gone!"** She had been so impatient with me but was glad I was there to talk to her. That way, she could tell me more about her life and what she wanted for her funeral. There was so much to know about

my sister in those few minutes that I had to share with the guests with clarity. I did the best I could in such a short time. I had to tell everyone about this new person, **"Tin Can Lizzie,"** and what that name meant to her.

I told the guests, "The book I am writing for Liz and our family is centered on not escaping our tribulations and emotions. She wanted us to face them with courage and dignity to **OVERCOME** them! Our Lord will help us and give us the strength to get through, but we need to think about how we will help ourselves! Liz wanted everyone to know the theme of this book: When life gets unbearable, there is always a way out! She learned how

Brother Richard gave a very moving presentation on how Liz influenced his life, giving him the drive and hope for a future of happiness and business success!

to **OVERCOME** her sadness and tribulations, even though she was at her end many times in life."

I explained to them how we had grown up in poverty, and I don't think they knew that side of Liz. I also talked about our conditions when growing up on Sophia.

I told the guests that Liz always had a special announcement as she made her grand entrance wherever she went. It was, "**I am here!**" I asked the guests to do the same to her to recognize her favorite saying back, and they all did! Now, we were there for her!

This was the final celebration of her new and peaceful life with her Lord and Savior and her dear departed family and friends. It was a time when Liz's chains of sadness, loneliness, and sickness she had experienced in her life, especially in her last days, were gone, and she was now released into the holy hands of our Lord. We told her we were all there for her and will never forget her. It was her day, and we are celebrating her final "**ESCAPE**" from the world and entering the gates of our Lord!

I asked them to look at their poker chips by their place settings, which were so special to Liz. I pointed out to the guests that Liz said the game of life is always a gamble! I told them that just as she pitched pennies, she wanted you to get a chance to launch when you needed strength and made choices by holding the poker chip. I told them she had said never to stop dreaming and never give up on your goals in your life! Pitch the last penny (poker chip) as you hold it, and go for it! She wanted you to have the "**BIG WIN**," as she always tried to do, even when times were so low for her. She held that penny in her hand, and now you have the poker chip to do it as she always did!

At that moment, John turned the celebration time of sharing over to my brother Richard, who was the last person to share about his sister.

Richard shared how Liz taught him to be the top in sales and their sales experiences together. He shared that they had some "amazing" times together when he lived with her. His presentation about his sister significantly moved us. Richard was robust and heart-warming as he shared the final tributes of his life with her. When he completed his short but powerful presentation, he said he would like to propose a toast to **"Tin Can Lizzie"** The staff passed out the pink champagne (purchased by Liz's friend, Donna) and Sprite. Brother Richard made a final toast to her in her new heavenly home with loving family and friends that went before her. We can hear them all saying,

**Here Comes Tin Can Lizzie! We were all waiting for your arrival!!**

Liz's going-home celebration was so gorgeous! She would have been so proud of her daughters for setting everything up and planning her big day. She would also be so proud of her friends and family members who shared special moments with her. I could feel her spirit as she looked down on me with gratitude for sharing her last words; she told me about being **"Tin Can Lizzie."** There was a small crowd, but it was mighty as Liz found peace in her new, gorgeous home with the pearly gates and sparkles around her! What a wonderful day it was! We will never forget **Tin Can Lizzie's Memorial Day Service** for the rest of our lives!

# Chapter 11

## A FAREWELL TO FLORIDA AS WE MARCH ON UP IN THE CLOUDS

### July 11, 2020

Yesterday was my birthday, and I always said, "It's just another day." Indeed, with my sister Liz gone this year, it was more than just another day. I was too sad. I was in Florida for this trip without getting together with my sister, Liz.

I never had a birthday party when I was a kid living on Sophia Ave. and living with my foster parents or even with my husband. I did have times when Dennis would take me out for dinner and have a cake with the kids, but I never had a significant and memorable party.

However, brother Richie took his wife Joann, my sister Dorothy, her girlfriend Donna and Kim, my sister's daughter, and myself to his country club pool outside the dining area. The dining room inside was closed, as many restaurants were nationwide due to the pandemic. It was very nice that he took us out before returning home to Ohio the following day.

Standing on the left: Dorothy, Donna and myself. Sitting on the left: Joann, Richard and niece Kim.

I have been to Florida so often with my children. Pam and Chris, when they were young, and with Dennis. We made it out to Florida again in February 2020. It was the last time I saw my sister Liz alive and the last time all five of us Stupavsky/Stupansky siblings were together. As I mentioned before, I did a PowerPoint Presentation in 2020 about our mother, Mercedes. The family just loved it! I discovered that our mother was in history books as one of the first babies who survived being born under 2 lbs. at that time. Our Mom was born in Bellevue, Ohio, in 1909.

Due to being such a tiny baby, Mom's eardrums never developed, leaving her deaf. Mom survived by being put in a newly invented incubator, barely even known in the medical Professions in 1909. Mom's story was significant, and because of her success, the idea of an incubator saved the lives of millions of babies. She was a famous lady and a Pioneer of surviving in an incubator. Now, Liz could tell our mother how proud we were of her in heaven! None of us would have been born if it weren't for our Mom's incubator experience.

Many thoughts were racing through my mind, especially during these last few days in Florida.

But this trip, of course, was far different than any trip I had in my life. Every time I left Florida, I would cry and miss my family, but not this time. I was so eager to get home! I missed my sister Liz so much, but I also missed my own family. I wanted to get home to them and share many stories and items I sent home.

This is me—my last glance looking out over the bay.

Looking back at the week's events, I couldn't believe how we cleaned out my sister Liz's clothes and everything in her bedroom. Dorothy helped me pack seven boxes of clothes, shoes, jewelry, and pictures Kim gave me. Everything I did and accomplished was racing through my mind, and I missed my sister. I was very grateful as I looked over the St. Petersburg Bay. I prayed and thanked God for the many blessings I had going to Florida over the years to see my family. However, I was sad that there were no gala shopping sprees or dinners with my sister Liz on this trip. It was like a lifetime going through my head, looking out at the beautiful view. I recalled silly little things and spats we had over the years, but also precious memories! I didn't want to leave those memories behind; no, not at all. I wanted those memories to linger on forever!

Mailing the packages home was expensive. I didn't care, for I had many precious pieces to remind me of my sister and give to my daughter, Pam, who loved her Aunt Liz. When we would come to Florida and go on cruises, Pammy always stayed with her Aunt Liz.

Pam always said those were the most memorable times of her life. Liz showed her the best time ever, and she always took her shopping and bought her things. I can't wait for Pam to enjoy the items given to her by her Aunt Lizzie. My sister even packed things and put our names on the boxes right before going to the hospital. She was so ready for us.

Pam will be so happy, and it will be inspiring to go through the boxes together.

My plane was leaving Tampa Airport at 10:45 AM, so I had to get up early to ensure I was at the airport to check in on time.

Sister Dorothy drove me, and before I knew it, we arrived at the drop-off area for outgoing flights. I made it to the airport, took plenty of time to check my two suitcases, and got through security.

My job was to get the two suitcases out of Dorothy's car trunk and be checked at the airport. Oh, the one big one was so heavy, and I kept worrying that I would be going over the limit of 50 pounds. Whew! I weighed my one big suitcase, and it was 49 pounds. God was so good to me! I kept my carry-on bag with my computer in it, just as I did on my trip to Florida, so I could pull it out if needed.

My seat on the plane going to Baltimore was perfect! Right over the wing. It was like that seat was calling me, "Sit here, sit here!"

I would soon be heading back to Baltimore Airport for a layover and then on a plane home to Cleveland.

I was ready to go through security again. Everything at the airport had tight security, more than expected with the COVID-19. Going home alone was strange like it was going to Florida, but Liz trailed me almost to Tampa. Yes, I traveled alone, but I felt Liz was with me. I don't think that will happen for the trip back home to Cleveland.

Liz followed me in the clouds on my way to Tampa, communicated through our spirits (Chapter Nine). We bonded so miraculously on her last days of life when she was in the hospital, giving me so many points to write in her book and so many secrets of her life. She even instructed me how she wanted everything written, and now I was here just for her on this trip. As I think back, I realize she wanted me to write down all the details of this trip in her book, which is what I am doing.

So, I wasn't alone; my sister, **"Tin Can,"** was with me and spoke to the echoes of my mind. But on the way home, I was looking for some sign from her and hoping she would be right there with me so we could exchange sign language, thoughts, and glimpses of her new life as she enjoyed in her early days before her final **"ESCAPE."**

## IN TAMPA AIRPORT GOING TO BALTIMORE

I looked out the Tampa Airport window, waiting to board the plane to Baltimore. It was nice and sunny, and the skies were blue with no clouds above. I kept looking for signs of my sister everywhere. I looked in strange places; maybe her shadow would pop out, and I would have pleasant thoughts of the trip ahead of me. I thought for sure I would have a sign, but no signs. I had no reminders of Liz anywhere. So maybe this time, I would be lucky to see at least a sign of her.

I boarded the plane to Baltimore and hurried through to find a seat right over the aircraft's wing. However, if I had any signs of Liz following me home, it would be by the plane's wing. I would still have a clear view of the wing. Then, I thought to myself, how silly! Just because Liz came with me to Florida, how can I expect her to follow me home to Baltimore and Cleveland? As I was walking down the aisle, I looked, and there were a bunch of seats near and over the plane's wing. Then suddenly I looked, and there was the wing of the aircraft, and I sat myself down. It was a perfect view out over the wing into the

Blue Skies. As the plane started to taxi off the runway, I said to myself, **"Goodbye, Florida; Goodbye, my Sister, Liz!"** I was so sad about everything that she was gone and up in the heavens, and I wouldn't talk or see her anymore.

I closed my eyes but couldn't sleep because I was too overwhelmed and anxious about this trip home. Then, before you knew it, we were getting ready to land in Baltimore, and I just accepted that I wouldn't have any experiences as I did on my way to Florida with my sister. I was sad, but I kept thinking of all the beautiful experiences and not-so-wonderful experiences I had on this trip. I was anxious to get home; I told myself I had to hold on to the memories of this trip, and if I hadn't gone to Florida for her memorial, I would never have forgiven myself, and I would be wondering what happened all the days of my life. It would not

I looked out the window; everything was clear, and the skies were so blue! I was sad that there were no clouds in the sky. I was always looking for one big fluffy cloud, but nothing.

be the same even if someone gave me pictures or a video as Kim did for me at her mother's 80th birthday gathering. I was there! I was happy Dorothy convinced me to come. I can write this book confidently, and I have many experiences, such as what Liz told me while in the hospital and what memorable experiences I had in Florida. I was thankful.

## ARRIVING AT BALTIMORE AIRPORT

When I got off the Baltimore plane, I found a seat in the Baltimore airport, which was a bit crowded. As Liz would do, I began talking to people around me, waiting to board the plane to Cleveland Hopkins Airport. Passengers asked me where I was heading and what I had done in Florida. I told them I had spent time with my sister Liz in the Clearwater Beach area.

They soon called seat numbers, and my number fell into the last group. I thought I 'd probably get stuck with a seat far back in the plane, nowhere near the aircraft's wings.

## BOARDED THE PLANE FROM BALTIMORE TO CLEVELAND

I boarded the plane from Baltimore to Cleveland and hurried through to find a seat right over the plane's wing. I didn't want to be pushy, but I did want a seat over the wing. As I walked down the aisle, both sides over the wings were occupied. I had to keep walking to the back of the plane to find a seat, and they were all taken.

I was anxious. I had to turn around and walk back to see if I had missed an empty seat somewhere. As I walked back toward the middle of the plane, I saw a teenager move out of one of the window seats and across the aisle behind his family—a father, a mother, and a little boy.

I rushed and sat down before someone else grabbed it! I knew I was in the middle of the plane, but not precisely where. I was quick! I put my carry-on bag on the floor under the seat, and I didn't even think of looking out the window, and the shade was pulled down. I didn't even pull the shade up, and finally, after I got settled and when we taxied around the airport and up into the sky, I pulled up the shade, and there I was! My seat was right over the plane's wing, just as I had on my way to Florida. I couldn't believe it! I couldn't find a seat; I got three seats right in the row over the wing. I thought being alone was very

I see something, I see her shadow right on the wing of the plane. It was **Tin Can!**

spooky, for I already knew that Liz trailed me on the way to Florida, but it wouldn't be the same going home to Cleveland. It was like this young teenager had saved the seat just for me and moved out of it as I walked back up the aisle. It was bizarre, indeed!

After I got settled in my seat next to the window, I pondered whether I should open the shade or leave it closed. I kept it closed. After we were way up in the skies, the stewardess passed out a little pop in a cup and a tiny snack. I decided to pull up the shade on the window, and I already had in my mind I wouldn't have any more **Tin Can** experiences. As I stared out the window, I don't think I even saw one cloud when we were in the sky. There was nothing but *bright, clear Blue Skies above.*

I continuously looked out of the window while in my seat.

Should I ask **Tin Can**, "Where are you?" But I wouldn't dare, for I knew the trip home would not be the same as heading toward Florida.

I didn't know if I should talk to her, for I accepted that there would be no gala appearances or showdowns from the **Tin Can lady**. I was so confident. Then, I kept looking up and out of the window, saying, "**Liz, I am here!**"—as she spoke to all of us when she made her late entrance where she arrived. I asked her again, "Lizzie, are you around in the Heavenly Blue Skies?"

I thought, "OK, **Tin Can**, I was blessed to have you share your last words with me before you passed away, live and in person, via phone." I must be grateful for the times we shared before and after you passed. I was up early in the morning, and I was happy. I made it on the plane safely and on **TIME**."

I was tired of trying to have her spirit speak to me, so I pulled down the shade. I thought I would nap or close my eyes and rest them. I was tempted to pull up the shade and peek, but I didn't. I laid back, closed my eyes, and thanked God for my blessed time in Florida, and I felt very thankful.

I switched my mindset to the future, and about the fun, I will have to open up those boxes that we packed and give the jewelry and clothes to my daughter Pam. How can I sleep? But I can rest my eyes and relax. Liz was out of my mind, with numerous other thoughts racing through my mind.

I thought, "I am going to forget about everything. I need to rest for a while before I get off the plane and be picked up by Dennis."

I was feeling peaceful, as I think **Tin Can** was as well. I decided to relax for once, and I was exhausted. I was trying to clear my thoughts and rest in quietness. Since Liz passed away, it has been a "Wild Ride," and I know I will have no rest once I get home. Now was the **TIME** for me to try to fall asleep.

Suddenly, I heard a pounding sound two rows above my row on the other side of the aisle. I stood in front of my seat and saw a small child kicking his feet or perhaps making pounding sounds with his hands. It was constant, and I could hear his mother holding him, saying, "March, march, boom, boom. We are flying high up in the sky and so happy. David, we are in a parade up in the skies."

They were pretending they were in a parade, I guess.

It alerted me to take note and see where the sounds were coming from again. Here, I wanted to sleep and rest, not hear all this aggravating pounding up high in the sky. I was getting a headache already! If it was bothering me, what did the other passengers think? The sounds became louder and louder, and I could hear the father's voice as I tried to stretch out to see, telling the mother and the baby to be quiet to soften their tones.

The mother said, "Daddy, we are in a parade, and it is so much fun!"

I stood up from my seat to see what was going on, for there was no other commotion. I was trying to rest, as I was sure other people were too. The voices were coming from the family sitting in two groups of seats, and the teenage boy who moved out of my seat was seated behind his father, mother, and, I would say, a child, maybe four years old. I could see the boy's light brownish hair bobbing up and down as I stood up. I never saw his face, only the back of his head. I knew I couldn't do anything, for

The big fluffy clouds circled around the wing of the plane.

the mother was trying to keep the child busy while he was stuck so long in a seat on the plane. I understand she would rather keep his mind active than have a crying, scared child to deal with. I could see that same teenager in the seat behind him holding his brother's police car up and making siren sounds to follow along in the parade. I could hear the teenager and the . saying, "It's a parade! David, let us keep marching." I think she was getting him some exercise by standing up in front of her while holding him.

Well, any thoughts I had about resting were done now. I might as well enjoy the ride and the view outside my window. I lifted the shade. As I then glanced out of the window, what did I see? I saw a vast, strangely shaped cloud. I couldn't determine if it would be a bright or dark cloud. I had to keep staring out the window. I was scared. I felt something would happen, but I didn't know what.

The clouds didn't float in the sky, but they rolled. I couldn't tell if they were going to get darker or lighter. I wasn't sure what was going on.

I stared out that plane window again, and I was so happy! I never expected to see any shadows of the **Tin Can**; I just enjoyed the view.

She wasn't even in my mind. I asked myself, "Is she out there, trying to message me?" Then, I saw that big cloud coming changed to a big, fluffy, white, irregular-shaped cloud; it encompassed the entire wing of the plane, and then I saw her shadow!

**There she was! It was Tin Can, and I could see her shadow of her Spirit!**

It was her shadow, right on the wing of the plane! A colossal, vast cloud was all around the aircraft's wing. The massive, unusually shaped cloud was moving along with the plane. I was shocked!

I was not expecting to have another Liz experience. Is my brain playing tricks on me?

I yelled out, looking up to the Blue Skies (only in my mind, for I didn't want to make a commotion on the plane). **"Tin Can, Tin Can, is that you? I am here!"** As she approached the wing, I could feel her spirit perched up high on one colossal cloud.

It's a parade up in the clouds. What does this mean? What is happening?

It was her! She wanted me to follow that cloud without moving my eyes. It was then that the marching sounds coming from the child started up again, or maybe I was just so enthralled at this scene; perhaps I didn't hear him right away. But sure enough, the child, his mother, and his brother were all singing and in sync, "Boom, boom, march, march." Then…

I saw the most amazing sight I have ever seen; there she was on that high cloud, and there were hundreds and hundreds of different-sized clouds behind her as she led the way. They were marching, and it was in a Beautiful Blue-Sky Parade! I never saw all those smaller spots of clouds on the way to Tampa, but only one big cloud, never all the little fluffs of clouds. Where did all the clouds come from?

I don't know if all those clouds were typical, but this was not normal for me to see. It was a parade, and it was led by "**Tin Can herself!**" In my mind, I asked her to reveal this to me aspiration, and she did. I felt her saying, "Listen to the little boy marching in the parade, yelling. Please listen and watch the band hear the music."

The music began to change. **Tin Can** led the parade as the heavenly band played a delicate harp-like tune I had never heard before. Every sound I heard was in sync with the little light-haired boy as he was kicking the seat in front of him. Liz even considered him as her son. The clouds of all different sizes were moving along with the plane. I asked, "**Tin Can**," what do these clouds mean?"

I could feel her saying, "Dr. Rita, it is straightforward; those clouds are all our family members and my dearest friends who went to the heavenly gates before me. I knew some of these people for years, and they left this earth and moved on to the next life. Daddy and Mommy, our niece Lisa, and our half-brothers. Louie and our mom's precious little "**Richie Boy** "were also one of those tiny little clouds."

She tried to tell me more about who was who, but I was in awe and fascinated that I couldn't get all the names. I did get that some of the names she said were the kids; she tossed the pennies in the cans in the streets. Those names were even down to every person she played with on Sophia Ave with the tin cans. She told me this time that she was winning all the pennies, as she always wanted to do, and now some were even playing with the yellow poker chips.

It was a miracle! Up in the skies! I knew she was up to this scenario and was waiting to set up the scene with the little boy marching a tune and kicking his feet on the free seat before him. No person was sitting in that seat, and I am sure the parents would never allow this commotion. Liz had a strange way of doing things and always came out with a "**BANG**!" I was in "**AWE** again"! I kept my eyes fixed, looking out the window, enjoying the fun and even the boom sounds from the little boy playing as he led the parade. How creative, wouldn't you say?

I asked myself, "How can this happen? Just when I thought I would not have any experiences this time going home, as I did as I went to Florida." I took out my phone and snapped pictures, thinking, *"How will I remember all this?"* But I knew I had no choice, and my excellent memory skills must be put to work. It was all "visual," and I had no time to pull out the laptop from my carry-on bag and write. By the time that I would get it turned on, I could have missed the parade, and no way could I do that! I couldn't take my eyes away

It is clear day and all blue skies! Where are all the small clouds?

from what I witnessed, the fluffy white clouds moving in the Blue Skies above, in sync with the boy pounding on the seat before him.

The pilot announced that we would land in Cleveland in ten minutes. The pilot said, "Make sure your seatbelts are fastened." I reached down from under my seat and pulled out my bag. When I sat up, I looked back out the window. What did I see? **Nothing**! The big cloud and the many little ones were gone! I couldn't believe it. The clouds had vanished in the sky! I wanted Liz's giant cloud and all those little clouds to follow me to the plane's landing. I wanted to see them and snap more pictures with my phone, but no clouds were in the skies. They were gone, and so was she! Where—where are those clouds? What happened to them all?

The kicking or pounding stopped, and I didn't hear any more conversations from the family. I figured the mother put the little boy in his seat or on her lap, kept him quiet, and prepared for the landing.

Oh, I made sure I had everything, and I eagerly waited to exit my seat and get in the rush of the other people in the aisle. When it was time to stand up to leave the aisle, I thought I wanted to talk to the family or get by them as they walked out and mainly speak to the little fair-haired boy. I wanted to see his appearance, for I had only seen him from behind. I thought they were only a few rows ahead of me on the other side of the plane.

**What! Where were they? They were gone, and so was Tin Can!**

Where did they go? No one was leaving their seats, standing in their row only. I waited until we were released from our seating area. When I went by the two rows of seats in front of me on the opposite side of the aisle, I asked some passengers if anyone had left their seats earlier, particularly a family with a little boy pounding on the seat in front of him. The people I asked said those seats were theirs, and no little boy was with his family. The people I asked thought I was a bit strange, or better yet, "**CRAZY**"!

In shock, I kept walking in the aisle to the front, asking myself, "Where were the parents, the teenage son, who gave me his seat above the wing, and the little boy? What happened to them? Where did they go? It can't be; it was so real!" I was walking very briskly until I got off the plane. I was in shock. Walking to the airport, I took my heavy carry-on and sat in the gate area. It was all such a surreal experience. I was feeling numb. I was crying but not sobbing. I just had to ask myself: "How can another phenomenon happen, not once but twice?" Plus, I thought I would not have any of these thoughts, visions, or possible mind-playing episodes with this trip coming. Then, it happened when I least expected it. I am in shock and disbelief! As you read this, I swear this was an actual episode of everything that happened as I wrote this to you.

No clouds were in the skies, only Blue Skies out above. After I composed myself, I got up and walked over to the gate's window. As I continued to look outside through the windows, a tune began to play in my head. As I walked, I started to sing it softly, audibly, staring out the window.

*Blue Skies, all out and above*
*Nothing but Blue Skies up above*
*No clouds up in the skies*
*Only Blue Skies shining down on me*

I never heard this tune before in my life. I started singing, and my spirit came up with the words and the melody. I kept singing repeatedly, using a low voice in the airport as I looked out the large windows in that gate. As I looked out the windows into the skies, I kept singing and repeating my made-up song.

I wanted to see the parade of clouds, not Blue Skies. I thought to myself," How did this happen? Where is my parade of clouds?"

Since I left the plane, I kept looking outside through the windows, trying to find the parade—but there were only Blue Skies. So, I kept singing this tune I had never sung or heard before. The funny thing is that I was singing it and would sing the words differently each time with the same tune.

*Blue Skies looking down at me.*
*Nothing but Blue Skies can I see*
*No clouds up in the skies*

*Only Blue Skies shining down on me*
*Blue Skies from the Heavens above*
*Only Blue Skies are coming down on me*

I kept singing this made-up tune repeatedly with a low voice in the airport, standing by the large windows, just staring out, looking for the parade in the skies, but nothing. I only saw Blue Skies. I kept singing the same tune over and over again, just staring out the big airport windows, thinking that one—just one—cloud would pop up. Yet, I called or chanted to my sister, "What happened to the parade you were leading?"

Suddenly, an elderly lady said, "Oh, Honeybee, I love that tune!" I was in such a state of shock I didn't even know where the tune was coming from in my head. I never heard that tune or the lyrics before. Where did the lady come from? It seemed she appeared out of "The Blue!"

Looking straight into her eyes while shaking my head, I asked her, "Is it a real song?" I wanted to tell her why I was singing this song and why I was disappointed to see Blue Skies instead of clouds marching in a parade.

She replied, "Sure is, and you sing it very nicely. You can sing! It has the same tune and almost the exact words, but it's your song! When I'm feeling BLUE, I sing that tune myself, and it always helps me feel better. You should try that sometime. I can't think who sings it, but it is a song, and thank God we got Blue Skies out there today. Aren't you glad? But if you want to know, here are the actual words:

*Blue Skies are smiling at me.*
*Nothing but Blue Skies do I see*
*Blue days, all of them gone*
*Nothing but Blue Skies from now on!"*

I wanted to say, "No, No, No, "but I couldn't tell her the story I just witnessed on the aircraft."

I wanted to see the parade of clouds, not Blue Skies. The lovely lady looked so strange to me and kept standing there. She asked me if I felt all right and said, "Sing it again, Honey!" I did as I looked out the window. Then, she started singing it with me. I can't remember, but I must have sung those verses repeatedly, and she was singing along with me. I wasn't alone. She sang along with me with my tune, and then we sang her tune with her words. It was nice having someone to sing along, even though I didn't know who this lady was.

Then, I thought I'd better get going. My plane arrived early, but I wasn't worried. I'd thought I better go and pick up the carry-on I had set on the floor. Soon, I would call Dennis to pick me up at the Cleveland airport. I turned to say goodbye to the lovely lady for being so sweet. I looked around, and *guess what? She was gone!*

After getting home, I kept singing the same tune but changing the words repeatedly. I searched my computer and found out that several different singers sang the song. The words may be slightly different, but the tune was the same. I think this was another remarkable miracle and fantastic phenomenon I experienced. What do you think? I couldn't take the clouds with me whenever I come across a tribulation, but I could take this tune with me! So, trust me, Liz and I would like to invite you to do the same!

Ever since my sister Liz passed away, I was in a state of shock for several days, and my mind was very overwhelmed! I couldn't comprehend some of my experiences, and I still struggle with them. But this was too surreal! Yes, I was drained and decided to keep the shade down on the window and rest my eyes, but maybe I did fall asleep, and possibly I was dreaming. But why and how would I whip out my phone from my purse and take pictures if I was sleeping? Was it sleepwalking but not up and walking around as I was confined to the compounds of the plane seat with limited movement? No, that can't be it at all, but it was something, and it was real! My mind was high up in a transient lucid "cloud," seeing many clouds moving out in the sky.

As a reader, if you know or can come up with some explanation for all of this, please write and let me know. There were just too many pieces that were revealed "**In Sync to Me**" within the echoes of my mind and happening. The family, the clouds, family members' names, the angelic music, and being "in sync" with the little boy kicking on the chair in front of him were all bizarre! Then, Liz called the little boy and said she loved him as her son…was that thought a figment of my imagination? Oh, my, what could all of this mean?

These experiences are all I have thought about, and finally, I decided I had to finish this chapter before the divine recollection would leave my mind. But the experience is lingering on, and so is the tune of the Blue Skies song above wherever I go.

Later, I prayed about this phenomenon, and the Lord put in my mind that the family could have been angels, which I strongly believe in. Standing up, I saw them in their seats across the aisle. They couldn't just disappear from their seats on the plane out into the clouds, could they? Was it a type of "**MANIFESTATION**?" But then again, maybe they were not only a few rows ahead of me on the other side of the aisle; perhaps they were further up the aisle, which could be a possibility. Who knows, but they were there, and there was a parade!

Yes, they were there as directed by the Lord, for He knew I needed one last experience before I faced my husband picking me up and my family waiting for me at home. I had to come back to my world where I have a family and the world where I live. The Bible says God created angels for many purposes, including guiding, protecting, and encouraging us. God wants us to know there are millions of angels praising God in Heaven. They do come down to earth "**ANGELS UNAWARE**." I know what the scripture says in Hebrews 13:2, "That some have entertained **ANGELS UNAWARE**," They could very well be sitting right on a cloud with **TIN CAN AND OUR GOD;** this possibility is constantly occurring.

Indeed, Liz did say that God would help me and encourage me to finish her book. I think she wanted these unique "**CLOUDY EXPERIENCES**" to be written so others could learn what she went through and what I am going through as I write each page of this book. Don't you think? I don't know the answer.

However, could it also mean that "Some were entertained by **ANGELS UNAWARE**? "This certainly could be the case in this phenomenal experience taking place within the clouds right outside my window and on the plane! Surely, we will never know, will we? Then, what about the lady at the airport who came out of nowhere and quickly disappeared? How would you explain that little "sing-along?" But it doesn't matter—our God knows what, real or unreal, dream or hallucination, fiction or nonfiction, fantasy or reality, sane or insane (maybe all of the above). It is just another miracle in life, and now it is in the legend of **"Tin Can Lizzie!"**

You can easily judge this by reading snippets of her life's accounts. She was quite a character and had pulled off the impossible many times. There is so much more, and of the **"SECRETS"** she never got the chance to tell. But maybe they will still be revealed to the other family members or me somehow! When we least expect something to show up, Liz might be perched up high on a cloud or looking in the bright beam of lights in our window as she did with me.

Maybe a stranger will come to us and tell us something about her life; who knows? We don't, do we? I wouldn't put anything past her—would you? This **"Farewell to Florida"** Chapter and this entire book are just the tip of the iceberg! Therefore, **"CLOUDY"** as it may seem to you, let me tell you I wouldn't put it past Liz! Think of the theme of this book: When life gets too overpowering to you, there is always a **WAY OUT!** Perhaps everything was getting too burdensome for me to handle, with her death and with everything else. But I know the only **WAY OUT** is to finish her book and get it published!

I think of all these stories, especially this chapter. Liz told me, "Rita, I will do what I must to make everyone believe this story of our family and me; it must be done!" She has pulled off many strange things throughout her life, but this story proves she still pulls off the impossible in heaven! As she said, while growing up on Sophia, she was not the family leader; our sister Dorothy was. But she is a leader in heaven, performing the impossible and orchestrating the band! As you read this story, you may **DOUBT** it is true, but I believe she holds us all up and strengthens us. She wants us to get through our problems and **OVERCOME** them just as she did when she was at the most troubled stages of her life! She is now a leader in our family from above the heavenly Blue Skies, speaking to us in our spirits!

She wants us to realize that now (primarily this is directed to me), she says, "You are almost to the finish line, and you can't give up now! I won't let you! Our family and others must read our story to understand who we are. It will give them the peace they need to make it through all their "***Trials and Tribulations***" until we can meet again in the heavenly parade of clouds and angels who watch over us."

I feel her saying, "Dr. Rita, thank you for all you do for our family and me. Please tell them to always look for me in the clouds and the heavens; I will show my love along the way!"

## MY ARRIVAL IN CLEVELAND "I AM HERE"

I took my time going to the luggage carousel and followed the crowd to find it. The plane landed early, and by the time I was staring out the window and talking to the lady, it was still earlier than the expected arrival time. I waited only a few minutes at the baggage carousel. I saw one suitcase go around and knew the other would be coming soon. Therefore, I thought I better spot someone strong to help pick up my luggage as I did in Florida. Sure enough, I didn't even have to ask, but a nice young guy approached me and asked if I needed help. I told him I got the first lighter bag, but the second was so heavy, 49 pounds, and he said, "Are you going to manage both this heavy one and the lighter one for your pick up?"

I replied, "I think I got to try. I think it will be ok." I had my carry-on bag around my shoulders and used one hand to push each piece of luggage. I called my husband, Dennis, and he was there in no time.

As I saw the car pull up, my Grandson Anthony waved to me in the front seat. I was so excited to see him and gave him a big hug. He quickly grabbed the suitcases and loaded them in the back, and we went home. On the ride home, Anthony asked me many questions about the funeral and his Great Auntie Lizzie. Dennis and my grandsons, Isak and Anthony, had a carryout chicken dinner with a couple of sides and a box of my favorite marshmallow-nut candy. Anthony carried my two suitcases into the house and wanted to see what was in the big one and if there was anything for him. I told him there wasn't, and he said, "Grandma, you know Aunt Lizzie always gave us things. Maybe she put away something on the side for Isak and me." I told him it was all Aunt Lizzie's clothes and things she packed for me and Aunt Pam. He was so disappointed but seemed to understand it was all girl stuff. I recalled how Aunt Lizzie bought him his first pocketknife with a nice leather case. He said he always loved that knife, and I told him she just knew you wanted that knife, and she surprised you and sent it to you. She loved you boys, and Christmas was always exciting with Auntie Lizzie and Aunt Dorothy's gifts to our house. Anthony said, "Yeah, Grandma, I will remember those days forever!"

In the following week, it was exciting to get one or two boxes from the mailman who drove up the drive to deliver my packages during the week. I didn't open them. I waited for all the boxes to arrive and planned to open them when my daughter, Pam, could come. The following Sunday, she came over for a casual Sunday dinner, and Pam and I opened the boxes together. My grandsons Isak and Anthony opened each box for us with excitement as Pam and I discussed each piece of clothing and item within the boxes. We were happy, but at the same time, we were filled with grief, and the shock of it all was so real. Liz and Dorothy had sent

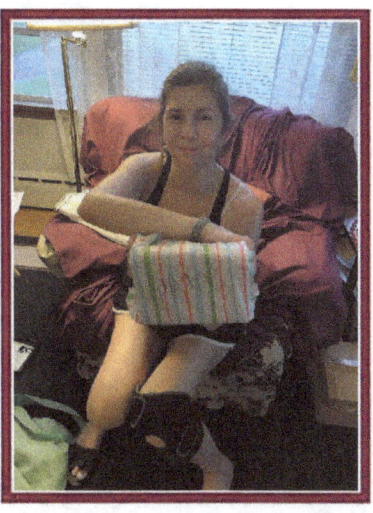

Pam opening up the wrapped presents from her Auntie Lizzie!

us so many boxes over the years, and this would be our last exchange from Auntie Lizzie.

I went over many details of the Florida trip with my daughter, Pam.

We were both very sad. Pam adored her Auntie Lizzie very much and started talking about their fun times when she stayed in Florida.

I did all I could to prevent myself from breaking down and crying again. So, I walked outside on my porch and looked up at the sky; it was so Blue, not a cloud in the July sky. I began to sing my "Blue Sky" song again.

**Blue Skies high above**
**Nothing but Blue Skies above**
**No clouds up in the skies**
**Only Blue Skies I can see**
**Blue Skies from the Heavens above**
**Only Blue Skies are coming down on me**

I believe that somehow or another, I have to move on with my family and keep writing Liz's book. After all, I made a lasting covenant with my sister, and I will follow through, keeping my promises to her to get busy, finish this book, and then publish it.

# Chapter 12

## A Final Farewell Life Moves On...

Well, here we are. We say a final farewell to all. The Stupavsky/ Stupansky family lives on! Liz wanted to tell not only her story but our incredible family history! Even though she didn't know that her conversations with me in the hospital were part of her last days, that **TIME** was so precious to me. She desired to tell everyone about her struggles in life and how she made it through those **Trials and Tribulations**. She hopes that when others experience terrible and rough periods, they will **OVERCOME** them, too.

Today, we who are left to carry out the family's legend of our sister Liz, the Tin Can Queen, and our family history live on! Our family's baby, Richard, lives in St. Petersburg, Florida, with his wife, Joann. Two of his children live in Ohio, while one son lives in North Carolina.

Liz's children, Kimberly and Gina, and my sister's grandchildren live in Florida. Dorothy is now the eldest sibling. She lives in St. Petersburg, Florida, and Victor lives with his wife, Jean, in California. Liz wanted me to talk about her life when she was young, our family members' lives, and how they managed to move on from that historical landmark, **SOPHIA AVE**, running parallel to Woodhill Road on the East side of Cleveland, Ohio.

I am the author of this book and a family member; therefore, I would like to introduce myself and my family. I was born on Sophia Ave. and raised in Cleveland, Ohio, all my life. I still live in a surrounding Cleveland suburb with my husband, Dennis. My daughter Pam, son Christopher, and grandchildren Isak and Anthony also live in the Cleveland suburbs.

October 2023, Our family cruise from the Left: Grandson; Isak, Husband, Dennis, Rita, Grandson; Anthony, and my son Christopher

2016, A cruise picture of myself and my daughter, Pamela. We took many family cruises together.

I was thinking back to Sophia Ave, where all our lives began long ago.

My grandmother Stupavsky purchased the Sophia house around 1910 when she had the family from the 9803 addresses, which, at the time, was a saloon.

2017, My daughter Pammy and I again, as we cruised together.

Within that house, we all survived through swamps of difficult trials, tribulations, and struggles. It took a long time, but we left that house as winners in a world that was too scary to face. We faced the inevitable future ahead of us and marched out strong! But one thing for sure—we did have a strong sense of purpose to make it through whatever life handed us so we could continue the upcoming days of our lives on earth.

1998 – 2000: The shell of the Sophia House after a massive fire that completely destroyed the inside of the house.

This book's theme becomes real here, *"When life becomes unbearable, there is always a way out!"* We all left that Sophia house, not knowing our paths in life, but we had hoped to follow our dreams. Just as in the beginning with our dad, mom, and niece Lisa as they passed away, and with **Tin Can** herself, it was Liz's **FINAL ESCAPE** as she entered the gates of heaven. How did **TIME** get away so quickly?

Things are much different today on Sophia Ave, but the house has a new family living there. The house looks much different than it was when we all lived there. Several years back, the house had a massive fire and was ready for demolition. I will never forget the day I saw **MY HOUSE** on the evening news on TV. I was shocked! Lives were lost in that fire! A couple of days later, visiting a school on that side of town, I went there, and sure enough, that was **MY HOUSE** on the news. All I could see were severely broken and covered-up windows and just the shell standing. On TV, reporters said nothing could be saved inside… but the news reports were wrong!

I couldn't wait to see for myself, picturing it much worse than it was. I thank the Lord, for the house was at least still standing!

The owner had decided that life could go on in that historic house, and the remains could be salvaged. The Sophia house was built in 1890. It was a two-family house, with one residence in the front and one in the back.

After the fire, the owner decided to rebuild the inside and restore the outside of the house.

It took a struggling inner-city father to have the faith to decide that there was still "**HOPE**" left in that house with its shortcomings, flaws, and living conditions.

This is the home where our lives took root and where we emerged into the real world! This is the Sophia house as it looks today. It still exists and looks great! I smile every time I look at this picture. Yes, the neighborhood is diverse, but the house remains, serving as a home for a very nice, large, young family. I am sure there is a lot of adventure within the walls, for history has a tendency to repeat itself, and I am sure there is still a lot of drama that exists.

The legend of that house will live on forever! It would be amazing to see how many stories and maybe even some nightmares are lingering in that house's framework, for it is still standing. I want to be a fly on the wall and follow the families who left that house and that neighborhood to see how they survived in their world. But there is no other house containing the legends the Stupavsky family created before moving on to their separate worlds. Where did **TIME** go? Several decades had passed, and I decided to return to that homestead someday to see **"life"** again amongst the many troubled and memorable years.

However, the Sophia house still had purpose and substance. One family finally rebuilt the house. Then, it was sold, and another family purchased and renovated it. A dormer was added upstairs, making it into a two-story home. Our attic, which used to be full of junk, had been made into a second floor, with bedrooms and a bathroom. There were so many improvements made to the house compared to when we lived there. The family tried to keep up the house and the yard.

I did go back to the Sophia house a few years later when I had gotten up enough nerve to drive by to see **MY HOUSE** after the fire... but found the house still standing, with a whole new fresh look! The legend of the infamous Sophia house lives on! The house looked so different, now! For me, it seemed to happen so quickly, as fast as the blink of an eye!

One day, after supervising my teachers at an old Cleveland City School nearby, I made another visit to the Sophia house. I bravely knocked on the front door and told the lovely lady who answered that I had lived in this house since I was born. She said she could see the excitement in my eyes upon returning to this homestead. She invited me inside to see their improvements and massive changes to the house's interior.

The lady was friendly and let me come inside. Oh, I was so thrilled but scared at the same time to walk into the house after so many years later! I couldn't believe it was the same house with an improved and modern look! The lady took me around the house. The room setup was much the same, but instead of a wide-open archway off the dining room, a wall had been added with a door to enter the bedroom. I told her how we had the house set up. The old bathroom that was turned into a closet when we lived there was now a stairway to the dormer's second floor. I asked how the upstairs looked and told them it used to be a dirty old attic. The young boy said, "Come on upstairs! I will show you. It is nice up there, and we have three bedrooms and a bathroom."

I said, "What? You have a bathroom in that old attic?" I was so surprised! I couldn't imagine it, for it used to be nothing but a collection of boxes and junk from my father that he was saving to sell someday. I dared not mention or ask if there were rats upstairs like we had in the days of old. It would have been an insult, and I wanted to show respect and gratitude for them allowing me to come into **MY HOUSE**.

But the mother said, "No, their rooms are a mess. I have to start dinner now."

I told them that my parents were **Deaf**, and the one older boy was so interested and asked, "Did they use American Sign Language (ASL)?"

I replied, "Yes, they did, and we all used ASL to communicate."

Then he very fluently signed to me. I was so happy! I had tears in my eyes. I asked the boy how he had learned about ASL and how to sign. The young boy told me he learned ASL in school, and it just so happened that my team and I started that program to teach hearing children ASL for credit! I was overwhelmed with joy that ASL was still entwined within this family and echoing within these walls.

I commented that I loved the house as it is now, and whatever they did to remodel, they did a fabulous job! I thought the house had lost its nostalgic warmness, but it had class, and my sister Liz would have loved it and been proud to bring friends home to visit. I could feel it was still **MY HOME**! I hated to leave, but the lady was anxious to return to her dinner preparations. I thanked the family for letting me enter the house to tour the "**New Look**" of "**MY OLD HOME**. "I told some stories of where everything used to be and a bit about my background and our family heritage. The young children thought what I told them was very interesting, and they kept asking me more questions about their house and my family. As I said, the young teenage children wanted to hear more stories of long ago! But their mother told them not to ask so many questions.

We went outside, and I took pictures of **MY HOUSE** and their yard. It was just so lovely and a dream come true compared to what it looked like when we lived there. My father had dreamed of building a garage someday with all that wood stored in the backyard. I commented, "Oh, there is still no garage." The young boy jumped in and said, "*We sure are gonna get one! We are gonna build it ourselves as soon we get us some money to buy the wood!*" I guess that was one of the hopes and wishes of the Sophia house occupants; they always hoped and saved wood or money to build their garage.

My father's dream was to build a garage in that yard, and I guess that dream still has not been fulfilled. But when it does happen, our father Fred will probably watch the process high above, with his family perched up high on a cloud.

I asked them if they used the basement, and the lady said, "*Sure do! We have a washer and dryer downstairs, but we hate walking outside to go down there.* The kids help me carry the baskets of clothes. It's cold in the winter, but I don't mind—even though the basement has no heat. The owner before we cleaned out that **Rat Hole** (I almost fainted when I heard that!), but it is a nice basement now, and we store our bikes and toys down there."

I told them, "We had an old wringer washer in the kitchen for years and years, and finally, my Dad and Mom saved enough money to buy a nice bronze-colored automatic washer and dryer that my father hooked up in the kitchen. The refrigerator was bronze, too, so the appliances all matched. Before that, my mom had to wash clothes for many people with the old ringer washer in the kitchen."

The little girl said," *An old wringer washer! You must be old!*"

The little girl's mother said, "*That wasn't a nice thing to say, and shush up, Missy!*"

I laughed and said, "Oh, no, please. I don't think I am old! My family and I spent much time living in this old house!"

The little girl said, "Yes, Ma'am, I bet you all sure did! Your life sounds fascinating, living in our house!"

I wanted to tell her, "No, Honey, it's **MY HOUSE**!" But I didn't because I wanted to show respect and gratitude.

But I did reply, "Yes, sweetie, it was fascinating, all right! I could tell you so many stories, but there is not enough **TIME** now, and I have to get back on the road before the work traffic starts."

The boy and the girl said they wanted me to come back again and tell them more stories of how life was with so many people living in their house.

I told the family," I would love to come back, and if I am ever in the area again, I will… if that would be OK with everyone. I won't let **TIME** race away without returning to visit again."

The little girl replied, *"Sure is, Ma'am! You come back again; you hear? We also want to hear more stories about when you were young living here in my house!"*

2013-2014: A Dream Come True! This is me! My dream came to fruition when I sat on the front step of the Sophia House at least one more time! It is something I just had to do. I wasn't there long, but in those few minutes, it seemed that decades had passed before my eyes. This was a miracle!

As we were talking in front of the Sophia house, I just said, "I used to sit on these front porch steps (as I sat down on them to demonstrate) for hours and hours to watch all the exciting action on the street. As I pointed to the front of the building where the store used to be, I told them it was so busy. Deliveries were coming, and people were going back and forth with kids hanging out on the street and store steps. Oh, there was so much to see and action going on! It was exciting!"

"Even today, I can remember everything! In my mind, I create a visual picture of what I see and snap it. I can remember all kinds of things as if they happened yesterday, yet it was so many years ago. It has always been my dream to return to Sophia's house and sit on these same front steps, and here I am, just sitting again! Your family made my dream come true! I can't thank you enough for allowing me to come to visit *MY* original home. Tears were rolling down my cheeks. I was trying to hide them as I put on my sunglasses."

The boy asked me, *"Would you like me to take a picture of you, Ma'am? I am good with taking pictures."*

I told the young teenager, "Oh, I would love a picture, and I will save it forever and ever! Someday, I will show my grandchildren how and where I grew up on Sophia Ave. I can look at the picture and remember some sights I saw as a little girl. I have wonderful memories of the days of old. I thank you all so much for this opportunity."

The little girl said, *"I sit on the porch sometimes, too, but I don't see anything good—just some bad old kids and gangs walkin' past my house. They better not mess with me, for I'll get my brother, and we'll gid them!"*

While looking up at the Klucho building next door, I had to ask her if anyone lived there now. I told them, "That building was a family-owned grocery store, in which it was very much a part of our lives. Years ago, it was a saloon, and my father lived there with his parents after he came to America from another country. My grandparents ran the saloon. However, after some time, they sold the business. Then it was just a memory and had to be discovered by a Klucho family member searching all the records."

2012, The side door of the Klucho Family dwelling—the store entrance of the Klucho Grocery Store was in the front on Sophia Ave. Little did I know this was my last view of that dwelling.

I was pointing up to the side of the Klucho Store building and saw some windows closed. I told the lady and the children, "My big sister Dorothy would go to that side door after store hours, sometimes very late at night, and she would ask to buy a few slices of bologna and slices of cheese because we had no food to eat. Mr. Klucho, the grocery owner, would give us some food, and my sister would ask him to put it on our grocery bill, and he did. The funny thing is, I don't think we ever paid those grocery bills, and Mr. Klucho never would ask my parents for the money— maybe because he didn't know sign language to ask my parents to pay our grocery bill. Everyone was nice to us in the Klucho Family Grocery Store."

The little girl laughed and asked, *"Why didn't you all have food to eat?"*

The young teenage boy asked, *"Didn't your mama cook you all some food? What's wrong with her?"*

I told them, "Well, remember that my parents were **DEAF**. My Dad was brilliant and a skilled electrician, but no one would give him any work. It was hard for him to take care of us and for my Mother to cook good food for us. But we all survived, and now we appreciate what we have, just like you children with such a lovely house.

The mother said, *"When the new owner bought the Klucho house from the former owner, no one lived there for a long time, maybe a couple of years.*

*I didn't know if the fire in our house blew over to the house next door and the back where garages and storage sheds were located. Maybe that is why the house was closed, and no one lived there. We moved into this house after it was restored from the fire."*

"So," she said, *"I hear the present owner may tear down the whole kit 'n' caboodle, garages in the back, the shed—all of it! We'll come home one day, and big bulldozers will knock it all down. I hope they can save the place and the property; it has some personality left. I hope it doesn't happen, but it can't be left alone standing there for kids to go a roamin' back there, and it could be big trouble! I called the police many a time!"*

After driving by the Sophia house several times a few years later, I had the shock of my life! The Klucho store building, back garages, and little buildings were all gone! I couldn't believe my eyes! The Klucho store had been demolished! I was shaking at the sight, asking myself, "Where is the Klucho Family store? Where is it?"

The little lady was correct because she said there was talk that the building would all come down. *She said it was just a matter of **TIME**, and it would happen, and it indeed did! I thought I was* dreaming and that it was a bad nightmare! I couldn't believe my eyes! That was my father's home when his parents ran the neighborhood saloon after he came to America from Czechoslovakia with his mother Katherine in 1903/04.

What happened to the Klucho Family Grocery Store building? It was gone and so was a piece of me gone with it! It is just memories now of a life that once existed!

I was in shock! The place that had been our second home was gone! Just like my sister was **GONE** today! I thought, "This isn't fair to the descendants of the Klucho family and our family. We had a joint family history of running and loving that establishment.

That store was a big part of our lives. I cried in my car and wept for our families."

The sad thing is that the famous Klucho Grocery Store is no longer standing, and its history is gone forever! **TIME just** slipped away like a *"Thief in the night."* It was unfortunate that the famous neighborhood Klucho Store had been razed. It was heartbreaking going past what used to be our family store on Sophia Ave. Now, the existence of that store and its legend were nothing but cinders, ashes, and overgrown weeds. This was a painful shock and a horrible sight to see! I wondered if the Klucho family knew what, when, and why their homestead was gone forever, wiped off the face of this earth! However, it will never be removed from our minds and hearts!

Later, I learned that the Klucho family knew what happened when their family grocery store and dwelling went down, and massive pieces of our early lives and families' histories were gone! Like my sister's body, only our treasured memories remain, as *"Ashes to Ashes and Dust to Dust."*

After writing all the words of this story, I have drawn very close to my sister as **Tin Can**. I will never forget her telling me her big secret of running out of the Sophia house on her way to **"ESCAPE."** As I traced some of her early beginnings to her mid- and older years, she was trying to seek and find a way of escaping the **Trials and Tribulations** she had been going through her entire life.

Does it all stem back to her beginnings living on Sophia Ave, or is there much more to her life? We can't point a finger at exactly what could have been her drive to succeed and face the challenges ahead of her. Today, we will never know, will we? What was the driving force of her life as she grew up on Sophia Ave?

Liz loved **"LOVE"** and always sought true love and happiness. Even when she had some bitter, rough rides in life, she was still on the run. We all have had some challenging rides to get us through the dismal times as we plodded along the pathways of our lives that God had set forth for us.

How can the family and I get through the holidays—Thanksgiving and then Christmas? How are her daughters going to make it through future holidays? I am discouraged as I think about writing these last pages of the book my sister Liz asked me to write. It is only me left to do all the writing—when it was supposed to be the both of us when she got home. I was tense as I kept moving forward, trying to complete this book—very anxious and struggling while reaching for the gold!

The first Thanksgiving after Liz passed away was our first Thanksgiving without Liz. I missed her calling me first thing in the morning. I thought, what can I do? Then, I had a thought. When I set the table for my family for the holidays, I will put a place for her. I know exactly where I will seat her—right next to the window where she appeared to me in the shadows with a light beam all around her while I wrote Chapter Eight in her honor. But I will remember her and her phone calls on future holidays, her birthday, and the date the Lord took her up in the Blue Skies.

2020, Our first holiday without my sister. We thanked God for her life! I set a place for her right by the window where I saw her shadows as I wrote her story.

Our Thanksgivings and all the holidays are sad without my sister, Liz. I say a prayer and set a place setting for her. I keep Liz's memory "**ALIVE**" for every Holiday.

But the real thought is, how will we all make it through our holidays without her? It will be unfortunate for Liz's daughters Kim and Gina and all of us. I wondered how I was going to make it myself. Plus, while I was in the process of writing this book, my heart was torn. She would never forget us on Christmas and all holidays with phone calls, cards, gifts, and spending our Christmas years together in Florida. She would shower us with gifts and bring some silly little presents to take home to my boys, Isak and Anthony. Liz would ensure that this first year when she's in the Lord's house would not be any different. She had her ways of doing things, but what she did for us the first year after will be a shock for the rest of our lives! I never expected a real gift from her that first year after she was gone, but she did it! She has passed away but still shows us signs of her presence! Her mysteries of life still linger on, and I am sure they will continue until we see her again in our Lord's house.

I am sure you wonder how this could be possible because my sister has already passed away. Yet, with Liz, there is always a way! Nothing is too complicated for my sister; she knew how to get around everything, keeping her eyes open for the best fit for us and looking for the best bargain! She couldn't resist a deal either to buy or sell something. She always wanted to find the best gift for us.

I never expected a package to arrive at my door two weeks before Christmas 2020. I was shocked! I wasn't expecting a package.

I opened the box that first year without Liz, and what did I see? A Christmas gift wrapped with a tag that said, "To Rita, Love from sister Lizzie." I thought, "OK, Kim, I know this is from you, for it has your name and address on the box. But no, this package was from Liz, the **TIN CAN QUEEN** herself!

After my sister was gone for the first Christmas, I talked to Kim. She replied, "That gift **IS** from Mom! Aunt Rita put it under your Christmas tree and opened it on Christmas day. You must wait, but it is from Mom. You will see. After you open it, I will tell you the story. You have to wait until then. Please put it under your tree until Christmas morning. Then you can open it, for it is from your sister!"

I replied to Kim, "What? That gift **IS** from mom?" I didn't want to say, how can this be? Mom is gone. So, I just kept my mouth shut. I was puzzled. What can that gift be? I felt and shook it like a little kid getting a surprise gift from Santa.

Well, that first Christmas day rolled around before I knew it. I kept staring at that mysterious gift on Christmas morning under my tiny tree. I was so depressed about not having my sister with me that I couldn't open the gift that first day on Christmas morning after all. Liz wasn't there to hand it to me or call me on the phone. If it were one of her corny gifts, she would buy it—not just for one person but for everyone in the family. Sometimes, we all got the same gift in some years, for she had made a deal with a salesperson she was so good at doing! She showed no partiality and was fair and reasonable to all. What can I say?

Liz was Liz, and she knew how to beat the odds even when she was not here with us anymore.

Finally, on that first New Year's Eve, Kim called me and asked what I thought of Mom's gift. I had to tell her I was so down and depressed that I didn't have the heart to open it on that first Christmas day. I kept touching and staring at that gift, wondering what could be inside. I told Kim I wasn't ready to open it yet, but Kim didn't accept that as an answer. She was a lot like her Mother, insisting on getting her way. She made me get the gift and open it. I was shocked! It was a special and unique butter dish for my kitchen, purchased by the **Tin Can** herself!

I placed Liz's gift under the Christmas tree as Kim had directed me to do and held it until Christmas morning.

Kim told me, "Aunt Rita, Mom purchased 12 butter dishes about six weeks before she passed away. Mom was so brilliant! She bought and shipped them to one of the neighbor's houses in **Top of The World,** where she last lived. She told the neighbor a delivery would come to her address and to keep the contents for her. Liz told the neighbor that if anything ever happened to her, she should give the package to her sweet daughter Kim and tell her what was inside for all the family members to hand out or send to everyone at Christmas 2020. Well, sad to say, the box arrived the day after my mom passed away. I was shocked, as was Mom's neighbor. I think you will think it is a very creative gift indeed and very useful. The butter dish will keep butter spreadable at all times, as well as to remember her every time we use the butter in the dish."

So here it is. **TIME** has robbed us of our **Tin Can Lizzie**, but Liz reminded me to think of her every time I use the butter from the dish.

I could hear Liz say to everyone who got a butter dish, *"See, me surprise you!"* just as my mother would say and sign to all of us. Liz was so thoughtful, kind, and generous, and she loved the element of "**Surprise**" when she gave us a gift.

I think Liz outdid herself on the butter dish gift idea. Don't you think? What can I say? My sister loved Christmas and ensured everyone had a gift to open on this first Christmas, with or without her. She always went out of the way and out of her means, but she gave willingly and from her heart! I will treasure that butter dish forever!

She wouldn't let that first Christmas of 2020 without Lizzie be any different, and she didn't. She did it with a bang! Now, I think of her every time I fill the butter dish and use the butter. Liz was so creative!

Through this book, we learned about who my sister Liz was, even though she seemed to make us think she was riding high in fancy cars in her successful real estate profession. However, she had difficulty making sound decisions professionally and personally. She was always hurting inside and searching for any indication of finding love and peace within her body and soul. It seemed she was often on the road to **ESCAPE** from something, someone, or life, for the burdens were heavy on her many times.

Reading the book's chapters, we got a small glimpse of **The Tin Can Girl** and the Stupavsky/Stupansky family. Some of us spell our name with a (v) and some with an (n), which started with Liz's idea. I am the only one who spells our name the original way, stupavsky. I hope you enjoyed the ride and took a visual picture of what life was like for all of us through the years. Yes, we all have moved on, and most still exist. But where is **Tin Can**? what is she doing today, up in the fluffy white clouds in the heavens? She is no longer physically with us, but her spirit and uncanny legend will remain in our minds and hearts forever!

As I write this final chapter, I am saddened that I couldn't write it with Liz and learn more about her and some of the secrets she wanted to tell me. But I think the more I write and draw closure on *"OUR BOOK,"* as she called it, I am learning and putting together the pieces of her life. She was with me throughout the writing process. I couldn't have completed this book without her! So, what does that tell us? She is here with me and everyone else as we seek her face, spirit, and connection with us.

As I write these pages, the only things left are our memories, heartaches, tears, pictures (as many are in this book), and confusion about how and why she passed away as she did. Her death was unconscionable and very sad for all of us. Yes, her health was failing, and she was 80 years young, but there was no excuse for how she passed away. She died without eating, drinking, or having IVs pumped into her arms for four and a half days before a routine procedure. This could haunt our family members for the rest of our lives and leave us uncertain and unrestful. We begged for peace, and we prayed for proper closure. My sister was so brave and wanted to be well. She tried to find a condo for her and Kim to move into together. My sister loved "**life**," and in no way did she want to stop it or was ready to stop it!

The hospital and the doctors all claim "no fault of their own" regarding Liz's death. Gina and Kim were dealing with the situation. Kim talked to the floor nurses on the phone as much as possible. I spoke to her several times a day to Liz so she could continue to tell me her story.

She did plead to go home. She wanted to finish this book with me and surprise her family. Liz wanted to be with her family and daughter Kim in the new living arrangement she hoped for. She, by all means, did not want to die.

No matter where Kim and Gina turned, there was controversy, including "pneumonia" being listed on her death certificate as the cause of death. In the state of Florida, a body cannot be cremated with such a cause during the COVID-19 virus time. The girls had to struggle with the hospital and doctors to get that cause changed. They would not change the cause, but her lungs were fine, as stated in the reports, and she never even had oxygen during the whole time of her pitiful stay! It doesn't seem very responsible to have a person go forth with a surgical procedure while being dehydrated and whose vitals were not very stable.

Therefore, at that time, the funeral home could not abide by Liz's wishes to be cremated—more grief and another tribulation the family had to go through. Liz, the famous "**Tin Can**," had to have that **FINAL ESCAPE**!

The family had to continually appeal to the doctors and the hospital to get the cause of death changed. The family was distraught, especially Liz's daughters, Kim and Gina. While this was happening, I never gave up, and I kept writing the pages of this book as I promised Liz I would.

Liz's remains were kept back in that **"cold room"** until the doctor would change the death certificate. He would not, but he did add "sepsis" to the cause of death, thus allowing the Health Department to permit the funeral home to go forth with Liz's cremation.

I would talk to the girls daily and ask what was happening. I would look out in the sky and pray and sing:

Dark clouds up in the sky
Nothing but dark clouds up in the sky
Dark shadows covered high
Nothing but dark shadows up high
No Blue Skies can be seen
Nothing but darkness can I see

Gina talked to several lawyers, who told her nothing could be done. She said that they could not go to the doctor or the hospital. The girls wanted no sums of money but liked the truth about what happened to their mother and were denied. An autopsy could have been ordered, but that would have cost a lot of money because the police authorities did not order it, and the girls would have had to pay out of their pockets. No matter where the girls turned, dark clouds were in their way, and there were no Blue Skies. It was one dilemma after another tragedy, just like the story of **Tin Can** all of her life. Here she was; she couldn't even have peace to have her last wishes honored to be cremated. The girls only heard of bits and pieces from the nurses' notes in their daily logs. Finally, several weeks after the memorial, our anticipated day was here!

Gina and Kim got calls from the funeral home that her mother's cremation and her last wishes would happen the following day at 8 AM. Kim informed the family, and we all were on a group text for the whole time of the cremation. We did not want **Tin Can** to be alone for her **FINAL ESCAPE**! We had no choice but to let her go. We had to feel that her spirit was at peace and let her be free to move happily in her **FINAL ESCAPE**! Liz had a rough enough time while she was alive, and she surely didn't need such confusion after she passed away!

It was a terrible **TIME** to pass away as Liz did. Why couldn't **TIME** keep ticking a little longer—at least until my sister left the hospital? Why did **TIME** mistreat Liz?

At that time, COVID-19 was an unconventional way of life; we wore masks everywhere we went, and our lives were so different. So many people have died of this virus. Now, we can only look for Liz in the bright lights, in the sunlight, or up in the clouds. My Florida vacations are on hold due to COVID-19, and nothing will be the same no matter how we look at things. Everything has changed, and we no longer have our Liz with us. **TIME** won out, and we didn't beat the clock as quickly as we hoped. The Coronavirus was whirling all around us, and there was no "**ESCAPE**" from **TIME** or the **VIRUS**!

This book must be published so others can have **HOPE** and learn of this marvelous woman! We can only remember who she was and how she lived as the **Tin Can Girl,** a Sister, a Mother, a Grandmother, and a Friend. Yes, she was guilty of doing many things with such remorse. She had so many more secrets to tell me, but she didn't make it. Now, we all have to remember the good she did on this earth before our heavenly father allowed her to make her **FINAL ESCAPE!** We remember her and are sad, but we remember all the good times, especially during the holidays. She just loved Christmas, and she had the gift of giving to all. I will honor and pay tribute to how she helped so many people every Thanksgiving and Christmas. Also, I will never forget her birthday by any means, and she was just so excited to be 80 years young and have a small family celebration!

Liz was so happy she made it to her 80th birthday party on June 3, 2020. Here she was, blowing out the candles on her birthday cake. It is hard to imagine that just 26 days later, she passed away! It was a matter of **TIME** the Lord took her home!

I yelled to my sister, "Liz, please know that you will be with us, and we will not and cannot forget you. This is the final farewell chapter of the book you so badly wanted to create, and now your dream has come to fruition. Many others can read and learn about you and our family. Upon reading this story of you and our family, many others can know that they, too, can **OVERCOME THEIR TRIALS AND TRIBULATIONS THROUGH CHRIST JESUS.** This book is our family's historical contribution. It is our legend to everyone that before leaving this earth, we will be with Liz again in a place where no virus and no clocks are ticking!

This book is our family's historical contribution. It is our legacy to everyone before leaving this earth and being with Liz again in a place where no viruses and no clocks are ticking!

I told Liz in the heavens, "You will be with us every holiday as you were with us since you left us to go into the Heavens. I miss the phone calls you usually give me every holiday, but we will not forget you. I was sitting next to the window to see you within the light beams when I needed strength to write. As our Lord said before he died on the cross, **"It is finished,"** I say the same message. It is all because you desire millions of others to read our and our family's stories!" Now, your book is finished and will continue to reach others worldwide!

Congratulations! Thank you, readers, for being with me. Writing this book involved many steps. I know many areas might be hard to understand, but I wrote it in the order Liz told me her story. So, please remember that fact, and that is how the Lord led me to write this story!

Thank you for following me along the paths I traveled since my sister passed away, going to Florida and back home again. It was difficult, and I had many problems, but God helped me get through the muddy swamps.

This book was written for all of you to know Liz better or to introduce you to Liz and our family history.

Oh, thank you for reading along and following the pathways of our lives. Each page has a special bond and love about my sister and our family.

At times, Liz's life was so discombobulated that describing her existence on this earth was challenging. We can probably identify with her somehow or in some fashion, but there has never been a more sincere and generous person than my sister. After talking with several people after her death, they said Liz would give away her last dollar, or her previous **"PENNY,"** to help someone in their own game of life. She always reached out to others, but sometimes people took advantage of her for a "handout."

She had many *Trials and Tribulations* in her early and later life; lots of pain, heartache, and struggles, but she had some joyous times, especially with her family and so many others. She wanted so badly for her life to be known to others so that she could help them in some unexpected way. She thought if folks learned of her life and her struggles, it would help them not go through their lives like being on a roller coaster, experiencing grief and hardships from one day to the next. She wanted them to know the theme of this book:

*"When life gives you trouble, there is always a way to* **OVERCOME** *it, and there is always a* **WAY OUT!"**

Hopefully, the suspense, excitement, joy, sadness, comical wit, and the amazing character of my sister Liz can be recognized, for she was so unique and special in this world. Liz's life was indeed amazing! We grant her a spot to rest in peace, up high on the clouds in the heavenly skies, sitting on *"Top of the World."* She may appear in the shadows or the bright beams of light at a window as she did to help me push and keep writing her book. But fill your mind of her, and look up, and when it is least expected, she may be out there looking down as peering in your dark window.

She wants us to remember her and how our family overcame all the struggles that we encountered in life and that we could endure and **OVERCOME. WE SURVIVED!** I am alive to tell her story! We lived too, and bits and pieces of our lives and who we are today can be read. Was life so hectic for us living on Sophia's Ave., or was it just in some bad times, another generation ago? Our fears were entirely different; we worried about how we would get our next bite of bologna and cheese, compared to now living in fear that we might catch COVID-19.

This pandemic has taken some of our loved ones, and because of it, Liz was not adequately attended to and cared for in the hospital. She was prepared and waiting for the procedure to be done before going back home. She had it done and went home all right, but not to her earthly home on **Top of the World Senior Community;** She went to her heavenly home with our Lord Jesus welcoming her. She deserves a chance to relax and rest in the arms of our Lord and Savior and to enjoy her new life in her new home with our family and loved ones who have gone to heaven before her. She needs a loud "**Deaf Handclap**" (hands shaking in the air as done in the Deaf Community) as she finally makes that **FINAL ESCAPE**. I applaud her; she is at peace, and her **MISSION IN LIFE IS ACCOMPLISHED!**

Liz knew how to do it! She pitched pennies, which she worked so hard for, just as a means of **ESCAPE** from the hard life she was going through. We, too, have to determine what our next move will be. We must pick up the poker chip and make a toss: life or death, win or lose? We could do it just as **Tin Can** did it! A happy-go-lucky girl with lots of spunk, vim, and vigor as she immersed herself in the game of life! Her game was a constant challenge with lots of dreams and visions. Everyone wants their life to mean something and contribute to themselves and others (living or dead). For Liz, her life unquestionably was just that! She desired that it was worth it if her story helped even one person! I hold positively in her belief that her story within this book can change a life and help many others. She said often that her story would go around the world, and I agree with her, for it certainly can!

No one is so impressive as Elizabeth Catherine Stupansky Seither, who has earned her seat in the heavenly kingdom. Our Lord would tell her, **"Tin Can Lizzie,** you did an amazing job and did it well!" **Your successful mission has been accomplished! You won the great race in the game of life!"**

Liz and I hope you loved the amazing story of **Tin Can Lizzie** and snippets of our family's life! To close this last chapter, I step outside into the light and the "Blue Skies Above." I can only see that my sister's life, **Tin Can Lizzie**, will resonate within your mind, spirit, and soul, as will our family members' lives. All of our lives are a **Living Legend and a Miracle as we trust our Lord!**

Thank you for allowing me to share snippets of my sister's marvelous life story and our family! Our families' enduring legend will remain forever! I walked outside, engulfed in sadness and tears, and looked high above in the skies, and what did I see?

*BLUE SKIES ABOVE*
*NOTHING BUT BLUE SKIES ABOVE*
*DARK CLOUDS GONE AWAY*
*ONLY BLUE SKIES ARE HERE TO STAY*

The final word from my sister Liz and myself is that we hope and pray that "Blue Skies" can also be seen in your life! Whatever you are going through, you can **OVERCOME**; hold on to the hope and love of our Lord Jesus with a positive attitude. Plan on overcoming any obstacles in your life. Please don't allow the enemy of **TIME** to take your peace away from you.

We thank you again for following along in my sister Liz's life and our family!

Love to all!

Dr. Rita Stupavsky Colasent and her sister, LIZZIE!

Liz wants you to remember:

*"When life gives you trouble,*
*there is always a way to overcome,*
*and there is always a way out!"*

**With love and sincere Wishes to you all! Lizzie and I hope in reading this story, you will be able to overcome your personal and family Trials and Tribulations as well!**

## JUST MY BIG SISTER, LIZ, AND ME

## LIZ, YOU'LL BE WITH ME FOREVER!

**THANKS FOR THE MEMORIES, UNTIL WE MEET AGAIN!**

# ASHES TO ASHES
# DUST TO DUST

July 21, 2020

*"The dust returns to the ground it came from, and the spirit returns to God who gave it."*

Ecclesiastes 12:7, New International Version

## TODAY IS OUR FINAL GOODBYE TO LIZ ON EARTH

A new group text was issued by Kim on July 20, 2020, saying that tomorrow at 8 AM, her mom was going to be finally cremated. I was so happy my sister could fulfill her wishes, but it was hard to believe. Kim asked if I could say a final prayer during that group message.

The morning came, and I was up about 5:30 AM. The words kept flooding my mind about what to say, and I thought, "How am I going to remember all of this when 8 AM comes?" Then I fell asleep and dreamed of Liz saying encouraging words to Kim, Gina, and the family.

I could barely see Liz's face, but she was perched high up on a fluffy white cloud as I had seen her before, high up in the sky when I was on the plane. She wanted me to pray for everyone to be strong; she was at peace and happy. She seemed confident that I would be OK and that she would always be with the family. In my dream, she sat with princesses, queens, and kings. She wanted everyone to know that the sad girl living on Sophia Avenue playing with the pennies in the streets is not sad anymore. Now, she is playing her toss game using golden tokens on the heavenly streets of gold with many new and old players. She wanted me to pray; she needed to hear the prayers and join us in our spirits. She was young again and so beautiful.

But today was the day she was returning to ashes. Kim and Gina fought so hard for their mom's last wishes to come to pass, and today, they will.

These are our actual conversations, as I prayed in the spirit as the process of her remains was changed to the heavens' dust and back to the earth.

July 20, 2020

**Kim** wrote: Hi, my family. I just got off the phone with the funeral home, and mom will be cremated around 8 AM tomorrow. Maybe Aunt Rita can pray so we can all say it to ourselves in the morning. Regina, I'll call you at 8 AM.

**Victor joined in**. Sounds good. I hope the crematorium follows through.

**Kim responded**: Prayers for momma: I love you, and may you rest and watch over me every minute of every day.

**Gina wrote**: Same, mommy. We love you!

**Kim added**: I just thought whoever wanted to join in at 8 o'clock could say their prayer, so if you, Aunt Rita, want to put a prayer on the group text, that would be wonderful.

**Aunt Rita responded**: Kim, thanks for asking me; you know I will pray as I have been. I am just thankful that Mom will be cremated and released as she requested. **THE TIME** is approaching!

**Gina wrote**: Please all pray for mommy to be free of pain, and I know she will watch over us. God bless her.

The following day, at 8 AM, July 21, 2020.

The group text begins:

*I let everyone know that I am tuned in to this group text.*

**Aunt Rita wrote**: Good morning, everyone. Well, it has been a struggle, but today is the day our sister, mom, grandmother, and friend will be sitting up into the clouds as her bodily remains are taken to her heavenly home.

**Rita started her Intro to the prayer for Liz:**

Dear heavenly Father, we are also praying right now. I have been praying since early this morning, dear Lord Jesus: Please give us strength and peace as we gather together for the final sendoff of your precious daughter, Elizabeth Catherine Stupansky Seither.

If you are with another family member, please hold hands to support and strengthen each other as I pray.

**Rich wrote:** Yes, Joann and I said a lovely prayer earlier this morning, and we will join together as one body of our family.

**Kim added:** Death is but a moment, but Love is Forever! I will love you forever, my mother!

**Rita started the prayer:** Lord Jesus, we pull together from all parts of the country across the miles in the unity of our beloved mother, grandmother, sister, and dear friend as her final remains on this earth are returned to you.

Lord, you said Liz was born in the dust of the earth. She will be taken back to the dust of the earth again.

Lord, she wanted this cremation to happen, and now these last wishes are finally taking place. We ask a special blessing for the family who fought to have her remains turn to dust again. We thank you for this opportunity to be joining our spirits in unison as her final "**Escape**" from this earth.

May we all be in one spirit with her spirit, for she is finally at peace. When she was born into this world, she wanted to be returned to ashes again, and as dust and dust, she shall return to her heavenly home.

Liz told me that when she walks through those gates, she will be greeted by her parents and niece, Lisa, when the Lord takes her home. This is what she wanted to happen; she wanted to return to her original happy self, and now she is! We thank you for that peace. We know that your servant Liz's life was a struggle, but she did make it through with your help and determination!

Heavenly Father, by your power, you brought Liz into this world and guided her life, and by joining together, we happily return her with peace and love to the dust again, Lord. We thank you for her life. Liz made it to be 80 years old—**Hallelujah**, now you wanted her home. She often told me that she looked forward to the day she could make that **Great Escape** again and make it to this birthday. **HALLELUJAH!** Thank you, Lord!

Her presence was felt during the cremation process through our thoughts and prayers.

**Rich commented**: Lovely prayer, Rita; thank you.

**Rita** continues praying:

Lord, you said in Genesis 3:19 in the Bible: "For dust you are, and to dust, you shall return." Now is the **TIME** for our beloved Liz to return to that state again. This is what she wanted. Now, through her family's support, she is being sent off as we continue to join our hearts and spirits together in prayer.

Now is the **TIME**! We give her a loud and happy sendoff—**HALLELUJAH!**, Hallelujah—for she wanted this! We are so happy she's at peace.

**Gina wrote**: Well said, Aunt Rita! Thank you so much!

**Kim replied**: Thanks, Aunt Rita.

*Rita continues: to pray in the spirit.*

Please know the following text was going on during her cremation: her returning to dust as our Lord said she would in the scriptures. I could feel her presence during the cremation, and we were deep in thought and prayer. I thought this process was worth savoring and being the concluding piece in her book *"The Trials and Tribulations of Tin Can Lizzie."*

Lord, as we are still holding on together in our spirits across the miles, give us all the peace that passes all understanding about our dear Liz. We believe she is looking down on us with her happy smile. Today, she is making her last sale. Today, she wants to sell us a good scripture verse from **John 14:3**, New International Version: "And if I go and prepare a place for you, I will come back and take you to be with me that you also may be where I am."

Liz wants us to know and never forget that our Lord said **HE** prepared a place for us. Her remains and spirit will abide in that sacred spot in the heavens forever since **HE** called her home. She would want us to be assured that when Jesus comes for us, she will be right there with **HIM**.

I am sure she wants us to trust in the Lord and his word. She will always be helping us along in life and will be united with our spirit forever until we meet again.

Donna wrote: (Liz and Dorothy's longtime friend)

To my friend Liz, who will not be forgotten, we traveled many paths together; some were good, and some were not. But we did it together, and one day, we'll be together again. I hope you find peace in your heart and enjoy heaven! I love you, and I'll keep you in my heart! Donna.

I can hear the gates of heaven opening up and Liz saying, *"I am here!"* Yes, she is in the "**Arms of the Lord!**"

**Kim added**: Open your wings, Mama, and fly, my angel.

**Rita wrote:** In closing this prayer, please let everyone know there's never a final real closing. Liz will always remain in our hearts forever!

This day is the end of her physical remains, but her life story and infamous legend get to be continued with every family member forever and ever; that's what she would want. She started us out by remembering her younger happy days back in the days of Sophia Ave as she pitched pennies. Now, she is pitching golden tokens up in the heavens.

**Gina added**: Aunt Rita, today she wants us to go on living and be confident in everything we do. She wants us to fly proudly with her and finish telling her story!

We will never forget her and think of all the good times we had together, but now it is **TIME** for her to return to dust, as our Lord said she would.

**Rita wrote**: Thank you, Gina, for saying. It was so nice of you. I need all the family's support and encouragement to finish her last wishes. I promise to finish telling her story!

To close this prayer on my part, I would like to share **1 Samuel 2:8**, New International Version:

"**HE** raises the poor from the dust and lifts the needy from the ash heap: **HE** seats them with princes and has them inherit a throne of honor. The earth's foundations are the Lord's; he has set the world."

Applying the scriptures about what our Lord has said, **HE** has raised Liz out of the dust. **HE** seated her with princes, princesses, queens, and kings. Now, she has inherited the seat of honor and the crown of **GLORY** on her head. As the scriptures state, she returned to the dust. Her job on earth is finished, and she has done her job well!

We pray all these prayers in Jesus' name as we continue this **TIME** of when she is **ASHES AND DUST.**

We then got an Amen from Donna, Rich, and Kim, who also sent us a picture of butterflies flying in the wind, and Donna sent us a huge heart of love.

Amen!

Amen!

Amen!

**Rita concluded**: Here is my final word: I love you, **Tin Can Lizzie!**

Thank you for letting us know that side of you, the **REAL YOU!!**

You said you had so much to say to me, and I am sorry we couldn't finish your book together. We are all here for you. You should have been here to finish writing **OUR BOOK**, but I will get it done, and the family will help!

We are saying we are here for you. "**HERE WE ARE!**"

Yes, you will rest, but I know you will have fun too, playing and enjoying all those new people you never met before.

Liz, please know that the game of life, of you playing in the streets of gold, is more significant than ever before!!

It is a **WIN-WIN**, and we are all by your side, flying with you!!

**Dorothy wrote:** Thank you, my sister, Rita, for all your comforting words about our sister Liz. This is a beautiful tribute to her!

I will miss Liz, as she was a big part of my life, good or bad. I will always love you, Liz.

Please give Mommy, Daddy, and my Lisa the biggest hugs ever and tell them how much I miss them!

**Amber joined in the group text:** (Liz's granddaughter from her second marriage)

Hello, everyone; as we conclude this final voyage for Grandma, I figured today would be a fitting day to share the new video tribute to her.

Amber put together a gorgeous collection of pictures showing Liz with family and friends. Beautiful, dreamy music is being heard in the background, which Liz wanted to play at her funeral. She loved that soft, dreamy music, for Liz was a dreamer throughout her life!

**Rita** wrote: Thank You, Amber. We will treasure this precious video for the rest of our lives and pass it on to many friends and family members. We will close this memorable day by viewing Amber's video of Liz's life. It was a wonderful tribute to her!

**Rita concluded:**

Liz's last wish was that her life would be told in a story; this is the best I could do. As I said, I could only write about what she told me, and

I filled in some pieces to make it more transparent and added more information about the family members.

So, my sister, you have your life story of **"The Trials and Tribulations of Tin Can Lizzie."** I revealed all about your **SECRET** life and your **ESCAPE** as **TIN CAN**. It was one big story you were eager to tell us all, and that is how you started your book with the title and the fantastic story of you running out of the house on Sophia Avenue. You said there were so many more **SECRETS** you wanted us to know, but the life of **Tin Can** was your biggest one. I know you had many more **SECRETS** to tell me to record in **OUR BOOK**, and I am so sorry that **TIME** ran away from you and you didn't get the chance to share so many stories. I am so sorry, my sister, Lizzie, that **TIME** gave you no justice!

You also made your final bow and got your favorite music, and Amber did an excellent job! So, I think this is where the story has to stop. I can only write what you said; folks may not agree, but that is how you told me. I thank you for trusting me with your **SECRETS** and your story. After this glorious day of you returning to the state of ashes, this is what our family members said, and I feel this is the end of the book *"The Trials and Tribulations of Tin Can Lizzie."*

**The group text concluded, and Rita wrote the following personal message to Liz:**

"Thank you, my "newfound" sister, **TIN CAN**! I am grateful that you trusted me to tell these powerful story snippets of your life and the lives of our family members. I will share it with many people, and as you said, it was your wish and dream to write a book and to be published, and we did it! It is what It is, and you started this process. On my part, it was a long, challenging journey with many complications in writing this book. But the family did help by giving me information and pictures. Liz, thanks for these last days of memories you gave me until we meet again. You always said, "**Rita, you can go on and on!** "But this **TIME**, you wanted me to go on and on and keep writing and writing!" However, I can't say that came from your lips anymore, for you are no longer here with us all, and we miss you so much!"

"Liz, I thank you for your love and trust. You sure surprised me and surprised yourself, too, by revealing as much as you did. Now, you have made a grand entrance into the Kingdom of Heaven! As our mother, Mercedes, would say and sign, **"Me surprise you, me surprise everybody."** Liz, you surely did! It was the shock of my life to learn all about you and you wanting me to write this book! I know you will lead me regarding what to do with this book. I know you will be with all of us forever! Thanks for the memories of all the fun times we had together, especially on the cruises! Now you are sailing again, and you have a crowd with you. I will never forget our cruises together! Until we see each other again! It is a luxury cruise you are on now, and I fondly say in tears, **"Bon Voyage**!" I am not yet physically with you this **TIME** on that cruise, but another one is coming up! Until we are together again, please be confident that we will be cruising out in the sunset with God's Son, Our Lord and Savior!"

"Liz, I will stress to all the readers as you wanted me to do: to never forget, when *The Trials and Tribulations* come, remember this book's theme."

**"When life gives you trouble, there is always a way to OVERCOME it, and there is always a way out!"**

We all thank you, our dear Mother and Sister, **Tin Can Lizzie!**

We must trust our God to find a solution with hope, faith, and confidence. Then, assuredly, we will make it through the darkest moments.

When the "**Cruise of Life**" is roaring, stop and think of Calm, Blue Seas and take TIME to look up and see the:

*Blue Skies above*
*Nothing but Blue Skies above*
*Dark clouds have gone away*
*Only Blue Skies are here to stay!*

After Liz's cremation, we all went separately and made it through what had to be done that day in each of our lives across the miles. We wondered how we would make it through life without our Mother, Sister, Grandmother, co-worker, and Friend—as our Elizabeth, Liz, Lizzie, and we cannot forget our "**Tin Can.**" Our only hope is to follow what she instructed us to do in the reality of this book's truths. It will not be easy to "move on"—especially for her daughters, Kim and Gina.

Reading this book might be hard for us, but as we read, we can know and love this sister of mine even more, no matter what we call her: Elizabeth, Liz, Lizzie, or the **TIN CAN**. For me, I know I kept the promise I made to her, as tough as it was. I can finally breathe fresh, warm sea air and imagine I am on a cruise sailing under the Blue Skies with her! My job is finished! I ran the final race and ultimately reached the golden final finish line! Thank you, Lord, and Sister Liz, for helping me reach our goal and this incredible miracle of finishing this book and publishing it for people worldwide to read, enjoy, and **OVERCOME THEIR TRIALS AND TRIBULATIONS!**

After that first 2020 holidays, Kim and Gina set up a tribute to their Mother, which included her ashes, a picture, a holy card, and Christmas decorations. We hold the memory of how much she loved Christmas. Kim and Gina make a toast to all the wonderful, precious moments they had together! It will be a new year, so we must all be strong, living without our Mother, Sister, Grandmother, and Friend. We will all miss her, but her life and legecy will live forever through this book!

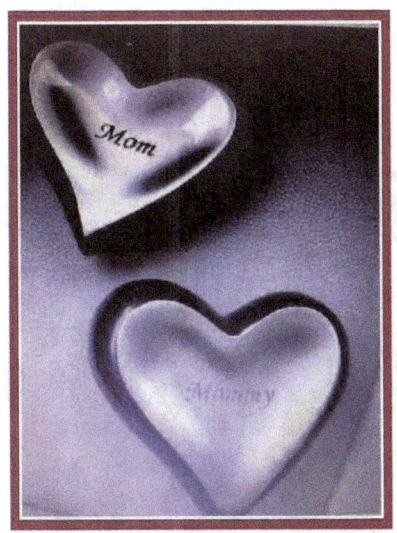

2020: After Liz's cremation, her ashes were given to Kim and Gina and they had little hearts made up so they can carry some ashes of their Mother wherever they go. Their Mom will always be with them and close to their hearts.

**New Year's Eve 2020.**

# PRECIOUS MEMOIRS FROM A DAUGHTER AS A TRIBUTE TO HER MOTHER!

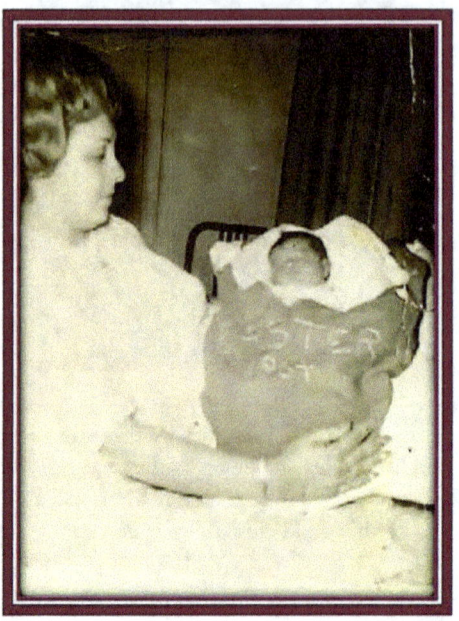

March 27, 1964: LIZ HOLDING HER NEWBORN BABY KIM, THE DAY SHE WAS BORN.

When I talked with my niece Kimmy, she said, "There were so many experiences and memories of my mom! Hey, I don't even know where to begin... But I do know my Mom was my ROCK!'

I said, "Kim, we should include some of your memories in her book."

"Yes, Aunt Rita, I can tell you some funny and serious stories, that is for sure. Mom was quite a character, without a doubt! Oh, she kept me busy, and she never stopped. Now, I miss that so much. I sometimes didn't have **TIME** for my children or me because I was always helping and doing for mom. I am lost without running for her now, for I was so used to it!"

I asked, "Hey, Kimmy, give me some examples because I will write them up and put them in her book, especially personal stories about her in her senior years. I know her, but not like you know her. You know her more than anyone. She told me a lot about her younger days, which was supposed to be a big secret when she named herself "**TIN CAN LIZZIE**" or the "**Tin Can Queen**." Mom would love you to add to the legend of her life and the family history. There are so many special moments to remember her by, and she loved you so much!"

"THERE SHE IS! CAN YOU BELIEVE SHE IS 80 YEARS YOUNG ON THIS DAY, JUNE 3, 2020? I THREW A LITTLE PARTY FOR HER, AND SHE SAID IT WAS THE HAPPIEST DAY OF HER LIFE!"

"Well, you know, Aunt Rita, Mom surely loved to go to dinner. She would dress all up so beautifully! She had everything matching—her clothes, jewelry, and shoes. She would ask me to fix her hair up pretty, and she looked so beautiful! She had to pick the restaurant for which she had always had a taste. She didn't ask me what I had a taste for. But I was always set on pleasing Mom, for she deserved happiness. And you know I loved to make her happy—that was a big part of my life— making my Mommy happy! Sometimes, it was just a drive-through fast-food place, but she said she was always starving. You know that from going on the cruises with her and visiting us in Florida. She would order a big meal and appetizer, and always say "My Treat" and pack the rest of the food in a carry-home container, which was OK because she had food to warm up when she was home."

"Mom wanted to treat me all the **TIME** when I should've been treating her, but I gave up a lot of my **TIME** and work so I could be with Mom, and she loved me for being with her."

I said, "Yes, Kim, but that was you, and you would always give her the small things that meant everything. Now that Mom is not with you every day and only in your heart, spirit, and mind, our Lord and Mom are saying, "Kim, my servant, job well done!"

"Hey, Aunt Rita, I am going back to Mom. She loved going out to dinner, the grocery store, and discount stores. She would pack that shopping cart so high, and I would look at her; she would get in line, and she wanted to buy it all!

I told her, "Oh, no, you get to pick out two or three things, and before long, she was calling me names. I had to take the full cart back to the customer service desk. Then, when we got into the car, we would laugh so hard about all the stuff she had wanted to buy and would never have been able to use up."

"MOM LOVED
TO SHOP!"

I replied, "Kim, when Mom was talking to me in the hospital, I told her about my air fryer, and she was so interested. She said she wanted one, but Kim wouldn't let her buy it. She wanted the big fancy one promoted by the famous chef on the TV commercial; he said, you can even cook a turkey. Your Mom said she was planning on a huge Thanksgiving Family Dinner this year, and she was going to get that air fryer!"

Liz said, "You'll see! Kim knows I don't have the money for that air fryer, but she has such a soft heart and will not disappoint me. She never does! I am so proud of her and love her so much! We have a relationship that is incredible, special, and very unique! She makes me feel "**ALIVE**," especially when I am not feeling well." I quickly added, "Kim, the family knows that Mom loved to go shopping—period! That surely got her in trouble with everyone, and I am not mentioning any names!"

Pam, my daughter, would come and visit her Auntie Lizzie to get ready for our cruise, and Liz would take her into a department store and pick out all new things for the family cruise. Pam would have to politely say," Auntie Liz, you save your money." But Liz would insist on buying her things to wear on the cruise. My Pam just adored her Auntie and loved to visit her. When Pam came to Florida to stay with my sister, she would say, "Auntie Lizzie and I have so much fun together! She is a character, alright!"

But Kim said, "You know, all the **TIME** she was a "big spender and a shopaholic," but I love her to pieces! I had to be very strict with her as if she were my daughter and I was her mother. When we went to get our nails done, oh boy, did she! Mom wanted a diamond sparkle on all of her toes and each of her fingers. Her nails would cost more than $125 by the **TIME** we walked out of there, but that was one of her many pleasures!

THAT IS MY MOM! OH, HOW SHE LOVED TO GO SHOPPING!

I asked Km, "So, what are some more stories I can write about in Mom's book? I used to call it "her book." Then, she knew how to "**Butter Me Up,**" and she would say, "Oh, no, Dr. Rita, it is "**Our Book**!" Then, she would say, "Just get it done and published so my family could read about me and a some of my **SECRETS** when I was young. They will be so surprised! I can't wait to show them what we are doing."

Kim commented, "Oh, Aunt Rita, I must remind you, as you already know, what a flirt she was with men!"

I said, "Kim, I remember you telling me that she would go to Doctor B's office and flirt with him, and she was old enough to be his grandma!

Kim said, "Yes, she was a flirt and so beautiful. She always wore perfect clothes, had perfect hair, perfect makeup, and everything would match. She was always dressed to Kill, and she had many men who fell madly in love with her! Her flirting got her in trouble and a few husbands, but she loved every minute!

"Oh, my gosh. " Mom was so friendly with everybody in her neighborhood of **TOP OF THE WORLD**, a 55-and-older complex. We had hoped to live there together when she got home from the hospital."

I responded, "Oh yes, Kim, Mom was so generous that she would give you the shirt off her back. She just packed so many clothes and other things for Pam and me. Now I have trouble wearing her things. It is so hard! I can see that piece of clothing on her, and Pam says the same thing.

Kim expressed, "Mom wanted to go on a cruise so badly, as you and Uncle Dennis had treated us to several cruises. I was only able to make one cruise. Boy, did Mom have a good **TIME**—and she spent lots of money on pictures!"

Hey, Kim, "I told Mom when we came to Florida in February 2021; if this coronavirus is over, we might go on another cruise with the entire family! I don't know where to get the money, but I will treat everyone to another cruise. I wrote about it in our book and that she and I spent lots of money in the picture studios on the ships. We are very similar in that respect. But it would be so wonderful to take another family cruise. I wanted that opportunity so badly. I can't believe it! Those were my hopes. A lot has changed since last February—the last **TIME** I was together with Mom and the family. I feel so lost, for she was with me on every Florida trip in my entire life. We hugged and kissed in February of 2020—who would ever think that was the last **TIME** we would see each other? So, I can imagine how you are feeling. You took her to the doctor's office, and then she had a mild stroke. Mom was admitted to the hospital and never came home to you. My heart bleeds for you so much, and she wants to give you the hearts of love she has for you."

JUST MOM AND ME WE WERE A GREAT PAIR, AND WE HAD SO MUCH FUN TOGETHER.
HEY, MY MOM WAS MY ROCK! NOW, SHE LIFT ME UP WITH THE WINGS OF AN ANGEL!

"Kim, as I am engulfed in tears now as I write up this interview for Mom's book, I can remember those cruises we took together, and Mom surely is sailing around as we speak. There is so much to say here about your mother! Words cannot express my heart of how much I feel for your loss, for I miss her so much, too. We didn't talk much in her last year. Whenever I called, she was in the middle of a TV show or something. She was often being Liz and crabby, and I would tell her to call me back, but she didn't. We made up for it while she was in the hospital. I spoke to her more than I ever had in my entire life. It was so nice to get to know this "**New Sister**" of mine. I didn't even know who she was during those conversations. She was so sweet one minute, and then she would get on me and say that I had better get this book published so her girls, family, and everyone could read it. They would know who she was and the sadness she had experienced in the "**Trials and Tribulations**" throughout her entire life!"

With that thought, I said, "Kim, your Mom just couldn't wait to surprise everyone, especially you, Kim, with this book. She wanted me to write about her and the history of the family. As I write, I feel her close to my heart, standing in bright lights outside my window. I had this feeling and experience when I wrote Chapter Eight about the day she passed away, and I am having it again. Thank you for sharing those precious, tender moments with your mother. I am sure there is so much more to tell. I felt her outside my window again, looking inside in massive bright beams of light as I wrote this story about you and her in a closely—knit bond of **Love**. I am sure she is so happy as you tell your stories to your Aunt Rita. She has **LOVE**, **LOVE**, and more **LOVE** all around her for you. I finished writing this out, and now I look up to the window, and she is gone! But she will be back again when we least expect her. She tends to do that from **TIME** to **TIME**.

## ANOTHER CONVERSATION WITH KIM

## AND HER SWEET ANGEL, MOM!

I started this conversation by saying, "Boy, Kim, your Aunt Rita is up to the wee hours of the morning writing what you are sharing about your Mom."

I said to Kim, "Believe it or not, your Mom and I are so different, but at the same **TIME**, we are the same. We love taking pictures wherever we go."

Kim told her Mom, "You always tell me how proud you are of me and what a proud daughter I am to you! So, no matter what happens with me and my marriage, I am a good Mom, and I thank you for being so good to me. I couldn't ask for anyone better. I love you to the moon, the stars, and back, my dearest Mom!"

Aunt Rita said, "Oh yes, Kim, Mom, and I always talked about Sophia as she is a pleasant reminder of her name to all of us as we grew up on Sophia Street when we were young. That makes her so special to the family. I told your Mom I think Sophia is a gifted volleyball player and will surely be in the Olympics someday! Mom always called Derek her favorite grandson, and Derek would say, "Yes, grandma, I am your **"Favorite,"** for I am your only grandson!" We would always laugh so much about that, and every **TIME** Mom would see Derek, she would say, "There he is—my favorite grandson!""

"Mom was so proud of Derek being a chef, using his culinary skills and what he accomplished with his company in such a short **TIME**. Derek traveled with his company as a trainer and was then asked to open his kitchen. He worked hard with little **TIME** off and said he didn't need college to get where he was in the restaurant business. He proved us correct! Then, I will always remember that horrible day I got the call from the police about Derek's boating accident. It left him as a person with quadriplegia, which was such a tragedy for all of us."

Kim said, "I then would get angry with her because I was so anxious to do something with my Mom, but then again, I'd have to let her sleep for a while. While Mom was sleeping, I would clean the kitchen, work on our laundry, and be very quiet on the computer to see where she was spending money that she shouldn't have been. I always caught her spending with that debit card; she couldn't help herself. But I was one step ahead of her at all times. She couldn't fool me! Mother, I love you, Mommy. I love you for who you are, who you were, and who you will always be—that person is my mother, Elizabeth C Seither, the greatest mother and friend I could ever ask for."

I replied to Kim, "That is so beautiful! Especially after all you and Mommy have been through—you still have a special love in your heart for her, and you will always be so proud of her. Not many people can accept some of the problems that you both went through. You are amazing, and I am so personally proud of you! Besides missing Mom so much and with all of the problems, including your health issues. You still have Mom shining in the windows of your life and your heart!"

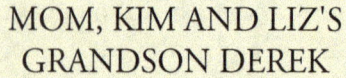

MOM, KIM AND LIZ'S GRANDSON DEREK

MY MOM AND HER GRANDDAUGHTERS, ALEXIS AND SOPHIA ON MOMMY'S 80TH BIRTHDAY PARTY I GAVE FOR HER. SHE WAS SO HAPPY ON THAT DAY. IT WAS A DAY TO REMEMBER!

"Good night, Mama, and good night, Aunt Rita—sweet dreams to you!"

Kim wrote on her Facebook page the following day, "It's hard to believe this beautiful woman has been gone for almost two months. It wasn't fair for Mommy, as she went into the hospital for treatment of a small (TIA) Transient Ischemic Attack stroke that she previously had in the doctor's office. The doctor said that he wanted to monitor Mom for a day or two, which ended up being five days, and then he ordered that darn colonoscopy. Dammit, Mom, I miss you so much, and you will always be the most beautiful, precious woman ever! I love you today, tomorrow, and forever! I love you, Mom. I love you, but *please stay out of trouble in heaven!*"

I replied to Kim on Facebook, "Hi Kim. It is early in the morning. I can't sleep, so I got out of bed to go to work on Mom's book. I opened my computer, and what did I see? This gorgeous picture of your Mom! Thank you so much! I take it as a sign from Mom when I see this picture of her that you just posted wearing the coat that I now have, and I am so proud to wear it." I believe she is telling me: Get busy on **"OUR" BOOK**, sister Rita!"

She looks so sharp, and I miss her so much. I say the same thing you did: "Stay out of Trouble in Heaven!" Mom is still meeting folks who went to heaven before her. Love, Auntie Rita"

## ABOUT THE DAY OF MOM'S MEMORIAL

Kim and I were conversing on another day, and I said, "Kim, your Mom's memorial was so beautiful! You and Gina did a beautiful job. I am positive Mom was looking down and was so proud of both of you. Everything was so nice, and she looked so gorgeous! She told me she wanted to wear this white outfit for her memorial that she wore at her 80th birthday gathering."

## THOUGHTS FROM KIMMY

Kim asked, "How can I go into our last days together? It is too difficult to even put into words. I have to ask myself what happened to her, that we are together for the last **TIME**? How can I handle this? It is beyond me, and it is more than I can endure. How can I continue my life without my dearest Mom?"

Aunt Rita replied, "Kim, Mom knows how hard this is for you—she does. Coming here today is unbelievable for all of us, and especially you. You were the life-giving thread that held you and Mom together. You were connected, as they say, "at the hip," and yet you had the same "heartbeat." She always asked you to do things for her, and you did! You loved being able to help her, and my heart aches for you. You no longer have that connection today, but please know she is always there with you. Oh, I bet you can tell me some unbelievable stories that you know about her, and not just the last few years when you were her caregiver, friend, companion, and run person. You were with her almost daily and knew her every move."

Kim replied, "Aunt Rita, Mom always called me "Her Kimmy," today is like no other day. I already miss her so very much! I miss her checking up on me ten times a day. As I look at it today and every day, it makes me smile. I am delighted right now, knowing and thinking of all the stuff I did for her—but she did so much for me and made me so happy—so I say to Mom, "You are my rock and my hero!"

Kim continued, "Mom never went down without a fight, and she made sure she had her last real estate deals down pat. In her last days, she told her client, "I am not going down till I sell your condo." On the day of her memorial, she did just that! This was the last sale of her career, and it was a beautiful ending. I can never forget that promise she made to that client."

So that is all I can say, Aunt Rita, "Mom made her last sale, and I am so proud of her, you can't imagine!"

I told Kim, "We are all so proud of your mother. She was the oldest in our family. She wanted to do so much for us and never could, but today, we give her Tribute for she did so much for us—more than she could ever imagine!"

"Yes, my sister, Liz, was a character, but she had "**Class and Charisma!**" She was a "**Goodhearted Person**" willing to do anything for you. Your Mom got along with everyone and made our lives much richer! Therefore, I am writing some of her final words for others to read and enjoy. Mom's last request was for me to write this book and our family's history. My mind and heart are filled with joy, which overcomes the sadness we are all going through."

We can never forget the story of **"THE TRIALS AND TRIBULATIONS OF TIN CAN LIZZIE"** as she grew older. Your Mom wanted everyone to know about this part of her and our family's history: how we grew up in poverty and struggled to survive! She wanted all her family to read this story, remember her legacy, and know how much she loved them.

In another conversation with Kim, I said, "Mom was the oldest in our family, and she felt it was her responsibility to get her and the family's story out for all to read and to understand. This book was another one of her big surprises. Yes, it surely was a surprise and shock, especially to me, as we move on in life without her—we will talk and share more stories of your mother and what she meant to all of us. What you did for your mother will always be held high in the heavens, and Mom will always watch over her family!"

She will be forever in our hearts! We can always read over, again and again, some of her famous moments and enjoy her experiences as her stories get passed down to her children and grandchildren.

I told my niece, "Kim, always remember, this story is your Mom's legacy. Her legacy was not for her. It is for those who come after her for many generations. Thank you for sharing these precious moments for all to read."

Love you, Auntie Dr. Rita

Here she is, your Mom, standing outside
my window just as she did once before.
But this time, she gives you hearts of love
and more love just for you!
Love You, Auntie Dr. Rita

# SPECIAL ACKNOWLEDGEMENTS

## A BIG THANKS TO ALL!

**I cannot thank my outstanding family and friends enough for their support and contributions to Liz and me throughout the process of bringing Liz's dream to fruition!**

**To My Siblings, Dorothy, Victor, and Richard Stupansky**: We must never forget that we had a **"ROUGH UPBRINGING,"** but **"WE SURVIVED!"** We miss you, our oldest sister Lizzie! Our memories of how our lives began on Sophia Ave will stay with us forever! We had the two most incredible parents in the world, Frederick and Mercedes Stupansky, who were both **DEAF** and loved us dearly! They always tried to do their best for us, and because of our wonderful parents and our early lives, we are the people we are today!

**We are strong, and we take pride in our Family Heritage!**

**To My Husband, Dennis:** I thank you for your patience and understanding while I was writing this book. It was a long journey, but it was necessary to keep my sister's promises, wishes, and my family legacy **"Alive!"** Then, when we all reunite in the heavenly kingdom with my sister, **"Tin Can Lizzie,"** we can hug each other and thank you for your incredible support. Please always know I love you dearly, and I am grateful for you being such a wonderful Husband, Father, and Grandfather.

**To My Daughter, Pamela Colasent Webb, and her Husband, Bradford Webb:** Pam, you were a tremendous help and gave me many ideas and suggestions, which I truly appreciated while writing this book. Please always remember that your Auntie Lizzie loved you very much. You were always very special to her, just as you are to me. I am very proud of my talented daughter for how you reach out to folks with Special Needs. You are truly gifted! Brad, thank you for being so excited about this book, and I know you couldn't wait to read it!

**To My Son, Christopher, and My Grandsons, Isak and Anthony:** Thank you for believing in me and encouraging me throughout the long process of writing this book. Always be proud of your Mother and Grandmother, Dr. Rita Stupavsky, who had parents who were **DEAF** and faced extreme poverty. Please remember how her family **OVERCAME** their **Trials and Tribulations** through our Lord Jesus in their lives, and you can too! When I am gone, know that I will always be watching over you and lifting you to the Lord. Please take care of each other. I love you!

**To Liz's Daughters, Kimberly Seither Kotsovolos and Regina Seither Subko:** My nieces love and deeply miss their mother! Your mother's prayer and wishes are that you will lead your children and grandchildren in continuing this tribute to their grandmother Liz, and to keep her memory and the family's stories alive for many years to come!

**To My Sister-in-Law, Jean Stupansky:** Jean, you have been an incredible support and have always been there for me. You believed in me and encouraged me to finish writing this book. I sincerely thank you for believing in me! When I was feeling down and wanted to "Give up," you were there to encourage me to keep writing and honor the promise I made to Lizzie.

**To Jim Sigmund of Houston, Texas:** Jim encouraged me not to give up on this book. He was always there to help me with my formatting questions. He is the grandson of the great Klucho Family, who owned the store next to the Sophia House. Jim assisted me with my family history research. A big thanks to you for all your help!

**To Amber Padgett, Liz's granddaughter in Clearwater, Florida:** She contributed and shared her many talents and skills to help my sister, Liz, in her real estate career. A big thank you from Grandma Lizzie and me!

LIZ AND I SEND OUR LOVE AND GRATITUDE TO ALL!

I am sure you enjoyed reading the story of "Tin Can Lizzie" and our family for many years to come.

Thanks to those who supported and cheered me on as I brought Liz's dream to fruition!

Hopefully, you'll enjoy reading Liz's Legacy and our family history for many years to come! Many people supported and cheered me on as I brought Liz's dream to life! God bless you, and thank you for your kindness and support!

Dr. Rita Stupavsky Colasent and her Big Sister, Lizzie!!

WE FINALLY HAVE A FAMILY CHRISTMAS PORTRAIT TOGETHER!
FROM THE LEFT: OUT MOTHER, MERCEDES, CHILDREN: LIZ,
DOROTHY, VICTOR, RITA, RICHARD AND OUR FATHER, FRED!

# THE INCREDIBLE JOURNEY

I kept my promise to my sister on this **INCREDIBLE JOURNEY** as I wrote about her conversations with me, her death, my trip to Florida, and back home again. This story was unexpectedly awarded the Golden Plume Award of Literary Excellence for contributing to humanity. This prestigious title is awarded to authors with exceptional and extraordinary writing styles to draw the readers' attention!

My constant plugging away and not giving up proved significant in bringing this book to fruition. Lizzie and our Lord were always behind me, helping me never to give up on getting this job done and reaching the finish line! I had a hard **TIME** on this journey, experiencing my sister Liz's passing, the trip to Florida, and returning to Ohio. Liz was with me on this **INCREDIBLE JOURNEY** every step of the way!

Writing Liz's book was a "**Life Line**" experience that constantly kept the threads of our connections with each other "**Alive**!" This book was an immense, long "**Journey**," taking many wrong turns and making many changes until I got the words correct. Liz wanted us to continue living with her through this book and our memories of her. But, most importantly, Liz wanted us to know that she would always be in our minds and spirits, loving us all until the end of **TIME**!

It was an **INCREDIBLE JOURNEY**! Writing her book was an experience I will never forget! I could feel Liz's spirit constantly prodding me to keep on writing! She never wanted me to "**Give Up**" or to be "**Discouraged**." Instead, she inspired me to describe our conversations and stories of her life and our family members. She was proud of her parents, siblings, children, and grandchildren.

Writing this book didn't end with me writing and submitting it to the publishers. Every **TIME** I read the proofs after receiving them back from the publishers, I had to **RELIVE** the whole experience all over again of losing my sister and her death. As I read her words, I can remember every one of them she said to me. It was so painful rereading the words that Lizzie inspired me to write.

It was stressful and painful to reread the entire book several times. I wanted to make this book perfect, as Liz would wish to depict herself and the family's stories. I had to relive my sister Liz's words, love, kindness, encouragement, death, and **FINAL ESCAPE** to Freedom!

I was my editor, and it was not easy to make changes and be an editor. So now, we are ready to re-submit the final changes and updates to get my sisters' and family's stories to readers worldwide! Indeed! Writing this book and the entire process has been a long, **INCREDIBLE JOURNEY** and a **TREASURE** for me. Liz and I are so happy the book will be available for all to read and **ENJOY!**

I reached my goal and completed the entire rough draft of the book by Christmas of 2021, and I was so happy! I wrote everything my sister Liz told me while in the hospital. She wanted me to feel proud and smile, and I shared her stories with others. On Christmas morning that year, I had a new assurance, confidence, and faith that the book would reach many readers just as Lizzie wanted. I had such peace within my entire being, mind, and soul that I had completed this considerable task just as I promised my sister I would reach the **Finish Line**. I felt peace and happiness because I had fulfilled my promise to my sister Liz and the goals I had set for myself to write our book!'

Thanksgiving 2021— So thankful that Liz's book is finished and off to the publisher!

On Christmas Eve, 2021, A new smile and sense of relief that I completed my journey to write my sister's final wishes!

Christmas Day, 2021— Merry Christmas to all our readers, from Lizzie and me! May God bless you as you enjoy our stories of **Tin Can Lizzie** and the Stupavsky Family.

As I read the final proofing from the publishing company, I started having Lizzie and her words in my thoughts and dreams again. I would tell her, "Liz, I did everything you wanted me to write and change! Now, what do you want me to do?" I had several nights when Liz was influential in the "Echoes of My Mind and Dreams." Finally, I yelled to my sister again, "Liz, I finished writing **OUR** book; what are you prodding me to do now? **Tin Can Lizzie**, what are you up to now?"

Then, I continued having dreams and thoughts about writing what you are reading. The **TIN CAN LADY** influenced a final short message: she wanted me to tell the readers to write a conclusion about how happy I am now because I have completed the task set before me to write her book!"

I kept getting the message that she wanted me to remind readers one last **TIME NEVER TO GIVE UP** when they are going through their **TRIALS AND TRIBULATIONS**, just as she and our family went through.

Then, a new prodding started in my mind. Liz wanted me to tell the readers that if they have a story, **GET IT WRITTEN**! Liz said, "Dr. Rita, I am so proud of you; the family will be proud of you! You never gave up, and you prayed and put up with me, prodding you to get the best quality and the story written! You did your best, and I am so grateful!"

So here I am, writing one last piece when I thought I had completed all book sections.

So, this is the final section, and it is about me and the process of writing this book! Our Sweet "**Tin Can Lizzie**" went into the heavenly Blue Skies in her new home to be with her loved ones again. So, Lizzie and our Lord helped me get to the "**FINISH LINE**," writing this book for her and our family. I give God all the glory for helping me through this long process and the constant pain of reliving my sister's words and her death. Now, it is **TIME** to celebrate Lizzie's life and her tribute, which will live forever!

In these last words, I felt **Tin Can** telling the readers: "Please, never give up on your dreams and visions to make it through whatever goals you desire to fulfill! There is **TIME**, and let **TIME** push yo u to the finish line and the last stretch! You can't turn back; please, don't let your **TIME** run away as a fast-moving freight train! You will miss the next train station!"

I hope you enjoyed reading the snippets about the life of **TIN CAN LIZZIE** and our Stupavsky/Stupansky family members! God bless you to accomplish your writing goals and fulfill your dreams to **OVERCOME**!

**TIN CAN** is telling all readers that you can be successful as a writer and publish your stories as you look to our Lord for strength, courage, and help to get you through! I know this book isn't written perfectly, but it was how Liz wanted me to write it, and I am so grateful! So often, I had to toss a coin about what I would write next when I had a few choices.

I am making it very clear that we need to relive the precious memories of our loved ones! The more we speak of their lives and words, the more they will live through us.

In the book, I wrote about my experiences, such as how I kept Lizzie alive during our holidays. Liz's daughters, Kim and Gina, also set up a tribute to their mom for the holidays. So, we all hold the memory of how much Liz loved Christmas.

The only thing I can say as I wrote the final words of this book is that I miss her as much as our family does! I know now that I did my job and kept her promise!

Today, Liz is still perched high on a cloud, sitting at the top of the world, saying, "Dr. Rita, I am proud of you!" Now, the book is out in the world, in the hands of millions of readers, so they can overcome their hardships and complete the tasks set before them. So Dr. Rita, thank you very much. **Job well done! Your mission is accomplished!**

# CRUISING IN CALM WATERS UNDER THE BLUE SKIES AGAIN

## TIME MOVES ON...

### OCTOBER, 2023

Where does **TIME** GO? I can't believe it has been so long since Lizzie left us on Earth and went to her heavenly home with our Lord Jesus. With Lizzie gone, life has been very different. My husband Dennis and I are no longer making our annual February trip to Florida to visit Liz and the family. The last trip I took to Florida was for Liz's Memorial on July 2, 2020. Will I ever go back to Florida? There are too many memories, and my trip would be dull, sad, and heartbreaking. After all, our trips to Florida with my sisters, Lizzie and Dorothy, were so exciting for many years. We never had a dull moment, and our schedules were so busy each day when we closed many stores and walked through flea markets. We went out for dinner to our favorite restaurants, and I knew all the spots we liked, for I had gone there enough times. It was also sad to see how, over **TIME**, our favorite places disappeared, many of which were due to the COVID-19 pandemic.

I have often considered going to Florida, but there were too many roadblocks. However, deep within my heart and spirit, I wanted to see if Liz and I could connect again and if I could have any inspirational moments with her. I had those precious moments before and was always sure we would have them again, but where and when I had no idea; it was always in my mind. I was positive I would have them. I will never forget working on the book, with the shadow of her spirit appearing to me by my window. Then, I had multiple dreams and visions of her trying to communicate with me.

Instead of our February trips to Florida, we stayed in our vacation place in North Carolina. My brother Victor and his wife Jean would fly from California to Florida, pick up my sister Dorothy, and visit us in North Carolina. We did a lot of thrift store shopping, took them to the surrounding sites, and had much fun together.

This last year has been tough on us. I worked on the book and then did marketing to get the messages to the readers. It has been a constant struggle and very frustrating! Plus, I had to manage my home and family while working as a part-time Sub Principal. **TIME** did me no justice to make things flow through the running waters, splashing my way for recovery.

Then, Tragedy struck again and my husband Dennis had a stroke, and everything changed for us. The stroke left him paralyzed; on one side, he was in the hospital for seven days, in rehab for seven weeks, and then as an outpatient for therapy for months. It was a struggle for Dennis, and the doctors could not understand how he had a stroke because he was a natural athlete in sports, an avid golfer, and he had no high blood pressure or high cholesterol, and he was on no medications. He was the picture of health.

Dennis' stroke hit us hard, and if there was a **TIME** I had to depend on God's and Liz's promises to get this book out, it was now. I know the book could help many people **OVERCOME** their **Trials and Tribulations.** My children Pamela and Chris and my two Grandsons Isak and Anthony were a tremendous help to me to care for Dennis. It was during this **TIME.** I had little **TIME** to continue my challenge to promote Liz's book. But by **God's Amazing Grace,** Dennis slowly pulled through his stroke and started progressing through much rehabilitation.

It seemed everything hit us at once, and I had to leave the book and give everything to the Lord and Lizzie in the Blue Skies above for help getting Lizzie's book out into the hands of readers. I was too busy caring for Dennis, maintaining the house, and working part-time. It was a lot for me, but as Lizzie told me, the opportunity to get the book out to the world will come, and I will not miss it.

Lizzie and my family had so many roadblocks and tough times growing up living in poverty and having wonderful parents who were Deaf. The odds were against us, but we all survived as **TIME** turned its course of direction!

My husband Dennis was getting along much better and regaining some of his strength. A year before Dennis's stroke, I booked a cruise for him, my son Chris, his finance, Missy, and my two grandsons, Isak and Anthony, along with myself. I would have lost a lot of money if I had canceled the cruise. The book was in the hands of the Lord; therefore, I had to decide, "Should we go on the cruise with the family or cancel?"

There is a piece of me that just had to go on this cruise. If I didn't try, I would never forgive myself!

In the days that passed, that was all I thought about: Should I go and make the kids happy, too, or forget it and take a money loss? I could not focus and was constantly troubled about what we would do. I yelled up toward the "Blue Skies," asking Lizzie to help me make a choice and to help me out here.

I had to see if I could still feel, see, and relive at least some of the precious, memorable experiences Lizzie and I had together. My entire being has longed for this possibility since she left us without notice or warning. We lived for those cruises and had some treasured memories to hold on to, but she was gone, and I was holding all the weight of getting book out on my shoulders. I needed a sense of calmness and assurance of my decision if I should go forth with the cruise.

Right after Liz passed away, in Chapter Eight, I wrote:

Today is the day my sister, **"TIN CAN LIZZIE,"** Lizzie made her **"FINAL ESCAPE."** I want my sister back—I do! I thought of all that would be missing in our lives, together with the excitement of this book, while she shared her life of **TIN CAN** with the family.

I told my niece Kim, Liz's daughter, in the "Memoirs" section near the book's end, I wrote.

Hey, Kim, "I told Mom when we came to Florida in February 2021; if this Coronavirus is over, we might go on another cruise with the entire family! I don't know where to get the money, but I will treat everyone to another cruise. I wrote about it in our book and that she and I spent lots of money in the picture studios on the ships. We are very similar in that respect. But it would be so wonderful to take another family cruise. I wanted that opportunity so severely."

Those were my hopes until Liz passed away.

But I have to put forth the effort, and going on this cruise could be the answer.

This is the last chapter I am writing to add to our book, and I wanted to see if Liz and I could connect again so I could share some of our cruise experiences for the last **TIME** as she is up in the Heavenly Blue Skies. We have always gone on many cruises together, so if I go on this cruise, perhaps I can feel her spirit and be at "Peace" that my sister, Tin Can, is gone.

A lot had changed since February 2020, when I was together with Mom and the family. I feel so lost, for she was with me on every Florida trip in my entire life. We hugged and kissed in February—who would ever think that was the last **TIME** we would see each other?

In Chapter Eight, on Page 148, when Liz passed away, I also wrote:

I have discontinued plans to visit Florida to see the family, partake in cruises, or engage in any activities involving her, due to the absence of **"TIN CAN."** What has become of **TIN CAN?** It is imperative that I see and feel her spirit again; I must, and I am determined to do so. Although I am uncertain of the method, I am committed to attempting. I must persist in my search for her, as I believe her spirit will manifest; I am confident she will appear when I least expect it.

Additionally, I mentioned that Liz's Spirit kept prompting and occupying my thoughts about the book's publication. At that time, her spirit had returned to my thoughts and dreams, again urging me to consider going on this cruise with the family and continuously occupying my mind.

Also, I wrote: In Chapter Eight, she continued to push and gnaw at my mind about publishing the book. Now, she's back in my thoughts and dreams, again gnawing at my mind as I think about going on this cruise with the family.

I fully remember those words I wrote, and I think of those words, and as I am trying to decide about the cruise, those words are haunting me.

**TIME** has passed, and I am still searching for her. I had many thoughts and recollections of her, but nothing as intense as I had when she prodded me to write the book. Therefore, I thought of possibly connecting memories again by going on the cruise, but I wasn't sure if that was right. As I prayed to our Lord, I asked him, what do I do next to get an answer?" I quickly got the answer from high above, and this was the only thing left for me to do, and it was simple!

This cruise would be the only way that I could possibly find her again and feel her spirit communicating to me like the days we cruised together on the Blue Seas under the Blue Skies.

Then, I thought, what would Lizzie do if she were in my situation? Would she go on the cruise or lose the money? As I wrote Chapter Eight, I remembered saying, "She is here—I know she is!" I prayed to the Lord and looked up to the "Blue Skies." I need to have that communication again to feel her in my spirit. I constantly prayed about it, then went out on the porch, and I looked up to the "Blue Skies" above, thinking I would get an answer, and then suddenly, I had an idea.

I just became "**Tin Can.**" I took on her persona, strong will, and challenge. I remembered what she would do next.

I returned to the house to retrieve two of her golden coins, which I had tucked away in an easy-to-find area.

After reacting as Liz would respond, I tossed up the tokens and caught them. I was assured and confident that it was a "**YES**" to go on the cruise.

When I came back to the house, I texted the boys, and they, too, were thrilled about another cruising experience. I was shocked when it was confirmed that it was a "**YES**" after I tossed her golden tokens toward the "Blue Skies."

I felt like a giant cloud had been lifted from my shoulders, and I could feel God's "Peace" flooding my entire being. So, with the boys' excitement and saying they would help with their grandpa, we decided to go on the cruise. I called my travel agent and booked our cruise for October 2023 out of Charleston, South Carolina.

I was careful when packing my clothes for the cruise because I knew Lizzie would want me to visit the photo studio, just like we did when the sisters (Dorothy, Lizzie, and I) sailed on the Blue Waters. together.

**TIME** moved quickly, and we ventured on our trip before you knew it. We first stopped to rest after a long drive from Ohio at our place in Ocean Isle Beach, NC. Then, **TIME** called us to move and head down to the cruise port in Charleston, South Carolina, to board our ship. Lizzie seemed to be calling me to "**hurry up!**" We took our new seven-passenger car, and we were all together. We left early for the two-hour drive to Charleston, SC.

It was a fun family adventure as we left North Carolina to drive to Charleston, South Carolina. When we arrived at the port, it was easy. We parked the car in the Handicapped parking lot, gave them Dennis' name, and they had a wheelchair ready for him. As his caretaker, they took him and me to a special boarding entrance. It was quick and easy.

**TIME** passed quickly while we enjoyed the calm Bahama breezes under the Blue Skies, the misty Blue Waters, the warm October temperatures, and the friendly people.

On the cruise ship, I sometimes felt like Lizzie; I became my sister, acting her role out on the Blue Waters under the Blue Skies.

Every step of the way, I could feel Lizzie's spirit hovering over me from up in the Blue Skies above, watching and enjoying our fun. I especially could feel her spirit while we were getting pictures taken. As I wrote in the book, Lizzie and I spent much **TIME** and money in the picture studios. When it came **TIME** to decide what photos I should buy, I would talk to Lizzie and ask her what she thought.

Whenever we cruised together, Liz asked me what pictures she should buy. After I told her which ones I liked, she would say, "I think I will buy them all!" sure enough, she did! My son, Chris, and grandsons, Isak and Anthony, told me to put the pictures down. They would shout at me, "Enough pictures already, Grandma!" Of course, I would tell them, "Don't worry about it, guys; I think I will buy them all, and sure enough, I did!

I remember telling Lizzie those exact words when she bought them all! I would yell at her and say, "Liz, you can't afford all these pictures, and what will you do with them?" She would tell me, "Sister Rita, don't worry about which ones I buy; if I don't use them, you will." Sure enough, many of the cruise pictures are in this book. Lizzie was right again.

Oh, I missed her so much on this cruise. I felt her spirit ever so close to me every step of the way. I could see her at our dinner tables as we would discuss our menu choices for every meal. Oh, how I remember our meals together. Afterward, I would dance in the dining room when the crew put on their shows. As I danced, I remembered Liz saying in Chapter Six, "When you and Pam come to Florida, you will have to teach me more Sign Language. You have accomplished everything I wanted to bring about but never got the chance to. But, for sure, I will be dancing with young people who are deaf when I get home—just like you can dance!"

I laughed and laughed and said, "Liz, when we went on the cruises, I begged you to get up and shake that body around, but no, you would not. You gave me so many excuses."

Looking at the dance floor, I quickly envisioned beautiful Liz signing to her young deaf dance partner. They were dancing away and enjoying themselves! This vision seemed so natural as if Liz had come down from the blue skies to teach people who are deaf or hard of hearing how to dance, as she had said she would do. Therefore, that quick insight I had of Lizzie teaching a young man how to dance was worth every second of going on this cruise with my family!

In closing, I never thought I would ever cruise again, especially since this year has been challenging: working on the book, marketing the book, working part-time, and then my husband's stroke. But by God's amazing grace, we made it, and we all enjoyed the calm Blue Waters, sunny hot days, each other, and Lizzie looking down at me in the October tropical breezes in the Bahamas.

We had to learn to **OVERCOME our Trials and Tribulations** and had memorable times with Lizzie when we cruised together. This cruise was a peaceful and precious **TIME** for my family to enjoy and be thankful for each other. It also allowed me to feel Liz's spirit above me as she cruised with us, and we relived our precious moments together.

My husband, Dennis, enjoyed and relaxed on this cruise after many months of hard work and therapy to regain his movement. The cruise was a tremendous natural healing experience for Dennis, and we were all so glad he went on this adventure.

So, I have many new memories of my family and some old and renewed memories of my sister, **TIN CAN**. I had to ask myself, "Would I be strong enough to endure the pain of her being gone and reliving all the memories of being on the cruise together?" When I tossed the coin, and when it was a go, I had to be strong enough to be ready for new and exciting adventures with my family and with Lizzie leading the way, and this cruising adventure was just that!

Now we are on a new pathway, still getting the messages out to others that there is hope for what you are going through as **TIME** moves on and you trust in our Lord!

This is the last piece I am writing in our book, and I wanted to see if Lizzie and I could connect again, and indeed we did! I will treasure some of our cruise experiences and memories of what we have always done together for one last **TIME**.

I thank my family for being patient and helpful with Dennis and me on this cruise, and most of all, I want to thank my sister, **TIN CAN LIZZIE**, for leading the way!

I want to finish this final added chapter in this book by thinking, "She is not gone forever. Her Spirit is out there. Someone so loving, kind, and inspirational to me and many others will ride above the earth again, up in the BLUE SKIES above and the CALM BLUE WATERS."

Therefore, the GENRE of the true story of **Tin Can Lizzie** and our family will still live on forever!

I will continue to sing the BLUE SKIES SONG, looking up and smiling at her when there are days when I miss her so much. I will continue to sing:

*BLUE SKIES ABOVE*

*WE HAVE BLUE SKIES TODAY*

*LIZ, I KNOW YOU ARE UP THERE,*

*I PRAY BLUE SKIES DON'T GO AWAY*

*LET THE BLUE SKIES FOREVER STAY!*

# Precious Moments To Remember

October 2023 from the left:

Grandson, Isak, My Husband Dennis, Myself, Grandson Anthony, and my Son Christopher.

October 2023: My Husband Dennis and I enjoyed the sunset view, looking out into the calm sea waters and enjoying each other as we thanked God for his recovery.

My Husband, Dennis, was so happy that he could make this cruise. We enjoyed being with the family and having every meal together. We will share our experiences on this cruise over the years. I was so delighted to have time with the family and to relive my time with Lizzie!

Thank God for giving me the courage to enjoy this cruise with my family and renew the special memories Liz and I had together when we cruised on the peaceful Blue Waters under the tropical Blue Skies.

October 2023: I am looking out at the evening view and enjoying the tropical calm breeze as sister Lizzie and I feel our Spirits united! I was sad without Lizzie, but I was thankful I could go on the cruise and relive such treasured, beautiful memories we had together!

October 2023: I look out at the evening view and enjoy the tropical calm breeze as Sister Lizzie and I feel our Spirits united! I was sad without Lizzie, but I was thankful I could go on the cruise and relive the beautiful memories we had together.

Sometimes, Lizzie reveals impossible tasks for me to do. I continue to look up and pray to our Lord, asking Him for strength, wisdom and courage, and peace to follow Liz's wishes and for His will for my life.

I feel happy and peaceful, and I tell Lizzie in the Blue Skies above that I will do everything to fulfill her wishes that our book will reach the farthest reaches of the world, just as Liz said it would in our last conversations together. I got it.

Well Liz, I can finally say, "**It's finished!**" We did it! I kept your promises, wrote the book, and published it. It was not an easy task, but I accomplished it with God's help and guidance and with your inspirational thoughts. I also renewed my wonderful cruise experiences with you, like we did when we cruised together! It was a journey of growth, and we accomplished it with the help of our Lord Jesus. We will meet again when we are together in the Lord's House.

## PLEASE TAKE THIS SCRIPTURE WITH YOU WHEREVER YOU GO!

James, in this scripture, says, "Blessed is the man who can remain Steadfast when they are under **Trials**. We can remain "**Happy**" when we undergo our **TRIALS AND TRIBULATIONS**, which can coexist with the pressure around us. We need to be **FAITHFUL** and **OVERCOME** those **TRIALS AND TRIBULATIONS** in your life, and Jesus will give you a **CROWN OF LIFE**, and he wants you to claim this scripture!

You will **OVERCOME** through our Lord!

### James 1:12

Blessed is the one who perseveres under their **Trials and Tribulations** because, having stood the test, that person will receive the **CROWN OF LIFE** that the Lord has promised to those who love him.

www.ingramcontent.com/pod-product-compliance
Lightning Source LLC
Chambersburg PA
CBHW071711120626
46550CB00001B/193